DINGHY BUILDING

DINGHY BUILDING

Richard Creagh-Osborne

JOHN de GRAFF, INC.
CLINTON CORNERS, N.Y.

First published in Great Britain 1963 by Adlard Coles Limited
Revised American Edition 1977
Reprinted 1978

Copyright © 1963 and 1977 by Richard Creagh-Osborne

John de Graff Inc.
Clinton Corners, N.Y. 12514

Library of Congress Catalog Card Number: 76–47918
ISBN 0 8286 0073 2

Printed in Great Britain

Printed in Great Britain by
Fletcher & Son, Norwich

Contents

Acknowledgements

THE author wishes to acknowledge the great assistance that he has been given in gathering material for the production of this book, in particular from the following:

W. A. SOUTER, (*Cold Moulding and Reinforced Plastics*).
SMALL CRAFT LTD, (*Single and Double Chine Hulls*).
CHIPPENDALE LTD, (*Cold Moulding, Clinker, and Chine Hulls*).
J. C. ROGERS, (*Cold Moulding and Composite Hulls*).
PETER WEBSTER LTD, (*Reinforced Plastic Hulls*).
KEITH PAUL, (*Composite Construction*).
TANGYES LTD, (*Space-frame Construction*).
THE TIMBER DEVELOPMENT ASSOCIATION LTD
MR. PETER BARTON, *who read the manuscript.*
MRS. CONSTANCE GARNER, *who typed the manuscript.*
MESSRS BOOTS, LTD, and MISS SERENA BROWN, *who processed the photographic films.*

All the firms listed in the Appendix and elsewhere who supplied information and assistance.

Introduction

THIS book is based on twenty years' experience of sailing and racing small boats, some of which I have built myself and nearly all of which I have maintained and repaired with my own hands. Thus, although I am not a professional boatbuilder or designer, I write from experience and I hope with enthusiasm, as I have always been interested in construction and fittings and have made a study of the subject. Even so the task of writing this book would have been formidable but for the co-operation given to me by leading designers and builders whom I have visited and consulted so that this book may represent the latest thought on methods of construction and the practical points arising in the details and fitting out of dinghies of all kinds.

In order to make a boat go fast—fast enough to win the biggest races—a great deal of attention to detail is needed. Because of this I have gradually found the most efficient and effective ways of achieving what we all desire, whether we are interested in racing or only pottering— a boat that sails well and handles well within the limits of its design. I know now that some methods of fixing two pieces of wood together are unnecessarily complicated, or possibly there are now new ways of fixing the pieces together if one uses new materials which are continually coming on to the market. Many of the old ways of building boats can be considerably simplified and improved.

I also know that many of the elaborations that are found on modern class dinghies are unnecessary. Many builders, designers and boat-owners cannot now see the wood for the trees, and become mesmerized by the clamouring advertisements to such an extent that all new fittings and boats find an enthusiastic market without their true worth having been assessed. Equally, in an effort to stop boats becoming outclassed within their own classes, rigid rules are framed at the time of designing. Classes therefore cannot take advantage of many new techniques and developments and all too often new classes are modelled on old ones with only slight variations. Advances are often slow to take hold as a result, and owners and builders often do not realize some of the short cuts that can be taken if the new techniques are studied. Examples in various fields are the ply/glass-tape joints, polyester paints, simplified wood joints using glue, and the use of terylene line instead of rigging-screws, shackles and other parts.

My aim in this book is to be severely practical, to consider only the essentials. I aim to try to explain in the simplest possible way and with the aid of many photographs how to build and fit out a dinghy efficiently and effectively so that it will do its job without failure. The reader can embellish his craft as he wishes, using fancy contrasting timber, and so on, but the boat will be sound and shipshape if he merely follows these directions.

I am an amateur boatbuilder. I write this book for amateurs. I venture to suggest that the amateur approach to the problem of building a boat is the one which will be most readily understood. In addition, I have used the maximum of illustrations facing the relevant text, because it is far easier to follow what is meant by looking at a picture than by trying to translate a mass of words into the necessary mental image.

BUILDING METHODS

I personally think that the various forms of cold moulding using veneers or plywood strips can provide the ideal method for the amateur wanting to build a boat. The method is extremely simple in conception, and the only tricky part, as in all boatbuilding, is in setting up the jig or solid mould in the first place. There is no doubt that round-bilge hull shapes are, in general, superior to hard chine. The sailing characteristics can be made better and the lines are fairer, and so the hull should be more easily driven and thus faster. Of all the round-bilge construction methods, I prefer cold moulding—it is very strong, light, rigid, easily accomplished, and is easy to maintain and clean. There are no traps for water to enter and it is completely leakproof and long lasting (Chapter 4, pp. 56–70).

Of the other round-bilge methods, glass-reinforced plastics (or fibre-glass as it is usually, but wrongly named) is the one which is on everyone's lips today. To read some of the manufacturers' advertisements one would think that this method entirely superseded all others, and that any boat not built this way is a dead loss to its owner.

There is no denying that there are some considerable advantages to having boats built of plastics, but, as is happening more and more in this new and fast-growing industry, commercial interests with their high-pressure advertising methods are trying to sway the public to buy only those things that are commercially profitable. The sale of plastics boats can be highly profitable, but the mould costs are high, and therefore long production runs are needed to keep the price down. The only way this can be done is by making a boat of interest to the widest possible market and then by pushing it in every way you can. Thus we are for ever having the virtues put before us, but never a hint of a disadvantage.

The obvious virtues include lower (but not negligible) maintenance costs, and the possibility of storing the boat out in the open without damage. For rigid one-design racing classes there is also the advantage of having every boat identical, and once the moulds have been made boats can be completed extremely quickly.

In my opinion that is as far as one can go with the unchallengeable virtues. It is frequently stated that G.R.P., to give it its abbreviated name, does not gain in weight through water soakage, but that is not so. A gain of up to 4 per cent can be found, and that represents about 10 lb on a boat such as a Finn. A cold-moulded boat if properly made out of the right materials need have no worse figures than this. Another advantage often quoted is that of having impregnated colour right through the laminate. I do not think it wise to pigment the resin in the main part of the lay-up, as it is extremely difficult in this case to see if a sound bond has been made with all air expelled and the glass thoroughly wetted out. This also brings up the problem of deciding whether a glass-plastics boat has been properly made. It is almost impossible for the buyer without technical knowledge to decide this. There are so many ways of making a glass-plastics boat cheaply by cutting down on resin or reinforcement and substituting an excess of various fillers, which cannot easily be detected afterwards. The effects of cut-price construction can be higher water absorption, free water getting into the laminate, poor strength and possible delamination of the lay-up.

There are also other disadvantages—G.R.P. has poor resistance to "scuffing" and also will be only about one-third of the thickness of timber panelling of equivalent weight, but the greater flexibility of the thinner laminate poses considerable design problems in small light boats to obtain the same performance. This is one feature which makes it rather less suitable for amateur boatbuilding, and another is the high cost of moulds. Other troublesome points are the difficulty of arranging for the fixing of fittings and the problem of carrying out alterations at a later date.

The builder must therefore weigh up the pros and cons and decide for himself if G.R.P. is for him.

Of the other round-bilge construction methods I feel glued clinker is second only to cold moulding for the amateur. It is a method hardly publicized at all, and if it was not for the class rules for our three main National "restricted" classes which demand clinker construction, it would now be almost unknown. Traditional nailed clinker is now hardly used at all, other methods having great advantages. But glued ribless clinker is another thing altogether, and for those who are experimenting with hull shapes it is the ideal system.

0.1

It can be seen how easily the shape of succeeding boats can be amended. A shows the original mould shape. B shows the extra piece which has been added on to alter the shape. (Chippendale, 12-ft National.)

The jig needed is very simple, and the moulds can be altered easily from boat to boat (Fig. 0.1). The resulting hull is watertight and strong, and is nearly as easy to clean and maintain as a cold-moulded shell.

The other main method which is gradually dying out, though it is still used occasionally for heavier boats, is carvel construction. It is usual for the single skin, fore-and-aft planking to be edge-glued, and ribs are screwed in afterwards to control splitting and assist in maintaining the shape. One cannot really use

0.2

The skeleton frameworks of two Eleven Plus dinghies. The accurate cutting of the parts of the framework controls the shape of the boat and all the pieces remain in the boat after it is completed. (Tangye, Eleven Plus.)

less than about 9-mm. planking for this system, and few modern racing boats are built as heavily as this. Its main advantage is that a very fair hull can be obtained which, if properly finished, can have a superior surface to any other method. It is not really very suitable for the amateur, but is mentioned here for completeness.

This leaves us with the variations of single-

and multi-chine hulls which form the majority of wooden boats seen afloat today. The sole reason for their continued popularity seems to be their suitability for mass factory methods of kit production. I cannot possibly believe that anyone who has had anything to do with round-bilge hulls would prefer a chine hull for its performance or its looks. There are a number of structural disadvantages to the chine hull such as excessive flatness of completed panels, and the difficulty of designing suitable shapes round which flat sheets of plywood can be bent. Sailing lines can never be entirely satisfactory even in the double-chine forms.

However, it can be extremely easy to assemble a boat by these methods and therefore I am sure that ordinary single- and double-chine construction will remain popular as long as commercial kit-set builders can sell their boats. Public opinion has already hardened against single chine, except for the newer jigless construction methods, which can show a real advantage in ease of construction.

These methods of building chine boats are going to take the place completely of conventional systems. The art of boatbuilding is going to be divided more or less sharply between the factory product, whether complete or in kit form, and the boat built truly from scratch.

It is quite difficult to decide where the true home boatbuilder will stand in all this. It looks as though there will be two very separate categories for some time to come. The factory product is already being designed and laid out in such a way that anyone who can use a screwdriver and a glue pot can build this particular boat. Labelling of pre-cut parts and fully comprehensive instructions mean that little can go wrong and a sound boat ought to result. The builder will not even need any jigs or moulds. The boat will literally take up its own correct shape as it is screwed together (Fig. 0.2).

I think that this book is going to be of some assistance to builders of these kit sets, but I hope it will also be a great inspiration to them to try their hand at something more individual and more refined as their second attempt at boatbuilding. The satisfaction to be had from building a boat completely from scratch is tremendous, and in this age of mass-production and sameness the greatest pleasure can be obtained from creating something completely individual.

Therefore there are really two ways for the amateur to build boats. We are not greatly concerned in this book with the most elaborate kit assemblies. All one has to do is follow the highly comprehensive set of building instructions.

But there are, of course, variations of kit-boat building, ranging from the simplest possible layout, giving accurately shaped pieces of wood, marked and listed, together with instructions of the "screw A to A'" and "B to B'" variety, to a much more worthwhile exercise. In the latter case one might be given enough of the right sort of timber to build the boat, together with paper patterns of the shapes, which the builder cuts out himself. In the first case the instructions are extremely comprehensive, and nothing is left to the owner's imagination, other than the colour of the paint.

Though the kit system provides the majority of amateur-completed boats now being built, and is a tremendous force in the new wave of enthusiasm for sailing, it is pretty certain that once a kit boat has been constructed any self-respecting amateur will want to build something more ambitious or which can reflect his own individuality, skill and ideas. One hopes also that there are still a great many people who want to start straight away on an individual effort, or perhaps who want to build a type of boat for which only normal skeleton plans or merely a table of offsets are available.

It is mainly for these people that this book is compiled. I aim to show the basic ideas behind the various ways of building sailing boats and to give enough information so that the amateur boatbuilder can work out how to solve his own problems.

There are many equally satisfactory ways of building boats, and we must keep a thoroughly open mind on the matter. Already, since starting this book, several promising new methods have come to light. One possible advantage of having a non-technical but enthusiastic handyman to write such a book is that such a person looks at the problems from the amateur's viewpoint. Speaking personally, I started building boats many years ago with an "utter perfection and time is no object" standard. Fairly gradually I have resolved a sort of compromise standard whereby absolute soundness of basic construction is my main aim, but where the actual finish and the method of arriving at the result is unimportant. I am prepared to try any method if I can convince myself that it is strong enough. Having been mainly engaged in high-pressure hard racing and also maintaining and often building my own racing boats, I think I have a very good idea of what will, and what will not, stand up to a really hard thrashing. Do not think, though, that I know nothing about knock-about boats. That is very far from the case, and I am fully aware of the sort of treatment that such a boat gets.

I will tell you how to obtain a first-class finish, but I will not think any the worse of you if you do as I do and don't bother to dowel screw-holes or scrape surfaces before painting. Frankly, I have not now the time to do much more to embellish my boats than is necessary to protect the wood or extract that last tenth of a knot which might win the big race. My view now, after many years of dealing with them, is that boats are there to be used, and there is just not time to fuss over them unnecessarily.

However, don't let me stop you treating your boat as if it was the finest antique Chippendale. I love to see such work and I greatly admire the patience and workmanship of the builders. I just want to get clear before we start that what mainly concerns us here is to demonstrate basic soundness and ease of construction.

PLANS AND PLANNING

The first consideration is how to interpret a set of drawings and table of offsets to be able to produce a hull of the right shape. Tables of offsets, when supplied, normally only refer to round-bilge hulls, whereas a large number of dinghies today are designed for the single- or multi-chine system. Nevertheless it is important to be able to go along with the designer to see how the moulds, jigs and frames are set up for the construction of a hull accurately to drawings, even though many of the plans for the simple dinghies for home building will have very detailed instructions and full-size drawings.

Some firms specializing in home-building kit sets will even supply on loan a complete jig, and sometimes parts are accurately labelled, cut and machined so that the building of your boat becomes a kind of Meccano-like process (Fig. 0.3). Large numbers of boats are built in this simple way and are perfectly satisfactory. However, only a comparatively small range of classes is catered for by this type of production or specifically designed for it. It is more likely that the intending builder

0.3
A typical numbered set of kit parts. Most of the pieces are accurately cut to shape and thus assembly is made extremely easy. (Tangye, Eleven Plus.)

will be faced with a set of lines and a relating offset table, or perhaps a rather skimpy set of construction drawings. A great deal may be left unsaid or may be left to the individual builder's choice or interpretation.

Designers frequently expect the builders to have a knowledge of construction methods and will thus leave out much detail from their drawings. This can give the amateur many hours of head-scratching, and he may finally throw the whole lot away in disgust.

The arrangement of the book is straight-forward, starting with a discussion on the lines plan and how to transform this into a jig on which a hull can be built.

The setting up of a jig (or stocks) is also similar for all boats; the difference being in degree. A moulded boat has to have a complete and more or less solid mould to enable the veneers to conform to the correct shape (Fig. 4.1, p. 57); strip-planked or carvel hulls need moulds only at fairly close intervals (Fig. 5.3, p. 73); chine hulls may need only three moulds, and in some designs even these eventually remain as permanent frames in the finished boat.

There is nothing difficult about making

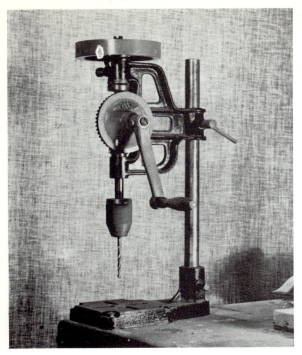

0.4
A small adjustable vertical bench drill which will take twist bits from $\frac{1}{16}$ in. up to $\frac{1}{2}$ in. in diameter, and is especially suitable for making holes in stainless steel, where heavy pressure and slow speed are required. (Keen.)

moulds and setting up a jig, however elaborate it may seem at first sight. Any handyman can do it, as long as extreme care is taken over the measuring and setting up. The common pitfalls are pointed out here, and the golden rule is always "measure twice and cut once".

Certain basic operations peculiar to boat construction are dealt with in Chapter 2. Certain difficulties are experienced in this field which do not occur when building a chest of drawers or a wheelbarrow, for instance. We are dealing with an object with compound curves. The fitting of seats and bulkheads presents some problems, and thus ordinary handyman methods which suffice to deal with the shelves in the larder waste time when used on boats. Though professional builders have certain special tools and jigs for dealing quickly with some boatbuilding operations, it is not essential to own much more than a good-quality set of normal woodworking tools. I use a vertical bench hand drill (Fig. 0.4) for wood and metalworking, and find that I seldom need a power drill. I do indeed own one, and also use it at times, but I would suggest for ordinary boatbuilding a fixed bench drill is probably of greater use. A tool that I find extremely useful and would always obtain if much work is planned, and which can save a tremendous amount of time and sweat, is a really good electric jigsaw. The Lesto model made by Scintilla has proved extremely satisfactory (Fig. 0.5).

An ordinary set of hand tools should include panel saw, hacksaw, heavy and light hammers (one with ball head), several screwdrivers (including a pump type), nail-cutters, pliers, spanners, chisels and gouges of various sizes, together with suitable sharpening stones, set-squares, vices, "G" cramps, hand drill brace and bits, padsaw, riveting dolly, files and rasps (including Surform-type tools), rules, and steel tapes, jack plane, and small rebating or block plane, spirit level, and plumb-bob.

Further desirable equipment can include the electric tools mentioned as well as other saws, such as tenon and rip saws, also bevel

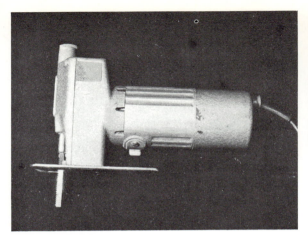

0.5
The Lesto electric handsaw made by Scintilla Ltd. A range of different saw-blades enables it to cut almost anything at maximum speed. An extremely useful tool for the home boatbuilder.

0.6
This small bench shears made by Hills can cope with 12-gauge stainless steel in sheet form. The replaceable cutting edges can also be sharpened.

and scribing gauges, scrapers, moulding planes. In fact, one can go on and on until one reaches professional standard or higher (Figs. 0.6, 0.7).

Many of the special jigs or tools needed can easily be made up, and, if one has funds to spare, time and trouble can be saved by adding new specialized equipment. Boats can be built perfectly well, however, with very simple tools and a little ingenuity. Specialized tools normally only save time.

Having thought about the building plans, and whilst you are setting up the jig, you can start collecting together the materials. The selection of timber can at best be a fascinating job for the competent amateur who aims to produce such a perfect piece of work that it

0.7
This small Burgess electric bandsaw could be invaluable for a home workshop where a number of boats are being built continually.

will be the envy of all eyes. Type and grain can be considered as well as the various possibilities of matching or contrasting colour.

However, even though full information and tabulated characteristics have been given for a number of species of timber, which will enable the perfectionist to select his material, it must not be thought this is the prime aim of Chapter 2. Due to the tremendous demand for high-quality timber and the unfortunate wartime gap when forests were not replanted, many types are in extremely short supply or are very high in price. The tables will enable a visit to the timber yard to be of considerable advantage if you ask for the names of the types available. You may be able to buy perfectly suitable timber, even though you may not have heard its name before.

The chapter also explains the main properties of timber, including plywood, and also deals with glues, screws, nails and other fastenings.

The principal types of construction already mentioned are covered in the chapters on hulls. These chapters explain in detail the various methods of producing a hull shell from the mould stage to the point where the deck and interior joinery can be fitted. In some types of construction a great deal of the interior can be fitted into the jig before the hull shell is planked up, and this can often be a great saving in time and trouble. So many of the compound bevels on centreboard cases, chines and bulkheads are more easily made from outside when the parts are already fitted in their final positions. Then the planking is glued to them as it is fitted, and when the hull is removed from the jig the interior parts come off, too, already fixed in place.

Some boats are now being designed so that they need no jig or mould at all. The interior of the hull, consisting of the centreboard case, spine, bulkheads, beams, thwarts, and knees, is assembled first, and this forms a rigid "space-frame" (Fig. 0.2, p. 9). Then the planking and decks are fixed last. This can be a great convenience as well as a saving in time and money. There is no wastage of materials and the assembly can be moved around at any stage in the construction. The plans will always show the method to be employed in building to these designs, because each is arranged differently. The resulting shape of the boat is entirely dependent on the dimensions and shapes of the interior framing. The boat is, in truth, built inside out. This type of construction will surely be developed further in the future.

1 *Building Plans*

THE most difficult way to start building a boat is to find yourself faced with merely a set of hull lines on a reduced scale plan together with a table of offsets. A tracing of such a set is shown in Figs. 1.1 and 1.2. The problem is how to translate such information into a shape.

The designer has put on paper in diagram form what he intends the outside shape of the hull to be. Of course, you will normally have more information than this to go on. The design will specify the method of construction, the materials to be used, the thickness of the materials, how the hull is to be fitted out, and so on. If the design is for a popular class there will undoubtedly be class rules and building instructions, which will give very definite restrictions and limitations on the construction, in order that the finished boat can pass the measurer and race on level terms with other boats in its class. There will, of course, be further sheets of drawings to assist builders in producing identical craft.

In this chapter, however, we are merely considering the outside shape of the boat. One may very well only be interested in this one feature. The completion of the boat may be to the builder's fancy.

The lines shown refer to an International Finn Class Dinghy which has a round-bilged hull 4.5 m. long (14 ft 9 in)*. The designer has used as a basis of his drawing lengths of half a metre (500 mm.). The length of the hull is

* There are Metric Conversion Tables on pp. **214–7**

therefore split up into nine sections. The transom is labelled Section 0 and each half metre from here to the bow is labelled from 1 to 9. Therefore the part of the drawing 500 mm. from the transom is called Station (or Section) 1, and the next one Station 2, and so on until the bow, which is called Station 9. The vertical lines on the upper and lower drawings in Fig. 1.1 are the station lines.

The outside line on the upper drawing shows the profile of the hull when looked at from the side. The outside line on the lower drawing shows the outside shape of the hull when looked down on from above. Only half is shown, because the other half will be exactly the same reversed.

On the lower drawing—the half-breadth plan—there are three lines marked A, B and C, parallel to the centreline. If you took a very big saw and sawed vertically straight down the centreline of the boat the resulting outside shape of one of the cut halves would be exactly the shape of the outer line in the upper profile drawing. If you sawed vertically down the next line outwards (line C), the shape of the cut area would be exactly the shape of line C on the upper drawing. Similarly cut along line B in the lower drawing, and you get a shape like line B in the upper. Likewise, lines A correspond. These are called buttock lines.

Similarly you will see a baseline marked on the upper drawing. This is a convenient line for scaling-off purposes and is usually parallel to the designed waterline, which in this case is marked W.L.4. Parallel to these are other

1.1

These are the lines of the International Finn Class racing dinghy, which are fully discussed in the text of this chapter.

The plans reproduced in this book, and the table of offsets on the opposite page are intended for illustrative purposes only and are not necessarily accurate. Builders of class boats are strongly advised in their own interests to obtain up-to-date copies of plans and class rules before starting any construction.

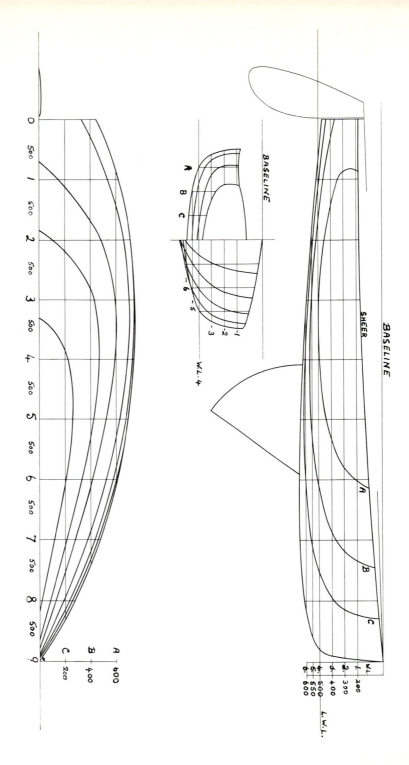

lines marked w.l.1 to w.l.6. The curved lines on the lower drawing represent shapes resulting from cutting horizontally along the respective waterlines. Only half the boat is shown on the lower drawing, because the other side is the same and you can quite easily see that if you cut horizontally along the waterline marked w.l.4, you will arrive at the shape depicted on the lower drawing by curved line 4.

A little further investigation will show that the buttock lines and the waterlines are all interrelated. This is made clearer by the plan of sections in the middle on the left. This shows the boat looked at from the remaining direction, which is along the fore-and-aft centreline. The left half of the drawing shows the port-side after quarter of the hull and the right half shows the port-side forward quarter. The curved lines represent the shapes of the sections if you cut down the vertical lines on the lower drawing.

The transom, which is Station 0, is, of course, exposed, and the inner curved line on the left half shows its shape. The next line outwards is the shape of Section 1, the outer line is Section 3. Then you turn to the outer

TABLE OF OFFSETS   DIMENSIONS IN MILLIMETRES

STATION		0	1	2	3	4	5	6	7	8	9
SHEER		182	185	180	174	157	131	112	80	45	
BUTTOCK "A"	FROM BASELINE	—	340	452	500	497	435	212			
BUTTOCK "B"		359	459	519	558	570	558	510	364		
BUTTOCK "C"		434	495	544	583	604	612	599	554	385	
KEEL		468	516	560	596	624	644	654	647	615	
SHEER		445	618	717	754	747	700	618	485	280	
WATERLINE 1.	HALF BREADTHS	451	620	717	754	745	690	603	462	259	
WATERLINE 2.		450	618	707	745	733	670	575	434	235	
WATERLINE 3.		319	535	663	717	695	627	520	375	140	
WATERLINE 4. (l.w.l)			148	484	599	593	519	414	275	124	
WATERLINE 5				125	442	469	420	325	206	72	
WATERLINE 6							260	196	110	13	

1.2
The table of offsets relating to the International Finn Class drawings.

line on the right half, which is Section 4, and which is also the midship section. The remaining lines are the succeeding sections forward.

You can now probably picture in your mind's eye the shape of various parts of the hull by looking at the curved lines on the drawings. The easiest drawing to start with is the Section Plan. You will see that the curves all come in to the centreline at different heights. You will notice also that a baseline has been drawn in the same position as the baseline on the upper drawing, and that it touches the top of the stem. The points where the sections meet the centreline can be measured from the baseline. You will then find that if these distances are marked on the upper drawing, each at its respective station, then the line representing the outer profile of the hull will pass through them all.

In the same way you can consider the next vertical line out from the centre on the plan of sections, which is buttock c, and is the same line as the buttock c on the lower drawing. Measure the distances from the baseline to where it cuts the sections. Transfer the points to the upper drawing and you will see that the curved line buttock c passes through them.

This shows the relationship between all the lines and curves on the three drawings. In actual fact, all the curves represent the outlines of imaginary plane surfaces, and they can best be imagined, as I have suggested, by thinking of a model hull sliced along the straight lines in the three different planes. The resulting areas are indicated by the curved lines. In this way one can represent a compound curved surface on flat paper.

You will be glad to hear that the amateur boatbuilder does not need to use all of these lines. The designer must use all of them, because unless all of them fair into each other, and match up with each other, on the three different drawings, the hull will be impossible to construct.

The main things in which we are interested in order to make a hull are the shape of the sections at each station and their relationship vertically and horizontally to each other.

If the drawings had been given to us full size there would be no need for a table of offsets. Sometimes one is given full-size drawings of the sections, which simplifies the making of moulds greatly (provided allowance is made for expansion and contraction of paper templates due to damp and heat). First, however, we will consider how to make the moulds from a small-scale plan and a related table of offsets.

The table of offsets for the International Finn is given in Fig. 1.2. This enables the builder to make templates the exact shape of the sections at the various stations.

What we actually require to do is make moulds which are the exact shape of the individual curves in the plan of sections less the thickness of the planking. We then set up these moulds 500 mm. apart exactly and keel uppermost. They are lined up so that their centrelines are exactly in line, they are rigidly fixed to a firm base so that they are absolutely vertical and absolutely parallel to each other, and also the centre points of each section must be at the correct height as shown on the plan of sections. Fig. 1.3 shows a completed jig for a double-chine hull partly planked up.

The planking is formed over the jig. If the boat is to be planked in longitudinal strips in

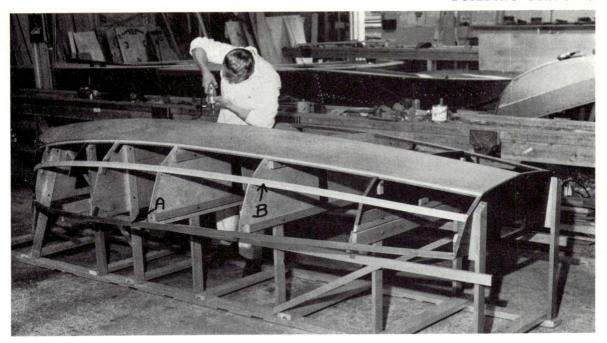

1.3

A partly planked jig for a double-chine sailing dinghy. The transom is fixed to the jig, but comes off with the completed shell. This also applies to the next mould forward, which is the bulkhead forming the after buoyancy tank. The next three moulds do not remain with the shell when it is lifted off. The upper chine (B) and the inwale (A) can be seen on the near side fixed to notches in the moulds. The worker is drilling the bottom plank for fixing screws. Notice the rigid framework of the jig, which enables it to be moved about from place to place, and also brings the boat at a convenient height for the worker. (Small Craft, 14-ft Leader.)

1.4

A fully battened mould on which a hull is to be constructed by the cold veneer moulding method. (Souter, Penguin Dinghy.)

1.5

A female mould in which a fibre-glass hull is being laid up. In this case the mould is for yachts' tenders of varying size. Shorter boats are made by inserting a temporary transom inside the mould, as can be seen in this photograph. (Souter, Penguin Dinghy.)

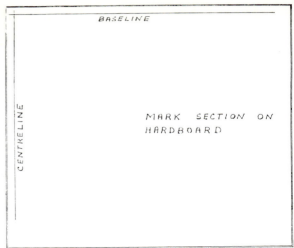

BASELINE

CENTRELINE

MARK SECTION ON HARDBOARD

1.6

the carvel or clinker fashion, it may not be necessary to do any more to the jig than this. If the planking is to be of glued veneers, then longitudinal battens will have to be let into the sections and run from one end to the other to make a semi-solid framework for the veneers to be tacked on to temporarily (Fig. 1.4). For fibre-glass construction a further solid mould will have to be made from this first one and this matter will be dealt with later (Fig. 1.5).

There are several ways of making the actual moulds. We will consider one of them. It is probably best to mark out the shape of each individual section on a sheet of hardboard. Fig. 1.6 depicts a sheet of hardboard with the baseline and centreline marked on it. Let us

assume that we are going to mark out Section 4, which is the centre section, and that the planking thickness will be 10 mm.

The upper half of the table of offsets represent the vertical measurements at various points on the curve we require measured from the baseline. The lower half represents the horizontal half-breadths, measured, of course, from the centreline.

We must now draw the vertical buttock lines A, B and C (Fig. 1.7), and the horizontal waterlines 1 to 6 (Fig. 1.8). We can then start marking off the offset points using the column under the figure 4 on the top line. Fig. 1.9 shows the points all marked in. Now get a thin batten and arrange it so that it touches as many points as possible. Tack panel pins at suitable points to hold the batten, but make sure that it lies absolutely fair. Now draw a line round the batten carefully. This is the

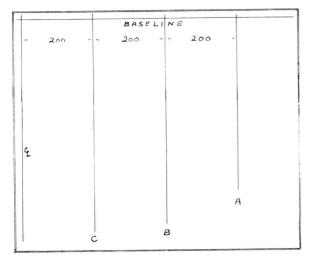

1.7

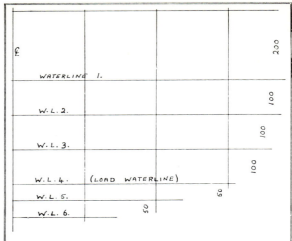

1.8

shape of half the section (Fig. 1.10). One can now cut round the outside of the line. Trim carefully to shape and then scribe a line parallel to the edge exactly 10 mm. inside. Trim off to this line and this will be the outside shape that the mould will need to be (Fig. 1.11), though, where the planking runs at substantially less than a right angle to the plane of the section, such as occurs near the bow, this shape will be slightly oversize unless an adjustment is made.

The mould itself can be made from any scrap timber of a suitable thickness. Half or three-quarter inch deal will be adequate for a hull of this size. Nail together a framework for a full width section including a centre piece and enough timber to go well beyond the sheer. In fact, it is just as well to prolong the two side pieces for a couple of feet. In this way they can form legs to raise the whole mould to

a convenient height for working. The legs can be cut to suitable lengths when setting up the complete jig and fixing to the base. Fig. 1.12 shows the complete mould for the section ready to have the shape marked on it. Make sure that one side of the mould is flat so that you can lay the hardboard on it and scribe round the edge easily.

Next mark a centreline and then lay the template so that its centreline lies exactly along it. Then scribe round the edge and mark the sheer height. Turn the template over and do the same the other side. Finally cut off the surplus wood and make sure that the centre and the two sheer heights are clearly marked both sides. This completes the mould for the centre section. All the others are done the same way. Usually the transom made is the actual one that will be in the finished boat, and so it will be made especially carefully out of the

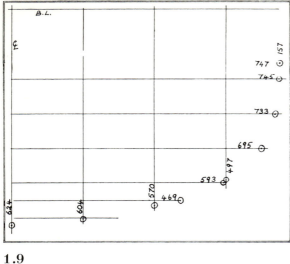

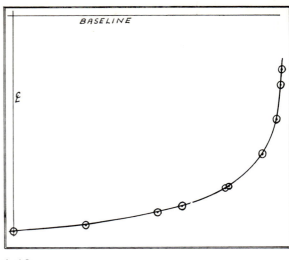

1.9   1.10

proper timber and will have legs temporarily screwed to one face.

The moulds can now be set up on a firm level base. The base does not have to be level, but it makes things considerably easier if it is. If the workshop has a wooden floor the matter is much easier. Small wooden blocks can be screwed to the floor and the legs of the moulds screwed to these. It is much better to screw rather than nail at this stage. The moulds can be clamped into position and then the screws driven before the clamps are moved. Nailing tends to shift things, and inaccuracies start creeping in.

If you cannot fix the legs to the floor it is probably best to make a sub-frame out of 4 in. × 2 in. deal and fix the moulds to this. Make sure that the frame is strutted rigidly. If planks are fixed over the jig later they will tend to pull the ends of the framework up-

wards and press the middle downwards. If there is any give in the framework, the hull may come out flatter than the designer intended.

Fix the transom mould to one end of the base. With a spirit level make sure that the two sheer heights are absolutely level. Fix one leg first. Cramp the other leg and gradually tap it down until the sheers are level. Then fix it. Strut the mould until the transom is absolutely vertical.

An essential operation is getting the face of each succeeding mould parallel to the first. If one makes the moulds out of timber of exactly similar thickness, and then screws the legs on to the back, one can then mark off on the base on each side the positions of the stations. Frequently cross-struts can be fixed on to the base so that one edge passes through exactly these points, and this helps to avoid errors.

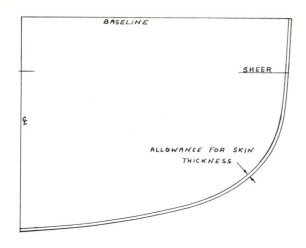

1.11

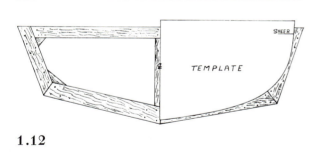

1.12

The legs can then be fixed level with these marks and all should be well (Fig. 1.13).

As each mould is set up the centreline has to come at the right height also. This is done with the help of a taut line running along the dead centre of the subframe low down. This is your baseline. It may or may not be the same as the designer's baseline, depending on how high off the floor you are going to have your jig. Some designers even use the actual water-line as their baseline and this is usually very inconvenient to use. In the Finn the designer's baseline is exactly 468 mm. nearer the floor than the centreline of the skin at transom. Remember to subtract the skin thickness and then measure 458 mm. down from the centre of the mould. If this comes at a convenient point, all well and good. Fix one end of your taut line at this point. If not, fix it to a convenient point and note the difference in distance. This difference will have to be added or subtracted when settling the heights of the other moulds.

You must have this taut baseline level, because it is essential to have the moulds at right-angles to it and then they can easily be plumbed. Therefore fix the other end and make sure it is level.

The next mould is then clamped as nearly in place as possible. By tapping this way and that, you will be able to get the centreline at the right height as well as the sheers level. Screw down and then proceed to the remaining moulds.

The boat will almost certainly have a hog or keel or some form of stringer along the keel line. This will connect with the inside of the stem. These will all be actual parts of the final boat and not temporary moulds. From the plans the keel or hog can be cut out to shape. It may need to have a centreboard slot cut in it and the dimensions of this will be shown also. The hog should be completely finished with the exception of its outside surface, which is usually faired in after fixing to the jig.

Notches are cut in the moulds to take the

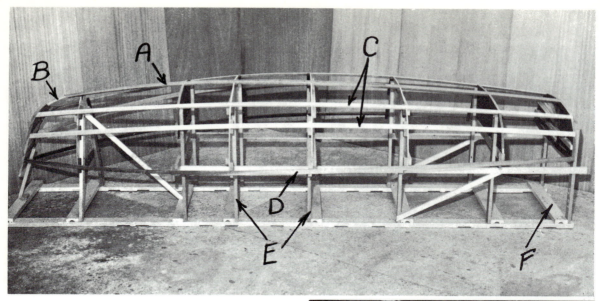

1.13

A completed jig with the hog (A), stem (B), double chines (C), and inwales (D) fitted to the framework. Notice the framework with cross struts at exactly the positions of the correct faces of the moulds. Notice that the legs (E) are fixed to the after side of the actual moulds forward of maximum beam position, and to the forward side of the moulds aft of the maximum beam position. Also notice that the legs are fixed to the after side of the cross struts (F) forward of maximum beam, and to the forward side of the cross-struts aft of maximum beam. The correct face for measuring the station positions is the after side of all the moulds forward of maximum beam, and the forward side of all the moulds aft of maximum beam. Notice also the diagonal struts bracing the whole frame rigidly. (Small Craft, Wayfarer.)

1.14

A permanent bulkhead fitted into the jig with the notches for the chines roughly cut. In this case the far side of the bulkhead is on the measured station point. (Small Craft, 14-ft Leader.)

1.15
The roughed-out stem and how it is fixed to the hog. It is just about to be pulled down so that the hog enters the notch in the top of the first mould. The point of the stem will then be screwed firmly to the base. (Small Craft, 14-ft Leader.)

hog and it can be laid and fixed in place. Due to the spring in the wood you must make sure that the moulds do not move in the fixing operation (Fig. 1.14).

The stem framing may be made up from two or three pieces of timber glued together or it may be a laminated member. The plans usually show a full-sized template of the stem profile and the shape can be got from this.

When setting up and fixing the stem one has to be a little careful, especially when dealing with class boats that may be very rigidly controlled on their overall lengths. Due to the

angle that the planking runs together at the stem the planks come to a point considerably more than the plank thickness in front of the inner stem itself. You may be required to plane a flat on the stem and then fix some half-round brass as a stemband. Check carefully that the position finally decided upon for the inner stem in the fore and aft direction will result in the final length of the boat measured to the outside of the stemband being correct.

The plans will usually show the angle that has to be planed on the side of the inner stem to receive the planking (Fig. 1.15). This can be done before fixing. You will then probably need to make a template of the outside of the stem which can be taken off the full-size plan. This will assist in getting the inner stem fixed in exactly the right place and screwed to the hog.

Apart from the fairing in of the outer surface of the stem and hog, this will be all that is needed basically to build a clinker or carvel hull. If a moulded hull is required, then the jig will have to be made into a semi-solid mould by means of longitudinal battens let into each section and finally all faired up smoothly (Fig. 4.1, p. 57). Use knot-free timber for the battens or there will be kinks and flats in the skeleton surface and it will be very difficult and tedious to fair them in.

The spacing of the battens is not critical as long as the veneers will bend round them fairly without a tendency to kinks at each batten with flatter areas in between. The first skin is usually laid diagonally at about 45 degrees to the centreline.

We now have a jig or solid mould which will produce a hull of the shape the designer

1.16

intended (Fig. 1.16). We must now consider the various methods of making the hulls.

A set of moulds for a 12-ft National Dinghy to be built clinker fashion. The transom is permanent. The centreboard case has been fitted into the jig between the halves of the centre two moulds. The hog and keel have been fixed in place and planking is just about to start. There are no notches in the moulds. The planking is bent round them and fastened only at the ends and to the next plank. (Chippendale, 12-ft National.)

2 Materials for Wooden Boats

DINGHIES that are "dry sailed" can be made from almost any materials. Materials which are not durable when exposed to the weather can still be used for dinghies kept out of the water and under cover when not actually being sailed. The modern paints and varnishes can protect non-durable timbers sufficiently to enable them to withstand normal sailing conditions. The only advantage in using non-durable timbers is usually cheapness, though it is sometimes an advantage to use a non-durable material for other purposes, such as better painting qualities, lightness, or extreme flexibility, or perhaps rigidity.

In the belief that some builders of dinghies will want to know the properties of the timber and other materials that they are going to use, I have listed a considerable amount of information which has been obtained from the Timber Development Association's pamphlets and other sources, and builders can select from these materials timbers to suit their particular purpose. Of course, not all of these timbers will be readily available, and there are others which are available and yet not listed here, so it is best to go to your nearest timber merchant and see what he has in stock. Builders of racing dinghies will be particularly interested in the weight of timber, and frequently one can save a great deal of weight by selecting a lesser-known but lighter material. This question of weight is particularly important when plywood is used in the construction of boats, as is so frequently done nowadays. I recently weighed samples of 6-mm. plywood in the

standard 8 ft × 4 ft sheets, and found weights varying from 20 lb to 30 lb a sheet. Now, a certain dinghy uses six sheets of 6-mm. plywood with a very small amount of wastage. Therefore by using the lighter instead of the heavier plywood one might save well over 30 lb in the all-up weight of the finished boat.

There is more to consider, though, than just the weight of the plywood. The lighter, less-dense grades of plywood will soak up moisture much more readily than the denser grades. Therefore builders using light plywood must take particular pains to ensure that all surfaces and edges, including the insides of tanks and the undersides of decks, are completely protected with at least three coats of paint or varnish. There is another consideration with regard to density of plywood, and that is its ability to take and retain paint and glue. The denser plywoods tend to be very hard on the surface and they are unable to accommodate the expansion and contraction induced by the considerable variations in surface temperature due to exposure to sunshine in the daytime and frost at night. This will cause small cracks and shakes to appear in the surface of the timber and the paint will suffer likewise, allowing water to enter with consequent delamination of the paint and possibly the plywood also. Many paint failures are caused by this effect, which is accentuated by the heat-absorbing power of some of the darker-coloured paints and also the effect of frost on timber which has soaked to a comparatively high moisture content. On the other hand, the softer timbers, which have a comparatively large volume of air space in their make-up, can absorb expansion and contraction of the timber within their own structures much more easily and movement and cracking of the surface is not so likely. Consequently paint is more likely to survive in good condition on these timbers.

As for gluing, the softer and more open timbers are more likely to take glue well than the harder and more dense timbers, because the glue can penetrate into the pores of the timber more easily. Some timbers are not easy to glue on account of their resinous or waxy nature. Teak is notoriously difficult to glue with the ordinary boatbuilder's urea glues. However, it seems to respond to resorcinol glue satisfactorily. Another waxy timber is cedar, and an example of a resinous timber is pitch-pine.

PLYWOOD
(See also Appendix H, p. 218)

Perhaps the most important material for the modern dinghy builder is plywood, and so we will discuss this in some detail.

Plywood is made from veneers stripped from logs, usually by means of a huge knife which peels off a continuous roll. This roll of veneer is cut into sheets of the required size and alternate layers are glued together at right-angles to each other, nearly always with an odd number of plies. A large number of different types of timber are used in the manufacture of plywood, as can be seen from the list in Appendix H. Frequently different types of timber are used in the same sheet of plywood, the core being of a different material from the face veneers. There are various grades of face veneers, depending on whether they are matched on one side or both sides, or unmatched, or whether certain small defects or blemishes, such as knots and shakes, are permitted. Obviously a builder who is going to have his boat painted rather than varnished need not buy expensively matched face-veneer plywood; he can very well do with a lower grade of plywood and can tolerate defects in the facing.

The thickness of the veneers can vary from about 1 mm. to about 4 mm., but for the normal boatbuilding plywood veneers of 1 to 2 mm. are usual. Thus three veneers are used in plywood up to 6 mm. in thickness, though some 6-mm. plywood will also have five veneers. Five-ply is used from about 6-mm. to about 10-mm. plywood, and thicker sizes have more veneers. There is almost always an odd number of veneers and the two outer plies are usually thinner than the core plies. With the thinner sizes of plywood it is important that the total thickness of the veneers running in one direction is approximately equal to the total thickness of the veneers running in the opposite direction, so that resistance to warping and twisting is maintained. There is, however, a type of ply with veneers of equal thickness which is designed to allow easier bending to gentle compound curves.

For boatbuilding purposes plywood is almost always bent into some form of curvature. Normal plywood will take a single curvature quite well and will usually curve better in the direction across the face grain than along it. Cross-grained plywoods with the face grain running at right-angles to the longer length of the sheet can be obtained if required. Also special plywoods with the core running at other angles than 90 degrees to the face can be obtained to enable special curves to be accommodated. Plywood will not normally accommodate double curvatures, and thus designers have to be careful to avoid compound curves in the panels of their boats. However, the effect of double curvature can sometimes be obtained in boatbuilding by making saw-cuts and then by reinforcing after the curve has been made with a backing piece behind the cut. It can be seen therefore that the cheap single-chine dinghies with only two panels a side can have only a limited range of shapes. The modern tendency towards double- or even treble-chine plywood boats enables a much wider range of hull shapes to be obtained, and consequently better handling qualities. Plywood can also be used in glued-clinker construction to produce a very strong hull which can follow very closely almost any compound shape used in dinghy hull design.

STANDARDS

There are various British Standards covering plywoods. One is known as B.S.1088, and to comply with this the maker's name, the thickness and an identification number have to be stamped on one corner. Also if any gaboon-type wood is used in the plywood this word has to be used also. Unless builders know exactly what they are doing in ordering differently they would be well advised to stick only to plywood conforming to the British Standard No. B.S.1088 or 4079.

However, the most important consideration from the amateur boatbuilder's viewpoint with regard to plywood is the method of bonding and hence the type of adhesive used.

Interior-grade plywoods (INT), are usually glued with animal glues, such as blood albumen, casein, or soya, and these will not stand up to moisture, and furthermore are easily attacked by bacteria and will decompose. No interior grade of plywood should be used in any boatbuilding. The next grade of bonding is moisture resistant (MR). This uses Urea-Formaldehyde (UF) glues, and though it will stand up to prolonged soaking in water at normal temperatures, and immersion in boiling water for short periods, and is suitable for use under most normal conditions, it will certainly break down under continuous exposure to extreme weather conditions. The next grade is boil resistant (BR); this is glued with a new type of adhesive called Melamine-Formaldehyde (MF) glue, which has a better performance than the moisture-resistant adhesive. Plywood glued with this adhesive will be quite suitable for dinghy building. Finally there is the weather-and-boil-proof grade (WBP), which can either be glued with a Phenol-Formaldehyde (PF) glue or with a Resorcinol-Formaldehyde (RF) glue. These adhesives are extremely resistant to weather, and will stand up to long-term exposure without delaminating or breaking down in any way, and, in fact, the adhesive is more resistant than the timber.

Whilst any of the MR, BR, or WBP grades of adhesives are suitable for dinghies that are dry sailed, it is recommended that at least the BR grade, and preferably the WBP grades are used for all boatbuilding. It is very important also that whatever grade of adhesive is used the plywood should conform to the British Standard Number B.S. 1203 (1963), which controls the adhesive, because the manufacturers frequently mix a resin adhesive of high resistance with interior-grade adhesives of animal glue or blood-albumen or casein, in order to extend their resistance. In the table concerning the principal types of plywood the column on adhesives shows the type of resin or glue which is used, and the term "extended resin" means that a mixture of resin and some low-grade glue has been used together. Plywoods containing extended resin should not be used for dinghy building or for any exterior use.

Many of the boatbuilding plywoods are made from varieties of mahogany of from makore, or sapele, which are mahogany-type timbers. These two latter are very dense and hard and produce durable plywoods, but which are difficult to handle in boatbuilding. At the other end of the scale is gaboon, or okoume, as it is sometimes called, which is very light and easy to nail and glue, but comparatively soft and easy to dent. It will be seen that a good compromise can be obtained by using plywoods made from agba, seraya, meranti, or African mahogany, but be careful when selecting the latter, because many timber merchants call all reddish-coloured plywood African mahogany, when, in fact, it is probably makore, or utile, or one of the other much more dense and hard types. A good guide is the weight. It is suggested that

for dinghy building a good plywood should have a weight of from about 23 to 26 lb per 8 ft × 4 ft sheet in 6-mm. three-ply. Five-ply will be a little heavier because of the extra amount of glue. This represents a timber weight of 34 lb/ft^3 (544 kg/m^3).

There are one of two other points to watch out for when buying plywood; one is that you should avoid plywood with a very hard outer veneer and a soft core veneer. If moisture enters through cracks or through end-grain it can travel right up the core and is exceedingly difficult to dry out. Another point to watch is that there are no hollows in the core. You can see this by looking at the end grain of the core along the side of the sheet to see if the cores are butted closely together on assembly; if there are holes, do not accept that sheet. Note that plywood is measured in metric thicknesses, which do not correspond exactly with equivalent English sizes in most instances, for one can get a considerable variation in weight·by not allowing for this. Another point is that one side of a plywood sheet is almost always better than the other side. When the work is to be varnished it is worth remembering this and selecting the best side for the top. There is a special type of plywood available to order for centreboards and rudders with the laminations running with the grain at a smaller angle than 90 degrees to each other; this gives greater strength and less chance of a fracture across the grain, and is to be strongly recommended.

SOLID TIMBER

It will be useful for prospective amateur boatbuilders to know something about the structure and treatment of solid timber so that they can choose suitable materials from timber yards, and know how to make joints and use fastenings, and how best to glue parts together.

Timbers can be divided into two main headings; softwoods and hardwoods. Softwoods are not necessarily softer to the feel than some hardwoods. The difference is a botanical one, and there are quite substantial differences in structure. To the casual eye the two types can easily be distinguished when growing, because the softwoods are all conifers and have cones as fruits and needle-shaped or sometimes scale-like leaves, whereas the hardwoods are all deciduous and have broad flat leaves.

The construction of the trunk of a tree can be thought of roughly as being a tightly strapped bundle of very fine tubes. This is not strictly correct in that the tubes are not continuous, but are really bundles of shortish interlocking tubes with pointed ends. There is connection between these short tubes or fibres by means of pores in the walls. The short tubes in softwoods are much longer in proportion than those in hardwoods. Also they are arranged in a much more regular geometrical pattern in softwoods than they are in hardwoods. They are, in fact, arranged in radial rows. Hardwoods also contain a number of tubes running the whole way up the trunk and branches called vessels or pores, and these conduct the sap to the leaves. These pores can quite easily be seen with the naked eye or a low-powered magnifying-glass in most hardwoods, and are particularly prominent in some types of mahogany and cedar (Fig. 2.1).

If you cut a tree across you cannot fail to notice the radial rings which are the annual growth rings. These are caused by the fact that in the early spring the tree grows fastest and the walls of the cells are thinner, whereas in late summer they are thicker and finally stop altogether, causing the dense ring. Quick-growing trees will have more air space in them when they are dried out after seasoning and will thus be lighter and softer to the touch. There are also other groups of cells called rays, and the veneer-maker uses these to display figuring by cutting them so that the rays form patterns on the exposed surface. The function of the rays is really to store food and sometimes resin.

The usable part of a tree in which we are interested grows by means of the outer layer just under the bark forming new cells by division and thus in a year making one more growth ring. A growth ring consists of a large number of rows of cells. The growth layer is called the cambium. The cells on the inside of the cambium act as conductors for sap going up the tree, whilst the cells on the outside of the cambium conduct the foodstuffs from the leaves, travelling back down the trunk (Figs. 2.2, 2.3).

PROPERTIES OF TIMBER

When considering the strength of timber one is concerned with:

(a) *Bending*. The resistance to bending is particularly important in such parts as the spars.

(b) *Compression*. This force also acts on the spars, and the timber used must be capable of standing heavy loads.

(c) *Shear*. This force is seldom of a very high order in the parts of a boat, but applies

2.1
Pores in a mahogany-type timber. Notice the size of the pores compared with the screwhead. (Rogers, Finn.)

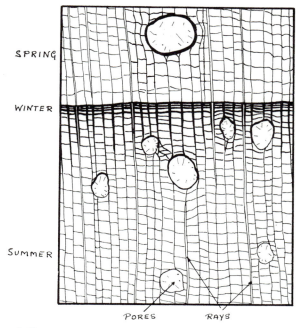

2.2

2.3

in a number of places, particularly at joints such as where the deck-beams are connected to the gunwale.

(*d*) *Hardness.* This quality is particularly needed in planking and decking and places where resistance to abrasions and heavy loads and knocks is needed.

(*e*) *Cleavage.* All parts of a boat need to be protected from splitting, and the advent of plywood and resin gluing has reduced the trouble caused by this fault.

(*f*) *Tensile Strength.* This is the resistance of the timber to being pulled apart in the direction of the grain. Most timbers are very strong in this direction, and it is not a great

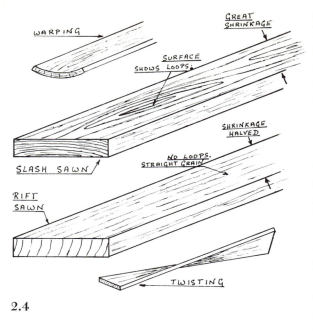

WARPING

GREAT
SHRINKAGE

SURFACE
SHOWS LOOPS.

SHRINKAGE
HALVED

SLASH SAWN

NO LOOPS.
STRAIGHT GRAIN

RIFT
SAWN

TWISTING

2.4

problem in boatbuilding, though it must be remembered that plywood is low in tensile strength compared to solid timber.

From the information given in the tables on pages 218–221 it will be fairly easy to pick a suitable timber for the purpose required. In general the timbers of higher density with a higher weight per cubic foot will be harder and resist bending and all the other forces except possibly cleavage. However, where lightness and flexibility and extra resistance to bending coupled with light weight are needed, it will obviously pay in general to use a softwood, because of the greater effect of the longer fibres in the timber which resist fracture due to bending stress. Thus, spars are usually

made of softwood. Another consideration will be water soakage, which will be less for the more dense hardwoods than the more open and porous softwoods. Therefore one will usually use a denser, harder wood where it is to be immersed for most of its life.

CONVERSION OF TIMBER

Growing timber usually contains a considerable amount of free water in the cell walls as moisture in the form of sap inside the cells. The first requirement for the timber converter is to remove the free water, which will evaporate quite quickly. After this the seasoning proper starts, and it is a highly skilled job.

Timber can be seasoned by stacking it under cover, or it can be dried in a kiln under controlled temperature. By and large, hardwood needs to be seasoned more slowly than softwood, and if the open-air method is used it is usual to start stacking hardwood in the autumn, so that it has the cool or cold winter in which to dry slowly, whereas softwood can often be seasoned in the spring and summer.

The degree of seasoning is measured by the amount of moisture left in the timber and is expressed as a percentage of the dry weight. A normal moisture content for timber used for boatbuilding is about 15 per cent. Dry rot is liable to start if the moisture content gets higher than 20 per cent. The initial drying of logs can be rapid, and one often sees logs kept partly in water to keep them from drying out too quickly. The usual system after the initial drying is roughly to convert it into thick planks and to stack these planks with air gaps in between them, so that the moisture can evaporate evenly from all over the interior. Uneven seasoning causes shakes and cracks, which are familiar to anyone using rough and cheap timber.

Timber can be plain sawn, by which is meant that the log is sawn through from end to end in parallel planks, or it can be quarter sawn with a number of minor variations which leave the annual rings running more nearly perpendicular across the planks. It is essential for timber used for planking, especially in carvel boats, that quarter-sawn (or rift-sawn) timber is used, because the shrinkage across the board is about half that of plain-sawn boards (Fig. 2.4). The amount of shrinkage from a saturated growing tree to a plank made from that tree and seasoned to 15 per cent can be over half an inch per foot of width for a plain-sawn board, and about half this for a rift-sawn board, and so it can be seen that shrinkage is a major factor in considering the type of timber to be used. Timber hardly shrinks at all on the length of the grain, and plywood shrinks very little in either direction.

A further consideration for purchasers of timber for boatbuilding is the straightness of the grain. Usually one needs considerable strength from the lightest possible weight of timber, and thus straight grain is essential for all strength members in building a dinghy. For framing of hatches and bulkheads and deck beams where they are glued to bulkheads it is not essential to have straight-grain timber, because it is really only there to provide rigidity and a fixing for something else. The gluing will stop any fracture caused by short or cross grain. For spars it is absolutely essential to have straight grain, or masts and booms will

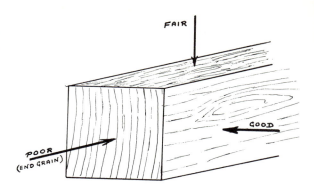

2.5
The relative holding power of screws according to the grain of the timber.

break immediately they are subjected to strain.

It is extremely important that all major pieces of timber are conditioned in the workshop of the boatbuilder after they have been obtained from the yard. This is particularly true of spruce and pine which are to be used for masts and spars, which are unsupported along their length by any other form of framing and therefore must remain straight and untwisted. It is recommended that the timber for making spars is obtained in solid baulks, partially converted, and stored for a period of at least a month before being broken down to the sizes in which they are finally to be used. Even then it is wise to leave the halves of a two-piece mast in the cut state for a couple of weeks to condition before being finally prepared and glued together. This will help to avoid the twisting and winding of spars after being made. Even after such careful treatment spars sometimes do take on a curve and these curves

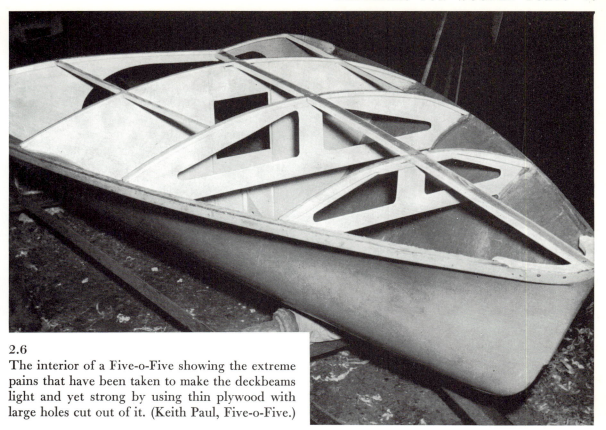

2.6
The interior of a Five-o-Five showing the extreme pains that have been taken to make the deckbeams light and yet strong by using thin plywood with large holes cut out of it. (Keith Paul, Five-o-Five.)

are extremely difficult to remove. Whereas a purchaser buying a spar from a spar-maker can reject a mast which is warped, it is very unfortunate for someone who has bought in just enough timber to make one mast only to find it taking on a severe twist after all the work has been expended. It is therefore very wise for builders to follow this conditioning advice as far as possible.

TIMBER TYPES

(See also Appendix I, p. 222)

The longitudinal pieces such as the chines, inwales, carlins, and the like can be of a light straight-grained timber such as spruce, pine or fir. Other timbers such as hemlock or mahogany or meranti can be used if desired. The main requirements for these parts are that the timber should be reasonably light, should take glue well and should be "clear" and free from knots and wavy grain. It must bend evenly without kinks and without the possibility of splitting.

The keel and hog are usually made from a harder timber, because more strength and resistance to water soakage and knocks are needed. Mahogany is suitable, or one of the mahogany-like timbers. Very hard timbers such as iroko and others should be avoided, because they are difficult to work to the required shape, and there is a good deal of planing needed here.

The frames for hard-chine boats are cut to shape and the planking is glued to them. Therefore nothing special is needed here. You can save a bit by using ordinary deal or pine, and knots will not matter as long as the timber is not too resinous. Similarly, where deck-beams are glued to bulkheads or frames there is no need to use anything special. For self-supporting deckbeams a clear timber is needed, and spruce is often used. Sometimes web-beams are made out of plywood with holes cut out of it to lighten it (Fig. 2.6).

The centreboard case will need a good-quality durable plywood or a solid timber such as mahogany. Thwarts and other brightwork can be of mahogany. For contrast, if the decks are to be varnished, one can use a white timber with an attractive grain such as syca-more. Rubbing bands are best made in rock-elm, as it is tough and stringy. Mahogany is not suitable, as it is too soft and looks terrible after a few knocks have caused water to enter and discolour the wood. Ash or oak can be used, but rock-elm is best. Rock-elm should also be used for timbers or ribs in carvel or clinker construction. It steams to shape well

and remains tough, whereas oak or ash tend to get brittle with age.

Rock-elm can be used for laminated parts such as the stem, deck knees and transom knees. Also it can be used to make very attractive and strong lifting handles.

All these timbers can be obtained through the boatbuilder's timber merchants who advertise in the yachting press. Most big timber yards hold stocks of timbers suitable for boatbuilding, and they can be visited and the timber inspected. If you bear in mind the purpose for which the timber is required you can often select a suitable type, even if it is of unfamiliar name.

GLUES

The next item is fastenings. Glue is used a great deal now for boatbuilding. It has the advantage that if the joint is well made there need be no other fastening at all, and thus one great source of introduction of water to the timber is avoided. Also there will be no cracks between parts in which water can lodge. A glued joint also spreads the bond over a wide area, but it is worth remembering, when deciding on a method of jointing, that the joint is only as strong as the surface of the wood. Though most glues are stronger than the wood, ultimate failure can often be seen to have been caused by the top surface of the wood tearing off. It is therefore sometimes worth while backing up a glued joint with a rivet if sudden heavy shocks are anticipated.

Two of the main types used nowadays are; the resorcinol and the urea glues. The former is usually a dark reddish-brown in colour and for the amateur has the disadvantage of costing more. It has to be mixed with a hardener before use. Urea glues are colourless, or nearly so, and can be had in powder or treacle form and can be either of the one-shot type, which will start to set off as soon as water is added to the powder, or of the separate application type which needs a hardener to be applied to one surface whilst the glue is applied to the other.

Cascamite One-Shot is an example of the former and Aerolite 300 is an example of the latter.

One occasionally gets failures in gluing operations, and it is sometimes difficult to pin down the reasons. One cause of failure is that the timber is too waxy or oily. The main timbers under this heading are teak, cedar and pitch-pine. It is sometimes necessary to wipe the prepared surfaces with a degreasing agent immediately before gluing. In my experience the resorcinol glues are more successful on teak than the urea.

Another cause of failure is too high a moisture content in the timber. It is strongly recommended that you buy in your timber well in advance and leave it in a dry, but not hot, place to condition for a few weeks. This particularly applies to spruce that is to be used for spars, for which this treatment is essential after they have been rough cut to nearly the right sizes.

Failures can also be caused by trying to short cut this operation by applying excessive heat during the curing period of the glue. It is necessary to glue in a temperature of not less than 45°F., and preferably about 65°F. for urea glues, and not less than 65°F. for the resorcinol. If you have to apply heat to get the temperature above 45°F., make sure that it is not too severe. Excessive heat can cause the timber to dry out and crack, and can cause the glue joint to crack also. A fan heater under canvas or polythene cover is quite a good way of distributing the heat.

I used to use the separate-application type of glue, but I eventually put several otherwise unexplained failures down to the inaccuracies of applying the liquid hardener to one surface. I found that if one wetted the surface too much then the glue from the other surface was unable to penetrate the already soaked wood and a failure resulted. Another disadvantage of this type is the staining of the timber that the acid hardener can cause. This is particularly marked on oak. Finally I transferred to one-shot glues and have had less trouble.

The operation of gluing is very simple, and failures are usually only rare. One can rely on the joints considerably if they are well made. They should fit well. Many of the glues are advertised as gap-filling, but this is only relative. When I started using them in my ignorance I thought that they would fill gaps of one-eighth of an inch. This is not so. They all contract on setting, and this will break the bond on a gap as wide as that. Some makers say that one-twentieth of an inch is the maximum. I would say that even this is risky. For the amateur builder I would say that you must take great care to fit the joints well.

One mixes the glue to a treacly consistency. Too thin and it will run out of the joint when pressure is applied, and if too thick it will not spread over the whole joint and may form lumps in places. Do not apply too much pressure, but an extra half-turn of the clamps

2.7

2.8

2.9

Three stages in the construction of a laminated lifting handle. Fig. 2.7 shows the various component parts, consisting of a plywood former, two pieces of rock-elm veneer, and a specially cut piece of scrap plywood which will be used for holding the cramp head. This is nailed to the bottom of the former, which will itself form the core of the handle. Fig. 2.8 shows the veneers glued in place and held by six "G" cramps. Fig. 2.9 shows the finished lifting handle in place on the stem. (Finn.)

may be worth while when the glue has gelled.

Spread the glue as rapidly and as evenly as possible. A broad knife or a rag tied to a bit of stick will help here. It is often best to apply glue very thinly to both surfaces to make sure it is well rubbed into the grain, and this is essential on oak and other dense surfaces. As well as double spreading for hardwoods and other dense surfaces it is essential to allow a few minutes for the glue to soak into the grain on hardwoods. Otherwise the cramping operation might squeeze out most of the glue and a starved joint would result.

It is always worth while to do a dummy run of the cramping operation before the glue is applied. It is surprising what a mess one can get into with the simplest-seeming gluing job. The cramps may not be big enough, or one hasn't got a piece of packing timber of the right thickness, or the joint slips and needs to be pegged temporarily. Time slips by, and before you know where you are the glue has started to gel and you either have to leave it as it is or take the whole thing to pieces and start again (Figs. 2.7, 2.8, 2.9). Scarfed joints need particular care to see they are properly pegged so that they cannot slip when under pressure. Other points to note are that it is not feasible to use resorcinol glues in temperatures under 65°F. Local heat almost always has to be applied for safety. Also, the label on the glue package will give the usable life of the mix once the hardener or water is added. This means the life in the pot. Once the glue is spread the surfaces must be brought into contact before the glue has skinned in the case of resorcinol glues, and before the glue has started to gel in the case of urea glues. This is of the order of ten to fifteen minutes for the former, and twenty to forty minutes for the latter depending on the air temperature. The pressure time for cramping should be double the "usable life" time for the prevailing temperature.

Liquid resorcinol glue is soluble in methylated spirit and urea glue is dissolved in water. Do remember to clean off excess glue before it sets hard. It is extremely difficult to remove when hard and can make preparation for varnishing impossible.

Cascamite has a rapid hardener that can be used with it if a quick result is essential. The C.I.B.A. glues, Aerolite and Aerodux, have separate application hardeners of varying speed of action.

Example:

Cascophen resorcinol glue: usable life of mix

Temperature	60°F.	70°F.	80°F.	90°F.
Pot life in hours	8–10	$3\frac{3}{4}$	$1\frac{3}{4}$	$\frac{1}{2}$
Bring surfaces together within these periods	25 min	15 min	10 min	5 min
Apply pressure before	60 min	45 min	20 min	15 min

Cascamite One-Shot glue: usable life of mix

Temperature	50°F.	60°F.	70°F.
Pot life in hours	9	3	1
Bring surfaces together before	30 min	25 min	20 min
Pressure time in hours	18	6	$2\frac{1}{2}$

Full information is given with the materials.

There are some other useful glues for boatbuilders including the so-called "woodworking glue". This is a ready mixed resin based whitish liquid which is spread thinly on the surface, or rubbed into both surfaces in the case of hard woods. The surfaces are clamped in the usual way and the joint has to be completed within about 5 minutes.

The glue is soluble in water before setting and so excess can be wiped off with a damp rag. It changes from white to transparent when it has cured. It is not so durable as a urea glue but is reasonably waterproof and could be used for all the less vital joints in dinghy building if well protected. I would not advise its use on boats which are left exposed or afloat.

On the other hand Epoxide glues such as Araldite are extremely durable and also have very good adhesive properties, even on difficult materials such as glass and metals. Their disadvantages are their cost and the long period of setting and building up to full strength. Some heat is usually needed to assist a good cure.

They come in two parts which have to be mixed thoroughly before application. Clean off the excess on the job and on tools before setting as it is extremely difficult to remove when hard.

There is a type of rapid setting epoxy which is very popular with home handymen and model makers. It starts setting in 5 minutes and is hard shortly afterwards. In my experience it is nowhere near so reliable in its adhesive qualities or durability as the standard Epoxide glue but it can be extremely useful on occasions to have a really rapid waterproof result. Very thorough mixing is essential as is the degreasing of non-porous surfaces with a liquid such as carbon-tetrachloride.

SCREWS AND NAILS

While we are on the subject of fastenings, I must say a word about screws and nails. Brass screws are used a great deal by the amateur boatbuilder. They are pretty expensive, though, and it is surprising how many boxes you will use when fixing the planking of a chine hull.

Moreover, brass reacts with mahogany and some other timbers and can cause local areas of disintegration round the screws in time. Screws are also the sources of entry of water into plywood, and so I advise that as few as possible are used.

I can recommend that "Anchorfast" or similar nails be used wherever possible. They are quicker to insert and hold just as well as screws for permanent fastening points. They are made with serrated shanks which grip the timber firmly. Screws need only be used in places where the "screwdown" action is needed to get the joint tight, such as occurs at the stem where the plywood is under stress. For areas that are very lightly stressed brass panel pins can be used. One-inch by 15-gauge is a useful size.

At some time you will have to decide whether to glue the centreboard case to the hog or to bed it in some sealing material. If the centreboard case is to be fixed to the hog before the planking is laid, then it is comparatively easy to get at it, and the joint can be made accurately. For the amateur it will be found quite easy to glue it in at this stage. If, on the other hand, it has to be fixed after the shell is completed, it is not quite so easy to see whether you have made a good joint, and bedding in mastic will be easier. Actually, there is another reason why bedding in mastic is likely to be more satisfactory. There is considerable sideways strain on the case, and this is quite likely to break a glued seam eventually. Future leaking could be forestalled by bedding properly in the first place rather than gluing. If the case is to be bedded it will be necessary to use rather more screws, because these will be the only actual fastenings. It will also be as well to use gunmetal screws in this position. Brass reacts with salt water and crystallizes, and the screws may snap in time. It is a damp part of the boat, and so it will pay to be a little more careful.

Do please drill holes for both nails and screws. Strictly, one should drill twice for screws. Once for the shank and a smaller hole for the thread. As this is a book for amateurs I can let you into a secret, and this is that, except in extreme cases, such as when preparing a hole for a very large screw or in very hard wood, I never drill twice, but always use quite a small pilot drill in soft timber, and a drill about the size of the shank beneath the thread for harder timber, and have never had any trouble yet. Panel pins need no holes, but copper nails do.

Also, on screws: I do not recommend using round-head screws, because the slot is of such a shape that it is very easy for the driver to slip and tear it off. Also it is very often quite difficult to remove an old round-head screw. Use raised-head screws instead. They have a head half-way between a round-head and a counter-sunk head and make a very neat job. Another point to remember is the danger of electrolysis between dissimilar metals. Never use brass or copper next to aluminium. Even the allegedly inactive stainless steel is not so when in contact with aluminium. It is better to use chromium-plated screws on aluminium track. Stainless bolts can cause aluminium to split. Watch out for this point in your rigging and your metal masts.

You may need to use some rivets. Copper nails with roves can be used. When riveting

the ends over the roves, cut the nail nearly level and tap lightly with a light hammer. Put a dolly under the head—this can often be the head of a heavy hammer. If heavy blows are made when hardening up you will merely bend the nail in the centre, and this will gradually straighten later and loosen the joint. For a lightly loaded joint, or where the nail is merely holding the timber while gluing, one can cut the nail point off and tap the end over into the grain of the timber. This makes a flush finish and it will be far easier to scrape and repaint later in the boat's life (Fig. 2.10).

This is about all that will be needed when building the hull. We will come to fittings and paint later in the book.

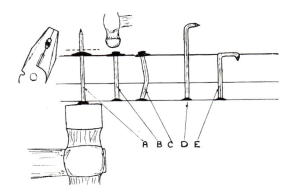

2.10
When riveting copper nails, the roves can be knocked down with a pair of pliers. The rove is usually a driving fit on the nail (A). Use a heavy hammer or dolly on the nail-head and tap lightly with a light ball-headed hammer to rivet over the end (B). Cut off the nail about its own diameter above the rove. Do not rivet too hard or you will bend the nail (C). Nails can also be clenched in the manner shown at D and E.

3 *Techniques in Boatbuilding*

THE reader should have a fair idea from Chapter 1 of how the shape of the hull of the boat is obtained and how the actual hulls are constructed by the various methods available in a very general way. We are now going to consider various special points found in building hulls by various methods and the best ways of dealing with them.

Necessarily this chapter will be concerned with many different types of hull construction, because certain methods are used in constructing parts of boats under all the systems which we are considering. Thus, spiling is a method used for getting the shapes of the moulded strips in a moulded hull and for getting the shape of the edges of planks in hard-chine hull, and also for obtaining the shapes of bulkheads fitted into any sort of hull. Similarly, the scarfing process is used in many parts of all types of boats.

SPILING

Spiling is a method of obtaining the shape of a curve, such as, for instance, when one is cold moulding by the strip veneer method and wants to fit the edge of the next strip tight against a strip which is already tacked down. One method of laying up the veneers for cold moulding is somewhat as follows, though there are variations. One can tack down parallel-sided veneers, usually at an angle of about 45 degrees to the keel, leaving gaps in between each veneer of approximately the same width as the veneer. Thus if one was using 2-in. wide veneers one would leave gaps between each

alternate strip of not more than 2 in. Due to the curve of the shape of the hull the gap will actually be quite considerably narrower at the keel and the gunwale than it is at the turn of the bilge. The problem is to fit new veneers into these gaps so that they are a tight fit.

A method of doing this is by spiling in the following way. One tacks down lightly the new veneer alongside the edge to which it is desired to fit so that it is touching this edge at at least two points. This will mean that, if the edge of the new veneer is straight originally, there will be a gap of up to $\frac{1}{2}$ in at the middle. One now gets a small block of wood or hardboard about the same width as the largest gap, and by running this along the edge of the already fixed veneer, and holding a pencil against the opposite side, a tracing of the correct curve is transferred on to the new veneer. By cutting along this line it will be found that the edge will then fit exactly (Fig. 3.1). It is quite a simple matter to untack the new veneer, move it over and then spile the opposite side. With a little adjustment with the plane one should be able to get a very tight fit indeed.

Another method of cold moulding is to start in the middle of the hull with a single diagonal strip and then work steadily from this to the end, which means that one only spiles one side of each veneer. The advantage of the former method is that the strips remain largely parallel to each other, whereas with the second method they can very easily get slightly and progressively at a greater angle to the centre

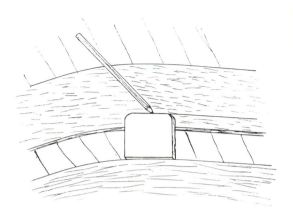

3.1

A method of obtaining the shape for a veneer to fit in between two already fastened veneers in one method of cold moulding. A suitably sized block of wood is run along one edge of a fixed veneer and a pencil held against the other edge transfers a parallel line.

3.3

A method of obtaining the final close fit of the bottom plank against a rebate in the hog. The block of wood runs against the edge of the rebate and the point of a nail underneath the block transfers a scribing line to the plank. This line is parallel to the edge of the rebate. (Chippendale, 12-ft National.)

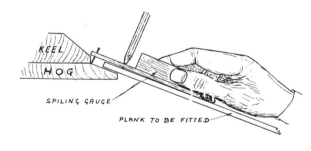

3.2

Another method of spiling the curve for the garboard plank where one cannot obtain a roughly close fit by other methods first. This method is useful for hard-chine boats. The pencil point passes through a hole in the gauge.

one, which though not harmful can look unsightly, especially if this is done on the outer skin of a hull to be varnished (see also Chapter 4).

The fitting of the bottom planking of a hard-chine boat where it has to lie in tight against a rabbet in the keel can also be done by spiling, in the way shown in the diagram (Fig. 3.2). The principle is the same. In the same way the fitting of a bulkhead or frame into

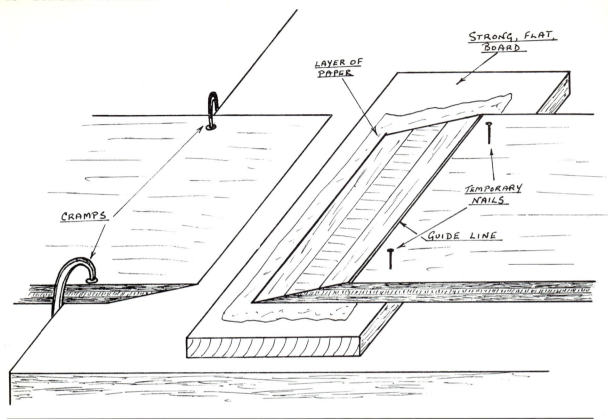

an existing hull can be done by spiling also.

There are many occasions in boatbuilding where spiling is the only method of getting a reasonably accurate fit quickly (Fig. 3.3).

SCARFING

It is frequently necessary to make pieces of wood up to a length which is unobtainable in standard sizes. One also frequently does not want unsightly lumps spanning the joint and therefore butt-strap jointing cannot be used.

The method of making these long lengths is usually by scarfing. In this way full-length panels to plank a 15-ft or 16-ft boat can be made up from standard 8 ft × 4 ft sheets of plywood, scarfed together, and also stringers can be made full length by scarfing two or more pieces. Masts also frequently need lengths of timber to be scarfed up to obtain the required full-length mast.

The diagrams (Figs. 3.4, 3.5) show how plywood is scarfed, and though great care is needed it is basically a simple operation, and

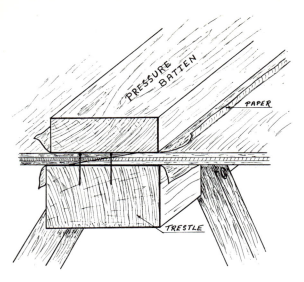

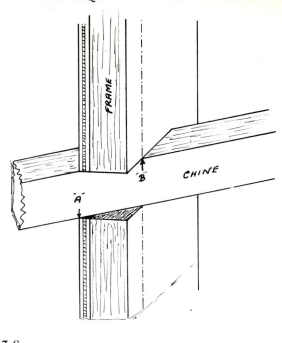

◄ 3.4, 3.5 ▲

Two stages in the operation of scarfing plywood sheets together. The faces must be absolutely flat and the pieces must be pinned together temporarily to stop them sliding over each other when pressure is applied.

3.6

anyone with sharp tools ought to be able to make a successful joint. The scarfing of other sizes and shapes of timber is basically exactly the same. The length of the scarf should be six to eight times the thickness of the plywood. Somewhat less is permissible using solid timber. The main things to remember about scarfing are to get the surfaces absolutely flat and the edges absolutely square, so that the faces of the joints meet evenly all over. Secondly, it is essential to pin the two pieces down so that they cannot slide over each other under pressure. Great pressure is not needed,

but it is essential to see that it is distributed evenly, otherwise there will be areas of dry joint where the glue has been squeezed out and failure may result. Though the angle of the scarf can be steeper when using solid timber, the length should never be less than four times the thickness of the timber.

FAIRING-IN

Another problem which crops up with all boats is that of fairing-in. This means correcting the angles and bevels of moulds and frames, so that the planking lies exactly across them and tightly down on to them. With glued construction it is particularly essential that the planks should lie tight to the frames and other members to which they need to be glued. It is essential when setting up a mould for making a hull, whether it be hard chine or round bilge, that the correct side of the frame or mould is used to measure from, and that the opposite side should be facing in the right direction. For instance, frames farther forward than the widest part of the boat should have their measured side the aftermost one, then one can fair off the corner on the fore side to match up with the lines. Similarly, frames aft of the widest point should have their measured side as the forward side, and then one can fair in by shaving off the after outer corner. The drawing (Fig. 3.6) will explain this more clearly. The measured side of the frame is the side marked A, so that when one lets in a chine or stringer which has eventually to finish up by being flush so that the planking lies tight to it and is glued to it and the frame, one has to bevel off the frame to the line B. Obviously if one had measured the frame as being the opposite corner to A, then the corner marked A would lie below the surface of the chine, and, of course, one would not be able to glue to the face of the chine as well as the frame. This is a point that must be remembered when setting up frames for building hulls.

Another easily forgotten point is that the bevel on frames is different at the top from that elsewhere because of the variation of curvature in the section and the amount of flare. Therefore one must be careful when fairing-in, and lay battens across the frames in the same direction as the planking is running and also at right-angles, to check that the bevel on the edge of the frames is correct in all positions. It is these bevels which cause some of the main errors in amateur boat-building. The idea is not difficult to understand, but it is frequently forgotten, and this is where the inaccuracies creep in. Essential equipment for correct fairing-in consists of straight-edges sufficient to span the distance between chine and keel, and chines and gunwale, where the planking is flat between the two points (Fig. 7.12, p. 98), and battens of knot-free material for laying along the length of the boat across the frames for fairing-in the supports for the long curved surfaces.

When fairing-in a fully built up mould for a moulded or fibre-glass boat, one will need light and flexible battens to try the fairness in all directions, both longitudinally and at an angle to the centreline as well as vertically. Fairing-in one of these moulds takes quite a time, and the whole finish of the hull can be spoilt by planing off too much and producing a "flat"; one needs to use a long plane for fairing-in built up moulds of this sort (see also Chapter 7).

REBATING AND JOGGLING

One does not normally need to use a rebate plane except on clinker hulls. Here one needs to rebate the last eight inches or so of one edge of each plank at each end, so that when the planks come together at the stem and the transom they lie flat and smooth together. There is also a method of joggling the planks at the transom so that they continue in a series of steps in the same way as they have along the rest of the hull (Fig. 3.7). The series of photos (5.23, etc., on page 81) shows how

3.7
Clinker planks joggled into the transom provide one method of dealing with this type of construction. (Chippendale, 14-ft Merlin.)

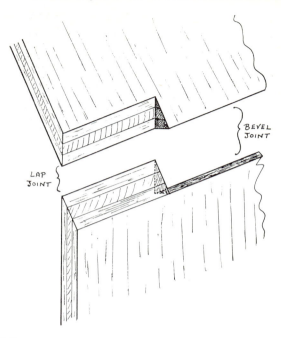

3.8

the rebate plane and chisel are used to make a progressively deeper rebate until it nearly breaks through the plank thickness at the stem. Care is needed to make this joint accurate and tight. A batten clamped or tacked along the plank the width of the rebate away from the edge will help to guide the plane. A groove made with a tenon saw can also help.

Joggling is needed near the bow of a hard-chine hull where the change of angle between the bottom and the next plank becomes too flat to be accommodated by the normal lap-joint. There has to be a change from a lap joint to a bevel joint somewhere near the bow,

and the drawing shows how this is accomplished (Fig. 3.8; see also Chapter 7).

CRAMPING

Another operation which has to be done in all forms of boatbuilding is cramping. One cannot have too many cramps, and the most useful size is the 6-in. cramp. One sometimes needs 2-in., 3-in., or 4-in. cramps, and one or two of these ought to be stocked, but one can usually do even the smaller jobs with the large 6-in. cramps (Fig. 3.9). It is quite a help sometimes to have large sash cramps, or cramp heads, for

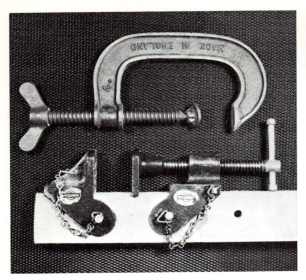

3.11
Gluing a breasthook into an International Fourteen. Strips of veneer and offcuts of timber are used to distribute the pressure of the cramp head. (Souter, International Fourteen.)

3.9
Two types of cramp in common use. The upper type is an ordinary metal "G" cramp which has a universally jointed pressure pad on the screw. Below are a pair of cramp heads which can be fitted on to a suitable piece of timber at any distance apart.

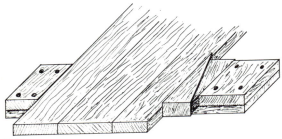

3.10
This shows how a jig for gluing together boards to make up a great width can be made. This method is sometimes used in the making of solid teak rudder and centreboard blades.

3.12
Here a thick piece of offcut timber is used to distribute the pressure over the whole area of the scarf. (Rogers, International Finn.)

3.13
These simple wooden cramps are easily made up and are not nearly so heavy as the metal "G" cramps for fixing planking. Arranged vertically like this, they have no twisting effect. (Chippendale, 16-ft Fireball.)

---

cramping together wide boards, but one can usually get away with making up a cramp out of timber and wedges in the infrequent cases when one needs to use a wide cramp (Fig. 3.10).

The main thing to remember about cramping operations, which almost always involve gluing, is to do a dummy run before the final operation. It is also essential to put packing pieces under the heads and feet of cramps where they are in contact with soft wood or parts of the boat which are nearly finished (Figs. 3.11, 3.12). They can cause considerable dents in the timber which are impossible to remove. When a gluing operation is under way it is also very well worth while tacking the parts temporarily together with panel pins which can be removed later, otherwise the parts will tend to slide about, and, before you are ready to screw up the cramps finally, the glue will have started to gel and it will be too late. When gluing up spars one really needs a cramp every foot, but one can sometimes get away with a wider spacing if one uses a backing piece of another sort of timber, and one can also make up temporary cramps for light work out of pieces of scrap plywood and wedges.

When cramping up a glued joint do not screw down one end of the joint hard and then continue along to the next cramp, screwing that hard, and on to the end. It is much better to screw all the cramps down lightly first, and then gradually take up half a turn on each until they are tight. It is also necessary to remember that the mixing of the glue is not always very accurately done, and in a case where it has been mixed a little on the weak side it will be very easy to squeeze it all out of the joint before it has time to gel. Therefore do not screw down the cramps too hard at first. After the glue has had time to gel and before it has time to set hard it might be advisable to give the cramps another half-turn. Remember the cramps are quite heavy and when one has a small object festooned with perhaps ten or a dozen cramps, it can weigh quite a considerable amount (Fig. 2.8, p. 40). If this weight is all on one side, it could twist an item such as a boom so that when it is taken out of the cramps the following day it could have a warp caused by this unequal weight. So make sure that the weight of the cramps is evenly distributed or otherwise supported (Figs. 3.13, 3.14).

LAMINATING

This is a very useful technique in boatbuild-ing. One often needs a structural member of peculiar shape which sometimes even follows double curvatures. The strongest and fre-

3.14

Various possible ways of making up wooden cramps out of scrap plywood and coach-bolts and wedges. They can easily be made for special purposes in the workshop.

3.15
A curved inner stem is being laminated up on a mould and cramped in place with coach-bolts and metal straps. (Souter.)

3.16
Here the keel and hog for a Flying Fifteen is being laminated out of several thicknesses of mahogany. A large number of cramps is needed to distribute pressure evenly. (Chippendale.)

quently the simplest way of making the part is to laminate it out of veneer strips. This technique can be used for making the curved inner stem (Fig. 3.15), fixing rails for bulkheads, lifting handles (Figs. 2.7, 2.8, 2.9, p. 40), knees (Fig. 10.51, p. 160), breast-hooks (Fig. 10.3, p. 141), cockpit coamings (Fig. 10.33, p. 153), and many other parts.

Usually one needs a former round which to tack the strips with glue in between, but sometimes one can arrange to laminate *in situ* (Figs. 4.19, 4.20, p. 67). As always with any gluing job, it is essential to make a dummy run dry first, and to pin the strips into position so that they cannot slip. Cramping pressure can be obtained with ordinary "G" cramps, wedges, or bolts and battens, or even as in the case of the stem capping, on p. 67, by screws and pads (Fig. 3.16).

Of course, the cold-moulded method of hull construction as well as fibre-reinforced plastics system are both also forms of laminating. The method is extremely simple and very strong.

DOWELLING

This is a neat and simple way of finishing off screw-holes, though there is a disadvantage to doing it in some cases.

It consists of countersinking the screwhead well below the timber surface by making a recess with brace and bit, and then filling the neat cylindrical hole with a matching plug of similar timber glued in (Figs. 3.17, 3.18). If properly done the hole is hardly noticeable, but care must be taken to match the grain. The disadvantage is that the screw-head has to be countersunk so far below the surface

3.17, 3.18
Dowels inserted into screw-holes in timber. If the grain has been carefully matched when smoothed off and cleaned up, they should be almost unnoticeable. (Rogers and Chippendale.)

that in some cases a great deal of the strength of the fastening may be lost.

The alternatives to dowelling are to fill the hole with putty or similar material or to file the screw-head flush with the surface and then varnish it. Dowelling is the most trouble-free method, as it is completely watertight and the surface coating remains perfect.

You can buy dowelling in various types of timber and of various diameters, but you can trim up a piece of suitable wood with a chisel if you only have a few holes to do. Be careful to get the grain running in the right direction. When you have cut the plug, just put some glue in the hole and tap the dowel home. The surface is planed off flush when the glue is dry.

STEAMING

There is not a great deal of steaming needed in any form of small-boat building nowadays, but you may require steamed elm ribs in a dinghy, or you may find a difficult chine or stringer which will not bend into place any other way. Floors which used to be steamed are now laminated, and you can deal with many tricky problem curves by this method.

The simplest steaming equipment consists of a suitable length of drainpipe blocked at one end and propped at an angle over any convenient source of heat. A little water in the bottom of the pipe sufficient for the purpose is allowed to boil gently. The lengths of timber are pushed into the pipe with string attached if they are short. Cover the open end of the pipe with a rag and wait (Fig. 3.19).

Dinghy ribs up to say $\frac{3}{4}$ in. $\times$ $\frac{1}{2}$ in. will probably be ready in about fifteen minutes,

but a chine about an inch square may need an hour. Give plenty of time, since it is not easy to reinsert a half-bent piece of timber.

When you judge that the timber is well cooked, it must be taken out of the pipe and bent into position with the absolute minimum of delay. For this reason place the pipe as near the work as possible and have enough help to enable rapid and certain bending. You will probably also need gloves to handle the hot timber. If the timber breaks then the cooking time has not been long enough.

If you have time it is often possible to cramp the piece of wood to the desired shape on the bench and to leave it for some hours or days. When the cramps are removed it will remain bent and it is easier to screw in this condition than when hot.

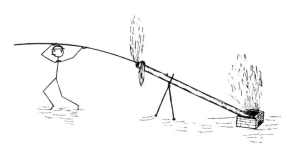

3.19

4 *Cold Moulding*

THIS is probably the neatest and strongest method of building a wooden boat. It can produce a really beautiful hull and is basically very simple to do; in fact in many ways it is the ideal method for amateurs to tackle. The main snag for the builder is boredom, for it can be a time-consuming method. At least three layers of veneer or strip ply will normally be needed to make most hulls, and the strips may well be no more than 3 in. wide. Thus the actual number of strips to be laid, together with the amount of fitting needed, makes this system a tedious one for the first-time builder.

Actually, there are a number of short cuts that can be employed to improve matters, and practice brings speed. If some helpers can be roped in, they can quickly be taught the simple operations, and one can then get on quite fast. There are also some new designs using only two skins of ply which can be built very quickly.

The main thing to guard against is that the seemingly endless repetition will cause the standard of work to fall off. This will show up with badly fitting veneers and edge gaps, and possibly badly stuck veneers and hollow areas.

The structural material needed falls into two types—strip veneer or strip ply. Veneer will be cheaper and can be obtained from specialist firms listed in the Appendix on p. 234. The use of ply may mean that less layers will be needed, but the shell could be a little heavier owing to the amount of extra glue. Also, owing to the extra stiffness of ply, one does not need a fully battened mould. One can leave inch gaps between the battens, because the ply will follow its own curvature quite easily. If one tried to build from thin veneers on a partially battened mould, one would not get proper adhesion, as there would be flat areas between the battens and it would be difficult to fair up the surface afterwards. Therefore the mould for veneer building needs to be more elaborate and carefully faired off (Fig. 4.1). Veneer comes in wide strip form and sometimes in random lengths (Fig. 4.2). With careful thought one can therefore arrange for the variations in length of strip required to be cut with little waste. Obviously with a diagonal lay-up the length of strip needed will be least at the bow and most around the point of maximum beam.

. If at all possible one should avoid having a break in any one strip. If it is unavoidable, then the ends of the butting strips should really be chamfered to some degree, especially if using ply.

For a painted hull it is easiest to use three diagonal layers—the outer one at the same angle as the inner, and the centre veneer at right-angles to these. If a varnished exterior is contemplated, then a fore-and-aft outer skin looks really good and has the added advantage of making it easier to get a fair surface without ridges and flats. The extra work involved in matching up veneers for length, colour and width, and the extra fitting, will mean that this skin will take a great deal longer to fix, but the final effect may be well worth the trouble. Note that for the outer skin plain butt-joints will be almost unnoticeable if the grain is carefully matched. Scarfed butts will be completely trouble-free, but the glue line will show more. The width of veneer needed can be varied over different parts of the hull. Obviously the wider the strip that can be put on, the less time needed per unit area. Beware of trying to be too economical, though; veneer is not very accommodating when it comes to going round double curves, and if too much is attempted there will be lifting edges that refuse to stay tacked down, and hollows will result. Also it will be impossible to spile the edges accurately.

A 14-ft boat will have a fair amount of curve to its sections, and it is probable that around 4 in. will be the widest strip that can be employed with safety, although, depending on the hull, one might be able to go as high as 6 in. Certain types of hull can be satisfactorily planked in a rather different way, which, if care is taken, can show a great saving in time. I have seen Flying Dutchman hulls which use one layer of 3- or 4-mm. three-ply and one layer of 2- or 3-mm. veneer. In this case the

4.1 ▲

A solid mould for the construction of a cold-moulded International Finn. (Rogers, Finn.)

4.2 ►

What the veneers look like when they come from the supplier. They must be sorted into lengths and those with any uneven grain will have to be discarded or used for small odd corners. (Souter.)

hull is very long (nearly 20 ft) and very flat, with only a gradual change of shape. The hull was planked with the inner ply skin in wide strips from keel to gunwale, arranged at right-angles to the keel, and with the outer plies parallel to the keel. Due to the very small fore and aft curve of the hull, wide strips of around 12 to 15 in. in width could be used. The outer single layer of veneer can be laid fore and aft or at a diagonal angle. In each case the strips can be up to 6 in. wide. The main points to watch are that the strips are stuck over their whole width, and that no hollows are left. I cannot say that I like this system greatly. It would seem that the saving in time could well be offset by the difficulty in handling such large floppy strips and in the uncertainty of getting a sound bond over the whole strip. A double skin lay-up cannot be so strong as one of three or more skins, and there is also the possibility of pinhole leaks where the strips cross. The three-layer diagonal system is very simple and foolproof, provided steady care is taken. Once the mould is built anyone could make a good job of the lay-up.

When making a mould for cold moulding a hull some thought should be given to short cuts in fixing interior joinery. Arrangements should also be made for letting the hog and stem into the mould so that the skin can be stuck to them *in situ* (Fig. 4.3).

The hog is simple, in that it merely means notching the frames so that a suitable-sized piece of timber can be let in and then bevelled off flush with the mould surface (Fig. 4.4).

The construction of the solid mould needed is somewhat different from that required for clinker, or carvel hulls, in that allowance must

4.3
This mould has been constructed so that the stem and the hog can be let into notches built into it, and then fastened down. The outer faces of the stem and hog are then faired off smooth so that they match into the outer surface of the mould. The veneers are glued to the faces of the stem and the hog, which then come off with the shell when it is lifted out. (Rogers, Finn.)

4.4
The transom and hog fixed into the mould. (Rogers, Finn.)

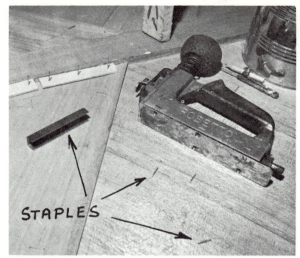

4.5
Hand stapling machines must be carefully chosen. Some of them are worked semi-automatically and can hammer the staples in far too hard, and they are thus driven below the surface of the timber and are difficult to remove. Make sure that the machine will take staples long enough for the particular veneer you are using. (Souter.)

4.6
The ply strip and panel pin system is probably best for heavy veneers and where there is a fair amount of pressure needed to hold the veneer down. Odd strips of ply are better than odd pieces of veneer for this purpose, because they do not split. Ordinary cheap indoor-grade plywood can be used. (Souter.)

be made when marking out the frames, not only for the skin thickness, but also for the thickness of the battens which are to form the surface of the mould. The battens should be thick enough to take the full depth of the staples or pins used for tacking down the veneers, and should be light enough to bend easily round the frames. It must also be remembered that some planing of the mould surface will be necessary to fair up minor irregularities, and thus $\frac{3}{4}$ in. $\times$ 1 in. batten might be a good

size for a 14-ft boat. Knot-free timber is needed for the battens or trouble will be experienced with flats and kinks in the surface caused by uneven bending.

Moulds will be battened fore and aft and thus there will be not much difficulty in allowing for structural members such as bottom rails of buoyancy tanks and floor-stiffening stringers to be let in. Make sure when planning the recesses for structural members such as those mentioned that it will still be possible to lift the completed shell off the mould. The stringers situated on or near the flat part of the bottom will cause no trouble, but those on the sides may cause too much difficulty in enabling them to clear the mould when lifted vertically upwards. The shell will be fairly flexible and once it has been started off the mould a certain amount of prising can be done, but not much. One does not want to have to start breaking up the mould from the inside to get the shell clear, when a little thought and preparation would have avoided trouble.

One cannot normally build the inwale into the mould because of this difficulty of lifting off. However, it is well worth considering building the shell without the transom and fitting this later. This will allow one to spring the shell a great deal more when removal from the mould is tricky because of fouling the built-in stringers or of tumblehome to the sections.

One of the most important of the small points to watch out for is that no glue can seep through and stick the shell to the mould. For this reason it is essential to lay paper or cellophane over the mould before tacking down the first layer. It could be a complete disaster if the shell were to stick to the mould. You might have to destroy the mould to get the hull off.

There are two main methods of fixing the strips. You can either use a stapling machine, as in Fig. 4.5, or you can tack with strips of ply and pins (Fig. 4.6). Each method has its points. Stapling is quicker and easier, but you must get a machine which will punch in large enough staples. If the veneer you are using is thin enough or flexible enough, the stapling method will probably be the best. If, however, your timber needs firm pressure to bend to the required curve, you may have to use the pin-and-ply method at least at the sheer and keel, and also at other points where you are a bit doubtful. The ply pads spread the pressure over a wide area, and the pins hold more firmly. Briefly, where only finger-light pressure is needed to hold the strips tight, then stapling is sufficient, otherwise use pins and ply. There is a snag to the use of staples on their own—if you possess a powerful tacking machine. It may drive the staples in so deeply that they will be difficult to remove later. Thus it might be best to use thin ply or even cardboard strips under the staples, as in Fig. 4.7. Staples are probably best in the end, because the holes they leave are so small that if the finished and faired-up hull is swabbed down with hot water, they will mostly close up and disappear. A tedious filling job will then be largely avoided.

Most mahogany or mahogany-like timbers are satisfactory for veneering. The grain must be even and straight. Try bending a sample across and along the grain to see if it will cope with the curves involved in your design. If you choose African mahogany be careful to inspect the grain; some is too wavy for easy veneering. The tendency for timber to warp is not important in veneering. The strips are flexible and when glued in place will be unable to warp. Meranti is a possibility, but watch out for the weight. It can vary tremendously in density from tree to tree. Aim at something between 32 and 38 lb per cubic foot. Soft timbers are very easy to lay-up and work, but may not be too satisfactory owing to poor resistance to knocks, abrasion, and also increased water absorption. It is essential to be particularly careful over the protection of light, soft, structural timber. Agba, whilst being highly suitable from the builder's point of view, can cause trouble in this respect.

There is a small point to watch out for when selecting veneer. Some timbers are comparatively stiff and a fair amount of pressure may be needed to get the strips to lie tight. Make sure that your staples are long enough to be able to hold the veneer tight without any suspicion of lifting. Also, if your hull has very tight curves in any part make sure that the veneer selected will be able to follow these closely.

In effect, one can make a hull out of almost any form of material which can be cut into strips and which will bend and glue. Reinforced plastics (or fibre-glass) is really only an extension of the cold-moulded idea. A Flying Fifteen was made out of strips of Tufnol a few years ago, and more recently a boat was successfully made out of glued newspaper. It is really only a matter of selecting your material and bonding it with a suitable medium. In the case of reinforced plastics one has moved from the position of using material such as wood, which has rigidity and strength only needing to be held in position with glue, to one where the rigidity is provided by the resin, and the strength by the glass. In the same way quite large yachts are now even made of concrete. However, we are now talking about cold moulding, using wood and glue.

The actual lay-up is normally done as follows: First decide how wide your strips can be. Start by cutting out, say, a 3-in parallel-sided strip of the right length for fixing in the

4.7

The operator here is using a compressed-air stapling machine, but the principle is exactly the same. The system used here is a good one: the veneer is tacked temporarily in place with plain staples, and then you follow up with strips of veneer stapled over the top. This spreads the pressure more evenly. (Souter, International Fourteen.)

maximum beam position. Try to tack this down at the point on the hull where there is most curvature. This may be somewhere between the stern and amidships. If it goes down tight without any kinks and hollows, then this width will be a satisfactory one, and you may be able to use wider strips in other places.

Fix this first strip carefully in the centre of one side at an angle of about 45 degrees to the centreline. Now cut out a number of strips of the right length and width to enable you to finish one half of the side. Arrange them in a pile so that the lengths are nearly right. It is a great help to have some sort of power-saw table for running off these parallel strips. Otherwise you must make up a jig to assist you

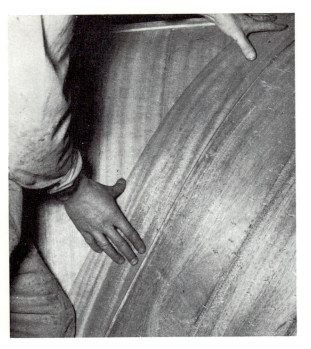

◄4.8, 4.9, 4.10, 4.11, 4.12 ▲
This series shows the sequence of fastening down a new veneer strip. It is first held firmly in place and tacked temporarily. The edge is then spiled, in this case using an ordinary compass and pencil. Then the veneer is taken off and the edge shaped up with the plane on the bench. Then spread glue thinly but evenly with a piece of offcut veneer both on the veneer strip itself and on the hull. Finally tack down the veneer firmly. (Souter, International Fourteen.)

in getting the edges planed straight and parallel. Actually, it is only really necessary to get one edge of each strip straight, because the other is spiled to a curve to fit the previous strip. This is due to the double curvature of the hull. Strictly it is not even essential for any edges to be straight, because the spiling will take care of the fit, but unless you do have parallel strips the angle of the lay-up will start to wander excessively as you progress. This could affect the strength of the shell and it also

would produce odd-shaped strips at the ends which could be tedious to fit and look bad if the outer skin is to be varnished.

It is normal for the outer layer, if diagonal, to be laid so that it slopes aft from the gunwale. This makes a neater finish with the stem of most dinghies, which is the area most noticeable to the eye when on the water. Therefore in a three-skin job the inner layer will be angled the same way.

There is also another method of laying-up the veneers which consists of tacking down alternate strips parallel to each other with a gap no wider than the width of the strips in between. Then the intervening strips are fitted by spiling both edges (Fig. 3.1, p. 45). For this method to be trouble-free it is essential for the alternate strips to be exactly parallel and exactly the same width. Therefore, unless the builder has some mechanical means of ensuring accuracy in cutting, it is probably better to use the consecutive strip method.

When using thin veneers you may find you are able to use shears to cut out the strips instead of sawing them. In any event do not cut the strips too close to the final edge with either saw or shears when fitting the inner layer. Trim up with a plane to remove roughness and splinters which can otherwise mar the jointing on the inner surface.

A good way of dealing with the trimming of thin veneer strips is to mark them near one edge with a straight edge; then hold the veneer on a flat bench with the edge just protecting from the side, using a board on top to maintain pressure. The edge can now be planed to the line with the veneer held steady and firm. Start fixing strips in, say, the middle of their lengths and work towards the keel and the sheer. But in any case, always fix each strip in the same way to avoid inaccuracies which might result in gaps. Fix each strip down properly for the spiling operation (Figs. 4.8, 4.9). Then remove it, trim the edge with the plane (Fig. 4.10), and spread the glue (Figs. 4.11, 4.12) (if it is the second or later layer) and refix permanently, pressing firmly with the palm of the hand, while steadily working along with the tacker (Fig. 4.7). The glue should be thinly spread both on the hull and on the veneer to assist in getting a complete bond.

The veneers can project an inch or two beyond the sheer, but at the keel there are two main ways of finishing off (Fig. 4.13). One can either trim off each veneer to fit into a hog and rebated keel piece, or alternatively the veneers can be carried over the centreline and planed off flush with the other side, before laying-up that side. Using the rebated-keel system it is not necessary to make a very tight fit until the last skin. Then it is necessary to run the rebating plane along the recess to clean up the edge (Fig. 4.14). Clean off excess glue religiously from each layer before it has had time to go really hard. If you do not do this you will have endless trouble later and many blunt plane irons.

If a group of people are building the hull it might be inconvenient to use the wrap-over method, since all four quarters of the shell might be under construction at any one time. Using this type of construction the glue has to be set before the excess veneer can be planed off.

However, it is much simpler, lighter, and quite strong enough, to build a hull just with a

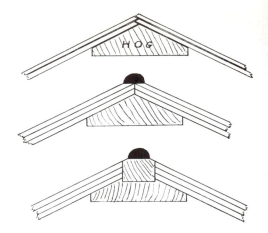

4.13

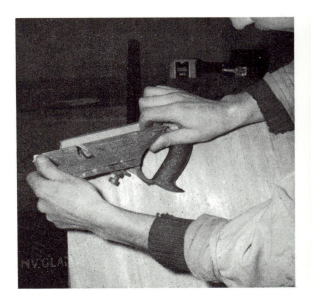

4.14

How the rebate plane is used to clean up the edge before the final layer of veneer is fixed. It is only necessary to make a really accurate joint at the keel for the last skin, as this is the only one which will show. (Souter, International Fourteen.)

◄   4.15

After the plywood pads have been fixed it is best to go round and tap them all over lightly with a light hammer. This helps to fill up the voids and expel excess glue. (Souter, Ocean Racer.)

▼   4.16

The veneering has now been completed on this hull. The plywood pads have been ripped off, but the nails have remained in the hull and the nail-heads can be seen projecting. However, they are $\frac{1}{8}$ in. clear of the surface and can be easily removed with a pair of pincers. The next stage is to clean off all the excess glue, and finally fair up the whole hull with a sharp plane. (Souter, Penguin Dinghy.)

hog and no keel at all. There is only one piece of wood to cut out for the keel and it can be fitted simply by planing it off flush with the mould. Also, the interlocking of the veneers near the bow can provide a strong tie against any tendency for the backbone to split. The other system is more massive and theoretically stronger, but in my opinion quite unnecessarily so even for knock-about boats, and extra strength can be obtained easily in other ways by adding reinforcement whether internally or externally. There is a difficulty with the wrap-over method where the bottom is very flat, and this may cause it to be abandoned when building to some designs. In this case one just butts the two sides together.

When you have tacked or nailed down a section of hull it pays to go over the whole area from the middle outwards with a light hammer. This is another good reason for

4.17 ►

This hull has been constructed of three layers of 3-mm. three-ply, which means there is a glue line every millimetre through the skin. In cleaning up this hull it has been necessary to plane clean through the top veneer in a number of places, in order to get the hull fair. (Finn.)

---

putting pads under the staples (Fig. 4.15). You can lightly hammer the pads and thus make sure that voids are filled with glue and that excess glue is expelled.

A word about the glue to be used; in my opinion it is easier to make a satisfactory job if one of the pre-mixed type glues is used rather than the separate-application type. It is not essential to use a resorcinol glue and also some people think it is difficult to spread this type properly. The type of glue consisting of a powder containing its own hardener, and which has to be mixed with water to start the reaction, is the easiest. Do not make the mix too runny or too stiff. A short period of experiment will show the right consistency. If too runny it may be too weak, and technical reasons may cause a poor bond. If too stiff one may not be able to press out surplus glue and fill up the voids.

The temperature of the workshop is another thing to be considered. If it is too hot the glue may gel before you have got the veneer stapled down tight. I have found that Casca-mite One-shot is very satisfactory for cold moulding. In cold weather some extra heat will be needed to help it to cure finally, as it has a rather slow hardener in its make-up.

Mix the glue in fair quantities, depending on how much you think you can accomplish in a

4.18
It has been possible to fair up this diagonal-moulded hull without going through any veneers because they are thicker. Bilge rails and external keels are being fitted. (Souter, Penguin Dinghy.)

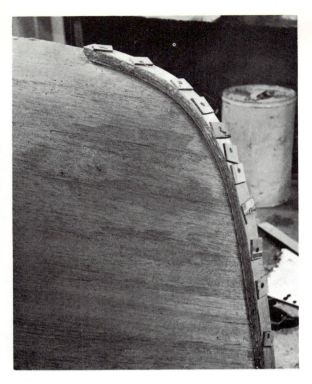

4.20
The laminated stem capping has now been faired off flush with the planking and it can be seen that a very neat finish emerges. Half-round brass is finally fixed to the flat on the outside edge, protecting the bottom and making a smart trim. (Rogers, International Finn.)

4.19
The stem is being finished off with a laminated capping. This has been moulded *in situ* by tacking strips of veneer round the stem with glue in between and then driving screws through the lot with plywood pads under their heads to distribute the pressure. (Rogers, Finn.)

4.21 ►
When a racing boat has to measure in accurately after completion it is essential to make a rigid jig consisting of accurate outside moulds. These must be set up in the correct relationship to each other. (Rogers, Finn.)

few hours. Half a pint might be a reasonable amount. Break off a piece of ply with a flat end about 2 in. wide, to act as a stirrer and spreader. Spread evenly on both surfaces and bring them together as soon as possible. Do not delay with the fixing down, but on the other hand, do not panic and get the strip fixed in the wrong position. When spiling, make a mark on both strips so that the new one can finally be tacked down in exactly the right position.

There is really nothing else to worry about in cold moulding, apart from maintaining a reasonable temperature for gluing. If you are building in draughty conditions in the winter, it is well worth making a tent out of polythene sheet to cover both hull and bench to keep the heat in.

Assuming that the lay-up has been completed satisfactorily, you must then carefully clean up the hull, pulling out all staples and pins (Fig. 4.16) and plane it all over with a plane set very fine. Try the fairness with flexible battens and when you are satisfied that no lumps or flats remain, give a good hard sanding with an orbital or belt sander, or sheets of garnet paper backed with a cork block (Figs. 4.17, 4.18).

There is one other operation which can profitably be performed while the shell is still on the mould, and this is fitting the stem capping. A boat with a rounded forefoot can have laminated pieces let in as in Fig. 4.19. It is perfectly simple to laminate this *in situ*, from veneer offcuts. They can be temporarily tacked in place, and then firmly cramped with screws having ply pads under their heads The screws can be removed later and the holes plugged (Fig. 4.20).

There is sometimes some difficulty in lifting a shell off the mould. If the transom has not been fitted, one can start by lifting the corner and working round to the bow. This should detach the shell. Failing this, broad flat battens or strips of veneer can be pushed up between the shell and the mould surface to release the sticking part. A boat with a vertical straight stem may be more difficult, as in this case each end must be lifted a little at a time to avoid jamming.

4.22
When the hull shell comes off the mould it must be dropped into the external jig to ensure that it is the correct shape. (Rogers, Finn.)

4.23 ►
The next stage is to clean up the interior of the shell. This can best be done by scraping and spokeshaving. (Rogers, Finn.)

Having removed the shell, lose no time in placing it in a jig consisting of at least two exterior moulds or frames, rigidly set up in the correct positions (Figs. 4.21, 4.22).

Scrape the interior clean (Fig. 4.23), and then cut out some inwales and clamp them in place whilst holding the side into the correct beam with cross-ties. The shell will not fit into the jig while the beam is incorrect, and it will be noticed that by squeezing the beam in the ends of the hull will drop and vice versa. Thus, if the boat is to measure accurately to a set of racing rules, it is essential to check and double check that everything is correct, before fixing anything permanently, and also a jig made of at least three exterior frames is a wise pre-caution. Juggle the beam ties and the inwales until both beam measurements and the sheer heights are correct according to the plan. The sheer heights can be measured from a straight piece of timber laid on the floor under the boat at right-angles to the centreline. Make sure that the jig is firmly positioned and level, and that the exterior frames are accurately set out. Measure up from the straight-edge (which must also be level), making suitable adjustments to allow for differing positions of baseline or keel heights on the plans to those of the straight-edges on the floor. Mark where the sheer height should be and repeat for each section for which you have information on the plans. The inwale position can now be adjusted

to be level with these points and then it can be glued and nailed in place (Fig. 4.24).

The hull should now be the correct shape. Check and double check again, because an error, if left after this stage, will be very difficult to correct. If all is satisfactory, then Chapter 10 will deal with the next stage.

4.24
The inwales have now been fixed and some of the deck beams also. In the foreground is a temporary tie to ensure that the hull is at the correct beam dimension before the interior framing is fixed. (Rogers, Finn.)

5 *Clinker Planking*

WHEN one talks of clinker planking nowadays one really thinks only in terms of the glued clinker-ply method. The old traditional nailed and timbered construction has become almost, if not completely, obsolete (Figs. 5.1, 5.2).

The glued clinker type of construction is very strong and quite easy for the amateur, as well as having the advantage of needing only a skeleton jig (Fig. 5.3). There is another big advantage to those trying out new hull shapes and those building to "restricted" class rules; the shape can be varied from boat to boat with only relatively minor alterations to the moulds, and no expensive basic jig costs are needed. One also has a hull shape that follows a set of round-bilge lines very closely without the elaborate jig.

Prototypes to test designers' ideas can very simply be constructed by this method, and when finally correct the lines can be transferred to a solid mould for cold moulding or reinforced plastics mass production. A number of "restricted" classes flourish, notably the International Fourteen, International Moth, National Twelve, Fourteen-Foot Merlin/Rocket, and National Eighteen-Foot classes, and budding designers might like to try their hand at boats built to these rules by this method. In addition there are one-design classes of the heavier type designed especially for this construction method, such as the *Yachting World* Fourteen-Foot Dayboat, and the National Redwing.

Glued clinker needs no ribs or timbers, as were essential in the older nailed method. The shell keeps its shape entirely by the rigidity of the planking curved and glued together at its edges, aided also by a glued deck assembly. Floor and centreboard-case reinforcements are usually fitted in addition, and sometimes built-in bulkheads and tank frames add to the structure. The effect of the double thickness at the overlap of each plank is that of a stringer to each joint, and this also greatly adds to the strength of the hull.

Points to watch are that the bevels on the plank edges are very carefully made so that the bond is sound; that only first-class plywood with a good bond between veneers is used; and that the sealing of the large amount of end-grain is well and truly done.

Because of the exposed end-grain and the difficulty of protecting this permanently from water entry the method is more suitable for boats that are dry-sailed than those left on moorings, or that are likely to take a hammering from being beached frequently. However, careful selection of materials can avoid trouble to a great extent.

There are many differences of detail which can be used in glued clinker hull construction, but there seems to be no real point in going as far as is required by some of the national class rules unless you are bound by them. The transition from nailed clinker to glued clinker made many problems for the rule makers, who were anxious to take advantage of the new method and at the same time avoid outclassing hundreds of boats at one stroke. Thus they were not able to use some of the best points of the

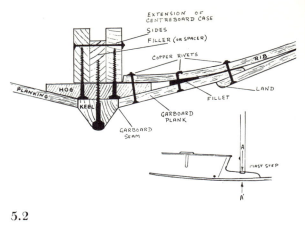

5.2

5.1
The traditional nailed clinker dinghy is a real trap for dirt. It is also extremely difficult to remove paint when it comes to need refinishing. With age the conventional nailed clinker dinghy starts to leak and it is then nearly impossible to rejuvenate it.

system to make the boats lighter, or to simplify the detailed construction at the keel, for instance (Fig. 5.2).

I think there are two things to consider when planning hull construction by this method, assuming first that one is free to decide the details oneself. Is the boat to have a light racing hull, the bottom of which will be treated with some respect when it comes to beaching and handling ashore, or is the boat required for knock-about purposes, and to

withstand the bashing of the inexperienced?

If the former, then there is no need to fit an exposed keel, and this will save one piece of solid timber. There is also no need to use a rebated keel or a two-piece hog and keel assembly, which comes to the same thing. It will be far simpler just to fit a hog into the jig and glue the garboard strake directly to this. There will also be considerably less bother in fitting the garboard seam; in fact, there will be no garboard seam. The garboards will simply butt on the centreline. The problem of water entry along the end grain will not be a problem with a racing boat which is dry-sailed, even should the gluing or filler in the centreline prove faulty.

For a knock-about boat I think I should still use basically the same method, but I would then plane a flat along the centreline and glue a keel piece on top, possibly screwing it right into the hog (Fig. 5.4).

If a really tough and wide keel is needed

5.3

The very light construction of the jig needed for glued clinker building. In this case the jig is arranged so that the centreboard case can be fitted into it before planking commences. The hog and the keel have already been bent over and fixed down. (Chippendale, 12-ft National.)

5.4

This gives an idea of how the hog planking and external keel could be constructed in a method of clinker building. This is a much lighter and easier form of construction than that shown in Fig. 5.6.

right through to the stem, then the hog can be suitably shaped and a possible section forward can be assembled as in Fig. 5.5. The keel can be fixed in two or more laminations should a single piece prove difficult to bend to shape (Fig. 5.6).

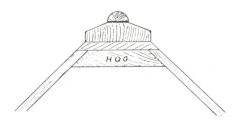

5.5

How a rather more heavily constructed keel assembly could be made. The keel can be made in two parts and fitted on last.

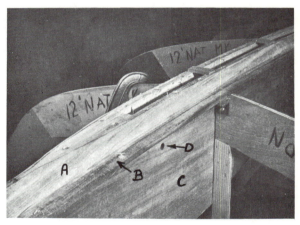

5.6

A close-up of the construction of the conventional keel and hog assembly in the 12-ft National Dinghy. A is the partially shaped keel with its centreboard slot already cut; B is the hog correctly bevelled to receive the garboard plank. C is the centreboard case which has been built into the jig. D is the centreboard pivot bolt-hole which must be drilled before planking commences. Notice also the temporary cleats across the centreboard slot in order to keep everything the right shape until held by the planking. (Chippendale, 12-ft National.)

The stem can be finished in several ways. Traditional practice was to rebate the plank ends into a solid stem piece. They were nailed or screwed down and the seams filled with white lead. Resin glues have allowed much simpler, neater, and more watertight constructions to be used. A straight-stemmed dinghy can be finished by screwing the plank ends to an inner stem and then by gluing a false stem over everything (Figs. 5.7, 5.8).

A boat with a rounded forefoot is not quite so easy. To start with, the inner stem may have to be scarfed up out of several pieces in order to carry the grain round, or it can be laminated out of several strips about 6 mm. thick (Fig. 3.15, p.53).

Secondly, the false stem will have to be laminated *in situ*, in the same way as described for the cold-moulded Finn (Figs. 4.19, 4.20, p. 67). It will have to be notched or scarfed at the lower end, so that it fairs in with either the planking or external keel, depending on the method being used.

The finishing at the transom can also be

▲   5.7
The plank-ends at the stem are normally rebated together so they finish up flush against an inner stem piece. (Chippendale, 14-ft Merlin/Rocket.)

◄   5.8
Then an outer stem is fitted on to cover the plank-ends and all is faired off smooth. (Chippendale, 14-ft Merlin/Rocket.)

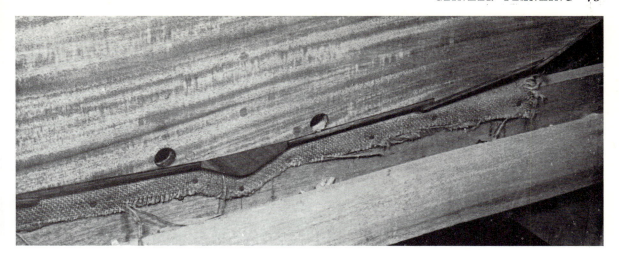

5.9
A simple way of finishing off the plank-ends at the stern of a 14-ft Merlin. The planks and the hog are merely screwed on to the edge of the transom and planed off flush. (Chippendale, 14-ft Merlin/-Rocket.)

made in various ways. The best looking and soundest system is to rebate the transom edge and to finish the planking so that the ends are concealed. This would be the preferred method for a knock-about boat. If you like you can glue the plank ends to a skeleton framework and then glue the transom on to the outside of this. The simplest methods involve merely gluing and screwing the plank ends to the outside edge of the transom and planing this off flush (Fig. 5.9).

PLANKING

The actual planking up is very simple basically, though it needs a fair amount of planning to avoid wastage.

The first thing is to decide how many planks to have and their widths. If you are building to a design specially prepared for clinker construction, the plans may give full information on this, and even supply full-size or reduced-scale templates of the plank shapes.

The actual shape of a plank will necessarily be curved. It may be of a flattened "S" shape, or just a simple "bow" shape, depending on the individual hull design, and the position of the plank. But in any case it will almost certainly be wider in the middle than at the ends, and will have to be cut from a sheet or strip of timber that may be wider than its greatest individual width (Fig. 5.10). Unless the plank widths are carefully thought out you may find that some turn out to be unwieldy in shape or size, and the finished hull may look odd.

It is best to start with a thinnish piece of

planking or hardboard about 6 to 8 in. wide, and the length required, to use as a trial template.

Mark on the edge of the smallest mould the number of planks you think you will need, and divide up the circumference of one side of the frame to give a trial spacing for the planks. The garboard and sheer planks can usually be quite wide, as can any other plank on a flattish part of the sections. At the turn of the bilge the planks must be narrower. If there is a considerable concavity in the sheer line, the sheer plank may have to be narrower, otherwise the curve in the plank might mean it would have to be cut from an impossibly wide blank. Extra flare to the topsides would increase the bow in the sheer planks.

When using standard 8 ft × 4 ft sheets of ply for planking suitable lengths will have to be scarfed up first. You can economize by scarfing lengths out of true to allow for the curve in the planks to some extent (Fig. 5.10).

Offer up your hardboard trial plank and roughly mark off how much curve there will be to the planks at various positions on the hull. You should then be able to decide how wide the various planks can be. They will probably vary from about 3 in. to about 6 in. exposed width. Remember to add the overlap at the lands which for 6- to 9-mm. ply will be about $\frac{3}{4}$ in. (19 mm.). Having decided on suitable widths, mark these accurately on the edge of the largest mould.

The next thing is to decide the positions of the plank edges on the other moulds. You will realize that the curves of the garboard seam and the sheer are fixed and it is usual, but not essential, to proportion out the plank

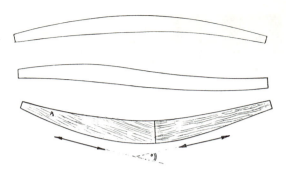

5.10

It will be found that planks can come out in a variety of shapes. One can sometimes economize in plywood when gluing together lengths to make up a single bow-shaped plank by scarfing the two parts at a slight angle to each other.

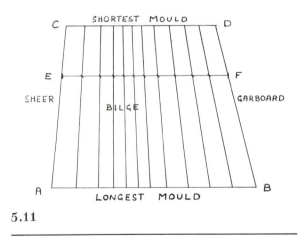

5.11

spacing on each mould in the same ratio as that decided for the largest mould. Therefore one has to resort to a piece of paper and draw a diagram (Fig. 5.11).

First measure the length of the edge of one side of the largest mould and draw this to a suitable scale across the bottom of your paper

5.12
In this 12-ft National Dinghy an attempt has been made to make the lands of the planks run more nearly along the waterlines by bringing the garboard seam out well abaft of the forefoot. (Chippendale, 12-ft National.)

—AB. Do the same for the length of edge of the shortest mould and draw it parallel to the first line but near the top of your paper—CD. Note that the stem might actually be the shortest mould, but it is best to use the first mould aft of this, if it is the next shortest, otherwise you might run into difficulties caused by the rounding of the forefoot.

Next join the two pairs of ends together. Now mark the plank-edge positions on AB. Then mark the plank-edge positions on CD, in as nearly the same proportions as possible. Now join up the corresponding positions with straight lines.

It is now a simple matter to measure the length of the edge of each mould in turn. Fit the length exactly into the grid so that its ends just touch the lines AC and BD, and at the same time is parallel to AB. Where the other lines cut are the positions of the plank edges.

You can, of course, plank up a hull how you like; even using straight planks for most of the hull. These will start running out at either the sheer or the garboard as you progress, and you will have to fit tapered part planks called "stealers" to make up the gaps. Not very satisfactory: but I have always wanted to try adjusting the run of the planking near the stem so that the lands run more nearly along the path the water travels. This would mean running the garboard out somewhere short of the forefoot (Fig. 5.12). There must be a fair amount of unnecessary resistance caused by the plank lands hitting the waves at an angle. A clinker boat is usually drier than a similar carvel one, because each land acts as a small spray deflector.

One usually starts planking with the garboard. If you are cutting direct from scarfed-up sheets of ply, you may find it easiest to make a hardboard template of each plank as you progress. The same template can mark off both the port and starboard planks, and you may also be able to trim it down for a further pair of planks later, and so it will not be too wasteful.

First get the curve of the garboard seam as nearly as possible. You may be able to scribe round the edge of the hog from underneath, as a first try. If the seam is a rebate in the hog you will probably have to finish off by spiling the curve (Fig. 3.3, p. 45).

Then offer up the template and while it is

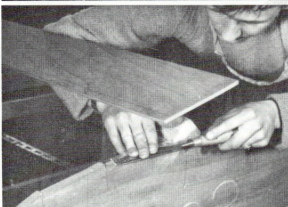

5.13, 5.14

The sequence of fitting the garboard plank to the 12-ft National Dinghy. 5.13 shows how the hog and the inner stem are connected with a knee and then the keel is fixed down on top. The rebate for the garboard plank can be clearly seen. Fig. 5.14 shows the garboard plank being held temporarily after the edge has been spiled to the correct curve. (Chippendale, 12-ft National.)

◄   5.15, 5.16, 5.17

Fig. 5.15 shows the after end of the garboard plank being held temporarily while fitting. 5.16 shows the notch for the garboard plank being cut in the transom. 5.17 shows the plank in its final fitted position ready for nailing and gluing. (Chippendale, 12-ft National.)

---

in place mark off the plank-edge positions from underneath, transferred from the moulds.

Draw a curve passing through all these points by springing a batten and pencilling along the edge. Cut out the template finally, and transfer the shape of your planking material. The garboards can then be cut and fitted, and fixed down with nails and glue (Figs. 5.13, 5.14, 5.15, 5.16, 5.17).

If you have decided that a ¾ in. (19 mm.) wide overlap is the most suitable one, then, using a marking gauge made up from scraps of ply and a pencil, mark a line ¾ in. in from the edge.

The bevel angle will vary all the way along the plank, but will in each case just reach as far as the ¾-in. line. The next step is to mark a rough guide for the amount to be bevelled off, and then to take this off. Lay a straight-edge across the mould and touching the corner of the plank. Measure A–B, and mark it on the edge of the plank at C–D (see Fig. 5.21). This is the amount to be planed off at this mould. Repeat for each mould (Figs. 5.18, 5.19, 5.20, 5.21).

There is one further operation to consider before the next plank can be fixed, and that is the finishing of the ends of the planks at stem and transom.

5.18

Subsequent planks are fitted in largely the same way as the garboard, except that the bevel to receive the next plank has to be planed first. Here the worker is planing the bevel ready to receive the next plank. (Chippendale, 12-ft National.)

5.19

A method of checking that the bevel angle is correct. This work has to be done carefully by eye. (Chippendale, 12-ft National.)

5.20
One must be very careful when trying the planks for fit, that they are cramped down evenly and fully over their entire length. Make sure that the edge of the plank is against the guide line on the already fixed plank all along its length. (Chippendale, 12-ft National.)

5.22
It can here be clearly seen how the planks are notched into the transom. (Chippendale, 12-ft National.)

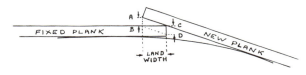

5.21
The method of calculating the amount of bevel to be taken off should it be found more convenient to do this on the bench. Sometimes this is the case, especially if the planking is rather thin and flexible in between the moulds.

Obviously, the planks must lie flush at the stem. One sometimes sees notched transoms with lapped plankings at the stern (Fig. 5.22), but it is also usual to fair them in flush here also. The best method of doing this is to merge the bevel on the lands into a rebate, starting about 8 in. from the plank-ends. It may seem difficult to do this for each plank-end, but it is really quite simple and quick, and by far the most satisfactory method. A short piece of batten can temporarily be cramped $\frac{3}{4}$ in. from the edge to act as a guide for the rebating plane. A clean shoulder is ensured by making a few strokes with a tenon saw against the batten. Do not run the rebate right down to a feather edge. Leave about one-sixteenth to an eighth of an inch of thickness and then rebate this amount off the face of the next

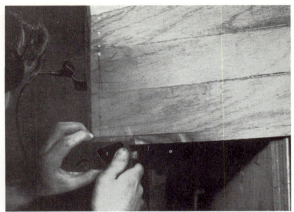

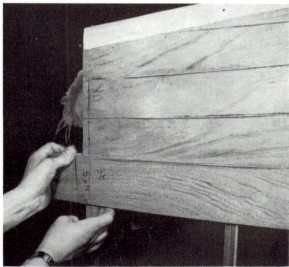

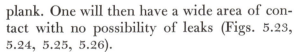

plank. One will then have a wide area of contact with no possibility of leaks (Figs. 5.23, 5.24, 5.25, 5.26).

Plywood planks do not, of course, split, but if you are using ordinary solid timber it is best to make the planks a few inches too long.

5.23, 5.24, 5.25, 5.26
This series of pictures shows how the planks are rebated together at the stem so that they lie flush. The first step is to make a cut with a tenon saw along the pencil line, marking where the land of the next plank will lie. Then the rebate can be chiselled out, tapering away to nothing at the stem. Finally it is cleaned up with a small rebating plane as in Fig. 5.24. The plank is then fitted and held in place with a nail bent over at the bottom. The finished series of planks at the stem should look as in Fig. 5.26. (Chippendale, 12-ft National.)

Nails and screws driven at the stem and transom should then cause no trouble and one also has a projection to enable the plank ends to be lashed down whilst being fixed.

The succeeding planks can be cut out in the same general way. Offer up the plank or the template so that it just touches the previous plank edge at the widest part (usually in the middle) and overlaps it everywhere else. Cramp it in place and then pencil in the curve of the edge of the previous plank underneath. Trim off the excess material and there is your first curve. Obtain the other curve with the springy batten in the same way as before, having moved the plank ¾ in. towards the fixed plank so that it matches up with the line of the bevel. Carry on a pair of planks at a time.

It remains to discuss the actual gluing operation at the lands. There is nothing very difficult about this as long as care has been taken to see that the bevels have been accurately finished. It is more fiddly than anything else, and at least one helper will be needed to make sure everything is right first time. As with all gluing jobs it is virtually essential to do a dry dummy run first.

You will need a large number of cramps.

5.27

The normal metal "G" cramps are not really suitable. They may not have enough horizontal clearance to span the plank width, and also their total weight will be so high as to risk distorting the planking. If you cannot borrow suitable wooden cramps, you will have to make some out of plywood and wedges, or scrap timber and coach-bolts. The sketch explains the features of a suitable pattern (5.27).

An electric hand-jigsaw is extremely useful in clinker building, not only for cutting out the planking accurately, but this cramp-making job can be done quickly and economically with a little planning and the use of such a tool (Fig. 0.5, p. 15).

Having assembled enough cramps for at least one per foot run, you can offer up the plank and cramp it in place. When all is right and firm mark on both planks so that the fore-and-aft position can be found again immediately. Drill at stem and transom for the screws or nails which are to be inserted here. It may also be wise to pin the centre of the planks together to stop any tendency for them to slide about later.

Then take the plank off again, spread glue evenly on both surfaces and cramp up again as quickly as possible. Fix the ends permanently this time, and that is that.

Professional builders use an electrically heated strip under the cramp heads to set off the glue quickly. We shall almost certainly not be able to do this, and so the normal polythene sheet and hot-air blower method will have to be resorted to if the air temperature is low.

If you have enough cramps you can fix the opposite plank, but this is as far as you can go until the glue is set hard.

5.28
The completed shell when lifted off is very clean and neat and strong, but still wobbly. In this case an exterior gunwale has been fitted to the sheer plank before it was removed from the jig. The centreboard case was in the jig at the start and has come off complete with the shell. It can be seen how the knee connecting the inner stem to the hog appears in the completed shell. (Chippendale, 14-ft Merlin/Rocket.)

That is about all there is to the principle of glued clinker, but there are a few general points to mention.

With clinker planking the surfaces of the planks must be finished ready for painting before they are fixed. This does not mean that sanding and minor filling cannot be done at all afterwards, but it is fairly difficult to do any finishing work at later stages, and so this must be borne in mind.

The outer veneers of plywood sheets are sometimes extremely hard, due to the influence of the manufacturing presses. Glue may not bond very well to such a polished surface, and so it is wise to take a very fine shaving off the unbevelled edge which is to be glued. This will also remove any grease or dirt which might affect the bond.

When planning a glued clinker hull bear in mind the effects of planking of various thicknesses. For any one hull shape there will be one thickness of plywood which will be most convenient to handle. In many cases this will also be the most desirable thickness for other reasons, too. For instance, a 14-ft racing boat would be built most easily with say, 6-mm. ply planks. This will also be a very suitable thickness for withstanding racing conditions and will produce a hull of conventional weight for this kind of boat (Fig. 5.28).

However, a 14-ft knock-about boat might call for heavier planking of, say, 10 mm. to withstand the rough and tumble of the conditions it will have to meet. This may not be so easy for the builder. The pressure needed to bend the planking into shape may call for stronger cramps and even a certain amount of steaming, and it will be more tricky to get a tight joint. A more rigid and elaborate jig may be needed to take up the bending stresses.

Going the other way, one may want to make a very light racing or experimental hull, using ply as thin as 3 mm. In this case you may need extra cramps to make sure that jointing surfaces are in close contact. Also you will have to be careful during the trial period that the plank is held down properly each time. It will be so floppy that errors could creep in unnoticed until the final gluing operation.

I DO not propose to go into great detail concerning carvel hulls but just to explain the principles. I do not consider it a suitable amateur's method, and it is fast falling out of favour everywhere, its place being taken by cold moulding and plastics.

The principle of carvel construction is that the fore-and-aft planks are laid edge to edge so that the finished surface is quite smooth. The skin is made of only one layer of planking, and the main difficulty centres on the problem of watertightness. Most large yachts are still built by the carvel method, and the seams are normally finished by squeezing a flexible caulking material between them. Dinghies that are dry-sailed, however, can employ the lighter and more watertight method of edge-gluing.

It is essential to use ribs and possibly built-in frames also in carvel hulls. The grain of the timber runs entirely fore and aft, and splitting would certainly occur if it was not for this cross bracing. Carvel hulls also tend to get narrower and deeper with age unless well braced, and it is also not practical to use ply-wood planking for carvel construction, since one cannot edge-glue this material satisfactorily.

The successful construction and length of life of a carvel hull depend very largely on the planking material selected. It is absolutely essential to use stable timber—a type that will not warp, twist, or split easily, and one with as little shrinkage across the grain as possible. Teak or other waxy timbers are a possibility, but the price and weight may rule them out. Resorcinol glues would have to be used also.

The choice usually falls on Honduras mahogany or cedar. Honduras is quite unlike ordinary African mahogany to work. It has a smooth and even grain, is light both in colour and weight, and is very stable. Cedar is also a pleasure to work with edge tools, but is often rather soft and brittle. Care must be exercised when driving nails that the right size of pilot holes (half the diagonal of square-sectioned nails) is used to avoid splitting. Trouble may be experienced in gluing due to the waxy nature of the timber, and so a resorcinol glue may be needed.

It is not practical to use less than about 9-mm. ($\frac{3}{8}$-in.) planking for carvel construction. Thus it is not a proposition for any racing boats other than heavy ones, such as the Finn. For hulls of a heavier type, one can employ the edge-nailed, strip-planked system, which is strong, and somewhat less prone to splitting, especially if "anchorfast" or similar nails are used (Fig. 6.1).

In dinghy work the ribs are usually fitted after the shell is complete, and they can be screwed from the outside. Screw-heads will have to be sunk, and the holes dowelled.

Ordinary carvel hulls have rather narrower planks than can be used with glued clinker, but the planks are set out in the same way. Alternatively one can use much narrower planks edge-nailed and glued. This is often known as strip-carvel building.

Strip-carvel is a very suitable method for an

amateur building a heavier and larger boat. There is very little shape to each of the large number of planks, and the construction can proceed even when one is single-handed. A power saw for ripping up the strips is almost essential, but individual strips will have to be scarfed if not of the full length. One will need a very long bench for planing the edges to be glued, and, of course, the whole surface of the hull will need considerable planing when complete.

The main disadvantage is in the time taken to complete a hull. Personally, I would still prefer one of the other methods if there is to be a choice. However, there is also the point that if the only timber available is a bit doubtful as to quality or stability, then it is almost the only method which is likely to prove really satisfactory.

The timber for normal edge-glued carvel should be very carefully treated and selected. It must have been well seasoned, and it must be rift-sawn to minimize shrinkage across the plank. It need only be planed on one side, since the outer hull surface will have to be planed by hand in any case. The planking should be very carefully conditioned and stored, so that it is not allowed to get too dry or too damp.

The method of making the glued joint at the plank edges shows some variation. It is probably quickest to use a pair of matched moulding planes. One planes a slight hollow cross-section on one edge and a matching convex moulding on the other. One then does not have to worry about the changing angle of the joint caused by the change of shape of the hull. The planks can lie at small angles to each other, without affecting the tightness of the

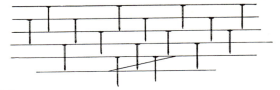

6.1

In the system of building known as edge-nailed carvel narrow planks are used and nails are driven vertically through them into the lower plank. Usually the planks are glued together and the nails have to be staggered.

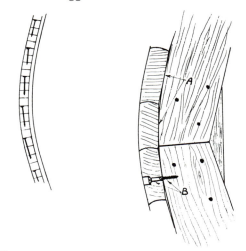

6.2

On the left is a section of edge-nailed carvel, on the right the more normal system of construction for small boats. The joint is radiused so that the planks can lie at a slight angle to each other without affecting the tightness of the joint. In dinghies that are to be kept out of the water the joints are usually glued, the inner faces of the planks can be hollowed slightly at A. The planks can be screwed directly into the mould as at B. Then, after the shell has been removed from the jig, ribs can be fastened through the same screw-holes. The space above the head of the screw should be dowelled.

joints. One has to prepare both edges of each plank before fixing down, and one may have to plane a slight concavity on the inside surface of some planks so that they can lie tight to the moulds (Fig. 6.2).

It will also be necessary to cramp each plank both edgeways against the already fixed plank and also inwards against the moulds. For this purpose small blocks can be screwed to the moulds in suitable positions to receive the cramp heads.

If you are able to fix more than one pair of planks in a day then you can screw each plank firmly into each mould. This will release your cramps for fixing down the next pair of planks. Finally, after removal of the shell, ribs can be positioned where the moulds came, and the same screw holes used for fixing them.

One has to be rather more careful when handling a bare carvel shell than that of other constructions. Get several helpers and turn it into an external jig as soon as possible after removal. Be particularly careful during this operation that the beam at the gunwale remains as constant as possible. Fit tie-beams at the first opportunity to keep the shell steady.

The ribs will best be made of straight-grained rock-elm and almost all of them will need some steaming to enable them to conform to the hull curves. Steaming is also dealt with on p. 55. The simplest way to steam is to obtain a length of iron water pipe which has been blocked at one end with a wooden or concrete plug. The length needs to be the same as the longest rib measured from the gunwale to gunwale and a bit extra. Prop the pipe so that the lower end rests on some convenient source of heat and the upper end is as near as possible

to the hull. Put some water in the pipe and let it boil. The steaming will take about a quarter of an hour for dinghy ribs, and then the first rib can be removed. You will need a helper and must work very fast. Use gloves!

As soon as the rib comes out of the pipe take it at the double to the hull, and force it rapidly into place. Bend it quickly to a greater than necessary curve at the points where these are most acute. These will usually be at the bilge and at the keel. Cramp the rib at sheer height on one side and tap the other side down as tight as possible. Then cramp this side and do the same with the other. The rib should now be reasonably tight to the hull and so start fixing it permanently from the keel upwards.

Put two screws through the hog and then work up plank by plank. The holes in the planking should have been prepared beforehand, and countersunk to receive dowels. Tap the end of the rib so that it lies tight, and then drill from outside and drive the screw. Continue tapping and screwing all the way up. Your helper may have to press the rib against the planking also.

Practise on the longest ribs. Should you break one, you may be able to use the pieces by the centreboard case or in the stem.

You may also have to fit some solid fitted floors in the stem and alongside the centreboard case to carry transverse loadings evenly. Each should be screwed and glued alongside a rib. The number of ribs for glued carvel construction can be less than for other forms, and might consist of one $\frac{3}{4}$ in. $\times$ $\frac{1}{2}$ in. (19 mm. $\times$ 12 mm.) rock-elm timber every 8 in. A strip-carvel hull can use even less in the way of ribs or frames. For the construction and fitting of floors see Chapter 10 (pp. 102–3) concerning the interior of the cold-moulded Finn.

Everything else is the same as for the other forms of construction described in Chapters 4 and 5.

7 *Single- and Double-Chine Hulls*

IN some ways this is the easiest method of obtaining a boat, but in other ways I think of hard-chine construction as an unattractive and tiresome system. I can best explain this apparent contradiction by pointing out that virtually the only way that boatbuilding can be made simple and also suitable for the maximum use of machine-cut parts is for hard-chine construction to be employed. In this way boats can be designed so that most, if not all, the frame pieces, stringers, keels, and even planking and deck panels, can be pre-cut to shape. It is even possible in many cases for the joints to be cut and even the correct bevels to be planed on the various parts. The planking and decks are cut from large flat panels and bent to the required shape over a previously erected framework.

If you are thinking of building a boat in the easiest possible way, then this is undoubtedly the way to do it. All the really tricky work will have been done for you, and it is only a matter of following the very detailed and comprehensive plans which are supplied by the factory. The builder and designer are interested in selling as many kits as possible, and thus it is in their interest to make everything as simple and foolproof as possible, so that only boats correctly shaped and constructed are put on the water. If you can also be persuaded by the simplicity of the system to recommend it to others, then they will be doubly pleased.

I think that the kit system is highly suitable for one's first essay in boatbuilding. It demonstrates the general construction of a boat very

well, but, of course, there is a great deal more to building a boat than assembling a set of parts. The kit system cannot show many of the basic principles of boat construction; for instance, the selection of the timber. Also, a great deal of the marking and setting out has been done for you.

I am sure that once having built a boat from a kit a keen and successful builder will want to try his hand at something more refined in shape and more of a challenge to his ingenuity.

If you are thinking of building a boat of some general description and for which kit sets are not available, then I do not regard it as so good a method as cold moulding or even glued clinker. The flatness of the hull panels does not allow one to make so strong or so rigid a structure as a moulded hull of the same weight. A fairly extensive space-frame is needed both to provide a fastening for the hull panels, and also to give extra rigidity to the whole. None of this interior framework is needed in a moulded hull and yet the skin thickness will have to be the same for both.

The large panels are also difficult to handle and the marking and cutting out is often infuriatingly awkward.

Double chine is one stage better in this respect, owing to the narrower width of the panels. It is likely also that there will be less twist and thus less strain on the panelling, but this system is already half-way towards glued clinker. The former is still capable of factory production, however, whereas this is not feasible for glued clinker. Thus I am certain in my own mind that one should regard ordinary chine construction as a factory system which can mass-produce kits that are extremely simple to assemble. It is an ideal system for a one-design class which is controlled and promoted by one factory or its agents.

I do not regard chine construction as the best or the easiest system for an amateur building from scratch, but a description follows because many prospective builders may want to do just this in order to join one of the several highly successful one-design classes using boats of this type.

But there are other reasons for my dislike of chine construction as an easy method for amateurs. There are so many different operations needed in the actual building process, dealing with frames, hogs, keel, chines, inwales, floor stringers, knees, and differently shaped hull panels, which may also require to be scarfed. The builder is always having to stop and think what to do next. There are many opportunities for errors and inaccuracies, which could mean that later joints cannot be made satisfactorily. Also, many differently shaped pieces of timber are called for. All this means constant largely unrelated measuring, planing, cutting and joint making.

In contrast, once the moulds are made, cold veneer moulding and fibre-glass moulding, and also, to a somewhat lesser extent, glued clinker ply, are gloriously simple methods, employing repetitive operations using the same materials and processes throughout.

There are one or two other general points concerning chine construction. If a group of amateurs is building several boats, then the parts of the first can be used as templates for

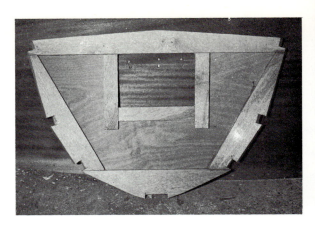

the rest. This gets over most of the construction tedium, saves a great deal of time, and goes part of the way towards the factory kit set.

Secondly, if one is to take maximum advantage of the system it is necessary to build as much of the hull interior into the jig before planking begins. In this way the centreboard case, bulkheads, floor stringers, knees, and even thwarts, can often be in place right from the start.

THE FRAMEWORK

Chine hulls are of three basic types, if one does not count the new composite construction methods using fibre-glass tape and resin.

There is firstly the fully framed boat where the shape of the sections is controlled by accurately made frames to which the chines and stringers as well as the planking are glued. These frames remain a part of the boat after it is complete and some of them could be in the form of solid bulkheads (Fig. 7.1).

◄ 7.1

A bulkhead which is also a frame. The whole assembly is inserted into the jig, but it comes off with the shell. Hatches, frames and deckbeams can be glued on to the plywood panel before assembly. (Small Craft, Gull.)

7.2 ►

The interior of a double-chine boat soon after it has been taken off the jig. It can be seen that the centreboard case and two bulkheads were built into the mould. The chines can easily be seen. Compare this with photographs later in this chapter of the hull being constructed. (Small Craft, 14-ft Leader.)

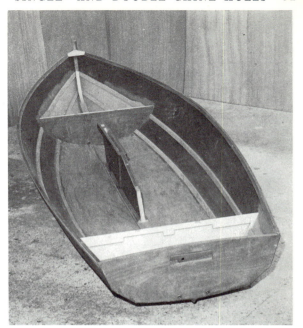

Secondly there is the frameless boat where the frames are set up into jig form. The chines and stringers are screwed temporarily to the frames and then the planking is glued to the former, but not to the latter. The boat is so designed that it retains its shape owing to the hull panels being curved and rigidly held at their edges. The frames do not remain in the hull and can be used again for another boat. The strength of glue and of materials such as plywood is now so much better understood that this method can be very satisfactory. It provides an interior which is much easier to paint, clean and maintain (Fig. 7.2).

The third type is what one might call the jigless boat. It is not really jigless, but one does not need the type of rigidly fixed and fairly elaborate jig that is normal. The boat is designed as a sort of self-supporting space-frame, round which the hull and deck panels are bent and fastened. The correct shape is entirely dependent on the designer giving the exact shapes of the frames and the exact length of the stringers. One may also need the exact shapes of some of the hull or deck panels. The boat cannot be made at all from a table of off-sets. It is literally built inside out. The whole assembly can be moved around or turned over at any stage during the construction, and will remain the right shape (Introduction, Fig. 0.2, p10).

Examples of this system are the Eleven-Plus, the 14-ft Scorpion and the 16-ft Fireball. The Fireball, in common with others, such as the Cadet and many simple pram dinghies, uses a bow transom instead of a sharp stem, and this simplifies construction still further (Fig. 7.3).

I suggest we quickly run through the construction of a fully framed single-chine hull as

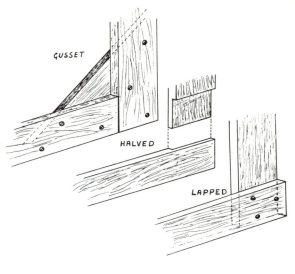

7.3

This Fireball Scow has been especially designed for complete simplicity for home building. The transom bow eliminates the difficult jointing at the stem, and the construction is on the space-frame principle, so the boat needs no permanent jig. (Chippendale, Fireball.)

7.4

being the most tricky of these types. If you can deal with this, then the others will present no difficulties.

BUILDING A FRAMED BOAT

Basically one starts as described in the second half of Chapter 1, though the moulds necessary for the round-bilge hull become the built-in frames of this hard-chine one. The only difference is that, since the frames remain in the boat and will be seen, they will have to be made carefully out of proper timber and not just nailed together out of scraps.

The shapes of the frames will be given in the plans. Mark them out by pricking through from the full-size drawings, or make paper templates from scaled-down drawings first, if only these are given.

The side and bottom pieces of each frame can be joined either by a halved joint and glued, which is neatest, or they can be lapped and glued, which is easiest, or they can be fastened by gussets, which is easy but messy-looking (Fig. 7.4). The final profile can be trimmed up after assembly, and there will also be some bevels to be planed on the edges. These can be roughly made on the bench and finished on the jig, but make absolutely sure on which side the bevel is to go. It is essential to mark the fore side on each frame, and also to mark which side of the frame is to be fixed level with each station. In many designs frames forward of the widest point have their aft faces level with the station, whilst frames aft of the widest point have their fore sides on the stations. This means that one edge of the frame is

7.5

How the frames are faired up in a hard-chine jig. This frame is actually a permanent bulkhead. A is the side frame. B is the plywood bulkhead itself. C is the inwale. The angle of the bevel on the outer edge of the frame A has to be faired in so that it matches the curve of C and also the curve of the chine at the top. (Small Craft, 14-ft Leader.)

bound to be proud of the correct shape, and hence it is easy to plane off the bevel (Fig. 3.6, p. 47). If the frame had been fixed on the wrong side of the station line, the bevel could not be planed without making the boat too small at that point. Therefore it is absolutely vital to make no mistakes about the positions and the bevels. Note also that the bevel may be

different at the top of one side from that at the bottom. Leave final bevelling until the fairing-in stage when the framework is complete (Fig. 7.5).

The plans ought to show what notches are to be cut in each frame to receive the hog, chines, and other stringers. If full-size templates are given, you can cut these at this stage, again making absolutely certain that you are marking out the correct face of the frame. Do not cut any bevels on these notches yet.

Some of the frames may form bulkheads and these can be assembled complete and any hatches or other items, such as drain-holes, can be fitted at this stage. You may also be able to fit deckbeams to some or all of the frames. Those frames without deckbeams or bulkheads (Fig. 7.1) will need some temporary struts to maintain rigidity.

The centreboard case can be fitted into the jig before planking begins, and you can cut the centre out of any frames through which it will pass, holding the sides together temporarily with a short piece of scrap timber screwed on.

Frequently the side pieces of each frame can be made long enough to act as legs to be screwed to the floor, but if there is a great deal of flare to the top panel this arrangement will be inconvenient, and an alternative method is to screw temporary vertical legs to the side pieces. If you do this, make sure that the legs are screwed to the face which is to be on the station line. Then one side of the leg will also be on the station (Fig. 1.13, p. 26).

Having made all the frames, the next step is to set them up. You will be lucky indeed if you have a rigid wooden floor to which you can screw wooden blocks. It does not matter if it is uneven as long as it will not move. You can, of course, bolt down to a concrete floor using Rawlbolts, but I honestly think you would find it simpler, if not as cheap, to build the subframe out of 4 in. × 2 in. deal (Fig. 7.6).

The subframe should have two parallel fore-and-aft members on edge connected by several crossbeams which have one edge exactly on each station. Diagonal braces will stop any movement horizontally, and squareness can be checked by measuring across the diagonals, which should be equal (see also Chapter 1).

A taut horizontal line must be strung down the centre to act as a baseline, and the frames are set up as described in Chapter 1. Use the plumb-line and spirit level carefully until all is square and level. The legs can be fixed directly to the edge of the cross-struts provided again that you have remembered to leave the correct edge level with the station line.

The frames will still be rather wobbly, and so it is essential to get at least one of them rigidly strutted in a vertical plane. It is not always convenient to strut the centre one, which would, in any other event, be the obvious choice. If you have to fiddle around fitting the centreboard case the struts might get in the way (Fig. 1.13, p. 26).

The transom, by the way, is usually fixed into the jig, and can either be a piece of solid timber such as mahogany, or it can be made in the same way as a bulkhead with a softwood frame and a plywood exterior.

7.6
This gives a very good idea of how the framework of a double-chine boat is built up. The subframe (A) can clearly be seen together with the legs temporarily screwed to the transom and the bulkheads and temporary moulds. The hog and stem have been fitted into the jig as well as two chines each side and the inwale. After fairing up, the jig is ready for the planking. (Small Craft, 14-ft Leader.)

THE STEM

Chine boats usually seem to have a rounded forefoot and the plans will show how the stem is to be constructed. It might be scarfed up out of two or three pieces, or you might laminate it as in Fig. 4.3 (p. 58). The straight stem is absolutely simple. The chines, hog and inwales will simply be notched into a flat inner stempiece. Then, after planking up, the whole lot is planed off flush, and an outer false stem glued

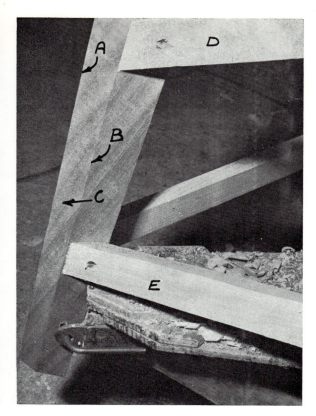

◄ 7.7

This close-up of the stem of a double-chine boat shows how the shape is translated from the drawings. A is the outer profile of the stem given on the drawings. Next you should mark the line B, which is the limit of the bevel, directly on to the blank of the stem. Then you should plane the bevel C just to meet line A and line B. This bevel, of course, varies along the length of the stem and this is calculated for you on the drawing. D is a chine which should fair into the bevel. E is the inwale which should also fair in. (Small Craft, 14-ft Leader.)

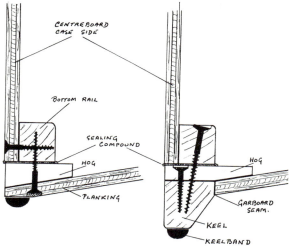

7.8

The drawing shows two possible methods of constructing the keel joint and the keel and centreboard-case assembly in this area. The sketch on the left shows a simple, light and neat method of assembling the parts. The drawing on the right shows a much more solid and massive construction suitable for heavier knockabout boats.

on. A curved stem will have its profile full size on the plans. A bearding line will also be shown. Cut out or laminate up a blank of the right shape, size and width and trimmed to the right profile. Then transfer the bearding line to the blank and plane off the bevel (Fig. 7.7). This will give you the correct bevel to receive the planking.

The plans will also show how the stem is to be connected to the hog. Frequently one can do this before fixing down (Fig. 7.13, p.100). The hog is usually a single length of solid timber and fits into the notches cut in the frames. Cut out and shape up the inside and both edges of the hog. Fix the stem and then start trial fittings. Cramps will have to be used to hold the hog in place, and bevels on the notches can be finally adjusted according to the curve that the hog takes up. A knee may be required as additional fixing at the transom. Make sure that the stem-head lands on the jig on the right place and tap the frames up to a vertical position. When you are satisfied all is correct, drill and countersink all fixing holes and mark in the position of the centreboard slot. Take the hog off and cut out most of the slot, leaving a short length in the middle to assist in keeping it straight. This can be cut out easily later. The best way of cutting out the slot is to drill holes at each end the size of the slot width, and then to use a jigsaw to cut out the remainder. If you have no jigsaw then drill several more holes and chop out in between with a chisel. Eventually a saw can be introduced.

A hog can now be finally fixed with screws and glue. Do hold it down with cramps while screwing. The screws themselves will not be able to draw the parts together firmly enough.

CENTREBOARD CASE

You might find it convenient to fix the centreboard case at this stage and before the jig becomes cluttered up with chines and stringers. Cases used to be made with solid mahogany sides about $\frac{7}{8}$ in. thick, and some classes still demand such massive construction. There is really no need for anything more than plywood sides about 9 mm. thick, together with a single diagonal brace. A bottom and top rail are also glued and screwed in place. The two

halves are made separately, painted inside and then screwed and glued together with vertical fillets of suitable thickness at the fore and aft ends. Solid timber cases are usually screwed to the hog with long screws from the outside. Ply cases can be fixed this same way, or alternatively can be screwed into the hog from the insides through the bottom rail (Fig. 7.8).

The curve for the bottom edge of the case to fit the hog can be simply obtained by making a hardboard template by trial and error. Make sure that you plane the bottom absolutely square. If you are very accurate you can glue the case to the hog, but you will probably find it simplest to screw it down on to a strip of sealing compound. One of the fabric-based strips such as Prestik or Sylglas is best. If you decide on this method and the boat is to have a long life, it is well worth using bronze screws, which will not crystallize like ordinary brass. After all, it will be only the screws which will be holding the case in place.

There is a simple trick for assisting in getting a really tight fit which can also be used

elsewhere. When you have got as close as possible by eye, rub chalk over the hog face. Offer up the case and tap it into place. Then remove the case, whereupon the chalk will have been transferred to the high spots.

It is also sensible to brace the case temporarily so that it is absolutely vertical. It may be possible to fix the thwart to hold it rigid later.

CHINES

The next jobs are fitting the chines, inwales, and floor stringers. They must be fitted in pairs to equalize the strains on the jig, otherwise you might find that the whole boat would be twisted and it would also be difficult to fix the planking.

Chines are not always rectangular in section even before fairing in, and some labour can often be saved by ordering them with the correct bevels already cut. There is usually little trouble in fitting stringers from midships aft. The difficulty arises forward, where more bend may be needed than the timber will con-

7.9, 7.10, 7.11
Here we see three stages in the fixing of the chines to the stem. The chines should be fixed from amidships aft first, and finally bent down to their required positions against the stem. In this position the angle can be cut fairly accurately and then a second cut made with the saw parallel to the face of the stem, and the chine pressed hard against it. Some help or steaming may be needed to bend the chines on to the stem if the curve is sharp. (Small Craft, 14-ft Leader.)

veniently allow. If so, and as much wood as possible has already been whittled off it, there is nothing for it but steaming (see p. 55). More time will be needed than for a thin rib as in carvel building—possibly an hour or more.

Chines will almost certainly need a good deal of twisting near the bow. This can be done by putting cramps on them to act as levers, and finally lashing them down. Avoid if possible putting any screws through chines except at the ends, for the holes will almost

7.12

How a batten is used to check the bevels when fairing up. In this case the worker is checking to see whether he has gone far enough in starting the bevelling of the edge of the already fixed plank. A long batten should be used for fairing up fore and aft. (Small Craft, 14-ft Leader.)

certainly result in kinks at these points. You will find that if the notch is a tight fit over the chine, the pressure needed to bend the chine into place should hold it firmly whilst the glue is setting, but, if not, it can be cramped. It is not desperately important that a sound glued joint should result at points where chines cross frames, as long as the whole assembly remains firm and unmoved until the planking is glued in place.

The twist and bend at the stem will certainly cause screws and glue to be needed to hold the chine here. It may be necessary to use temporary struts to the jig and fastened or cramped to the chine in order to absorb the strains until the planking can hold them (Figs. 7.9, 7.10, 7.11).

Do not fasten the chines down permanently until the joint at the stem has been made satisfactorily. The easiest way of doing this is to project the chine past the stem, but held hard against it. With a saw held parallel to the stem face, cut through the chine. This will result in a nearly correctly angled cut being made. Bend the chine round and adjust its position until it is just touching the stem face. A further cut across the end using the face as a guide should now result in a close-fitting joint. The chine can then be cramped into the right position and drilled for screws.

When fitting chines make sure that there is enough wood standing proud above the frame edges to allow the full bevel to be made ready to receive the planking. Remember also to work from the correct side of each frame. If it has not already been done the frame edges will have to be bevelled as well as the chines during the next process, which is fairing in.

FAIRING IN

It is now necessary to fair in all the frames, chines, stringers, and inwales, stem and transom, so that the plywood can lie flat and tight everywhere. Use lengths of springy batten or lath to test the fairness. A batten long enough to span three frames is needed for the fore and aft direction, and another slightly longer than the widest part of any panel for the cross testing. You must be very careful not to plane the frame bevels too far, because the edge against the station line is the exact shape of the boat, less the planking thickness at this point, and this edge must not be reduced at all. Therefore start the fairing in with the frames, and then take a little off the chines and hog and continue in this order. Try for fairness by springing the batten across two or more faces in the same curve as the planking will adopt (Fig. 7.12).

Your plane iron needs to be very sharp. If you have to use pressure to make it cut, it will be impossible to do an accurate job, and so do touch it up frequently on the stone.

When you are satisfied that all the framing is fair you can think about the planking.

PLANKING

The first problem is the joint at the keel. If there is to be a rebate formed by the bevelled hog and a separate keel piece, then now is the time to fix the latter (Fig. 7.8). Cut it to shape according to the plans and try it for fit. The centreboard slot will have to be cut to match that in the hog, but do this last after final fitting for length. In some types of construction the keel at the bow continues as a laminated stem capping, in which case the exact length is not critical, and a simple scarf joint can be left. Alternatively, the planking might be notched round the end of the keel where it finishes, and it can finally be faired in afterwards (Figs. 7.13, 7.14, 7.15). The keel can then be fixed with glue and screwed from underneath through the hog.

The normal sheets of ply available in Britain are 8 ft × 4 ft, and this means that joints are needed to make up the required length of planking for all but the smallest of yacht tenders. Chapter 3 (p. 44) explains how plywood is scarfed, and if you decide to use this method, now is the time to plan it out. The plans frequently show you how to lay out your sheets most economically, but if they give no help on this there is nothing for it but to make trial templates. You can make a rough skeleton template out of thin springy battens or laths by tacking them temporarily to the framework along the keel and chines, and then strapping them together with other battens across and at angles. You will finish up with a flimsy skeleton template, the outer edge of which will be the rough shape of the whole panel. Lay this on the plywood and transfer the shape with a pencil. By laying sheets end to end and shunting your templates round you can soon find a layout with minimum waste.

You need not bother to scarf the sheets if you do not want to. Butt joints are nearly as neat and perfectly satisfactory—some say better. In this case measure where the end of the sheet will come on the framework and then let into the chine and keel a cross strut at this point. Then the end of one sheet is glued down on to this up to half its width, and the beginning of the next sheet is glued down on to the other half (Fig. 7.16). It is best to arrange matters so that the butt strap comes at the part of the hull which is as flat as possible and where there is a minimum of twist in the panel to avoid a slight kink showing on the final surface. The butt strap is usually just notched into the two stringers and then it will have to be faired in flush in the usual way.

If you have done your job with the skeleton template carefully you should have a very good fit to the panels at the first attempt. Offer up whichever panel includes the lower

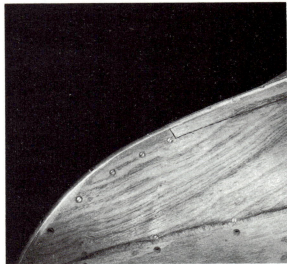

7.13, 7.14, 7.15
Three stages in the construction around the area where the hog and the stem meet. In this case the stem has reinforcing pieces screwed and glued to its side at the base, which provide a firm fixing for the end of the hog. The outer keel is glued on top of the hog, and the planking is notched round it as in Fig. 7.14. Finally the fore end of the outer keel is faired off flush with the planking. A keelband of metal is then screwed along the whole length of the keel and round the stem. (Small Craft, Gull.)

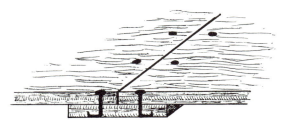

7.16
A butt strap joint which many people consider to be more satisfactory than a scarf joint for planking.

part of the stem first, and cramp it down firmly or screw it temporarily with steel screws. The joint at the keel is the first consideration, and you may be able to trim this

7.17
Planking should start with the panels nearest the keel. The operator is using a pump screwdriver to drive in the large number of screws needed for fixing the planking. The next stage is to bevel off the edge of the ply flush with the chine if a lap joint is to be employed. (Small Craft, Wayfarer.)

7.18
The boned joint is the soundest both for resisting knocks and for stopping water entering the end grain of the ply.

BONE OR FILLET

up straight away with the plane. If the trial cut is a long way adrift you can get a very close fit by spiling which is also explained in Chapter 3 (p. 44). When you are satisfied that the keel joint is as close as you can obtain, then cramp the panel down all round and start drilling the rest of the holes for fixing screws or nails.

Brass screws are expensive and also take a fair amount of time to drive even with a good pump screwdriver. It is well worth considering copper or copper alloy "Anchorfast" nails or similar ribbed nails. You may still have to use a few screws around the stem, in order to get that last tightening effect to bed the joint down firmly. You must drill pilot holes for copper nails and then temporarily run a few steel screws through some of these to hold the panel in place. Nails may go right through the chines, and in that case there is no need to use the "Anchorfast" type, because they will have to be clipped and clenched over in any case. (See Chapter 2, p. 29) If the thickness of the chines is such that the nails have to be clenched, then the amateur may find that screws are less trouble after all.

There is no need to get an accurate fit to the plank edge at the chine. Leave a quarter of an inch or so to spare. Fix the panel down evenly both sides together, starting amidships. As you near the stem the pressure needed will increase and you will have to resort to cramps, with a pad of soft wood under the heads. Even this may not be enough to deal with the twist and a kettle or two of boiling water poured over that part of the panel can often work wonders.

In single-chine boats the forward part of the lower panel has to be twisted through almost 90 degrees, and this is often the most troublesome part of the whole job. Double-chine boats are much easier, since not only are the panels narrower and much easier to manage, but the twist at the stem is about halved. The disadvantage is that there is an extra set of chines to fit and an extra set of joints to fit, nail and screw (Fig. 7.17).

CHINE JOINTS

The next problem is the type of joint to be used at the chine, and there are several possibilities. The soundest and most satisfactory long-term joint is undoubtedly that using a rebated fillet or boning piece. Unfortunately it is also by far the most difficult to make (Fig. 7.18). Some kits will supply chines already rebated and shaped,

and in this case you will have to use this type of joint, but also most of the tricky work will have been done for you. The boning piece protects and seals the ply edges, and also takes the first knocks of grounding and other minor damage. If you are faced with having to cut the fillet yourself, the easiest way is to fit the bottom panel and then to trim the chine edge exactly to shape, using a rebate plane. Then using the edge of the panel as a guide and holding the plane against it, you can plane out the rebate, but be careful to hold the plane hard against the edge, because the rebate must be exactly a right-angle. If you allow the plane to wander, the bone will be a sloppy fit (Fig. 7.19).

The next panel has to be fitted to the chine and then the plane can be used to trim that edge flush with the rebate. Finally the bone is fitted into the angle with glue and pins and then faired off flush with the planking. You can run the rebate out near the stem where the planks flatten out.

A much simpler and very nearly as satisfactory a joint is just to use a plain bevel or lap and then to plane a flat along the joint. A piece of batten is then glued on to the flat and finally faired off as before. This also protects the ply edges and seals the grain, and it will also have to run out near the stem. Where the chine angle is fairly sharp it is not even necessary to make the panels meet, since the flat to receive the capping will cover this area (Fig. 7.20).

The two simple joints, bevel and lap, both have slight difficulties, and it is a matter of personal preference which to use (Fig. 7.21).

The bevel joint needs a great deal of careful

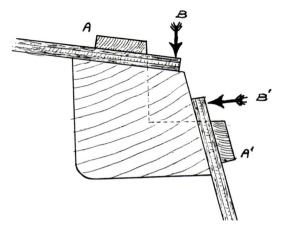

7.19
How the bone is fitted. It is best to tack battens along the edge at A and A′, and then to use the rebate planes in the direction B and then B′.

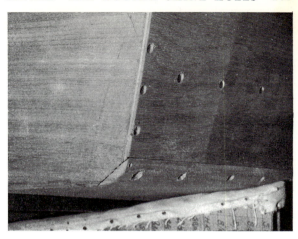

7.20
How a capped joint is finished off. This is nearly as satisfactory as the boned joint.

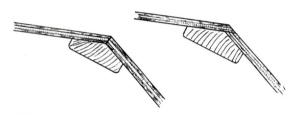

7.21
The two simplest joints used in chine building are the bevelled joint on the left, and the lap joint on the right.

planing of edges with the rebate plane, and also requires the edge of the next panel to be spiled to enable it to fit tightly. On the other hand, it is straightforward and the same from stem to stern, and also the ply edges are fairly well protected (Fig. 7.22).

The lap joint is basically simpler, but it has the disadvantage that as one approaches the

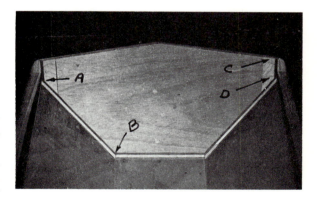

7.22
A Fireball stem transom before painting, showing A, a lap joint along the upper chine; B, a bevel joint along the lower chine; C, the inwale, which in this case fairs off and is glued on to the chine D, where the planking becomes very narrow at the stem. (Chippendale, Fireball.)

7.23

Near the stem of a chine boat the width of a lap joint becomes impossibly wide and therefore one has to change over to a bevel joint. The worker is chiselling out the start of the bevel and it can be seen where the lap is changing over to a bevel joint. (Small Craft, 14-ft Leader.)

7.24

Now the lap-joint can be seen to be completely faired in and the worker is cleaning off the edge of the bevel part of the joint up near the stem. The change-over can be clearly seen on this chine and also in the already completed chine just above. (Small Craft, 14-ft Leader.)

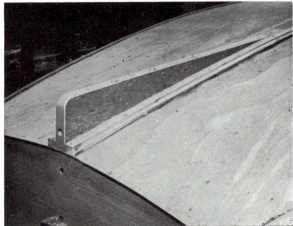

7.25

If one wishes to avoid having a rebate at the garboard seam one can use the construction shown here where the centreline is planed off flat after planking, and an outside keel glued on then.

stem the lap starts to get impossibly wide, until eventually it has to be changed into a bevel joint for the last couple of feet or so (Fig. 3.8, p. 49). The edge grain of one panel is also exposed, though in some designs a bilge rail can be fitted to cover this (Figs. 7.23, 7.24).

The remaining panels are perfectly straightforward to fit and will have far less twist than the bottom panel.

It may be that the plans call for the keel, if any, to be fitted after the planking, and in this case one simply planes a wide flat along the centreline and glues and screws the keel to this (Fig. 7.25). Other designs have no exposed keel, and still others ask for it to be fitted before planking as just described.

Before turning the hull over it would be as well to fit keelbands temporarily to protect the bottom, even though they will have to be removed for painting later. Make sure that the flats to receive them are the right width, and always bend the stem bands to the right shape *before* drilling the holes. They will never bend smoothly otherwise and may break at the holes (see Chapter 13).

A small point, but which, if not attended to, could cause much trouble later—remove all surplus glue from joints while it is still soft. It will be very difficult to get off when hard and will blunt plane irons quicker than anything.

◄   7.26
How an outer keel has been glued on after a flat has been planed along the centreline. Additional protection has been given in this case by a short skeg glued and screwed on top of this. (Small Craft, Gull.)

8 Composite Ply-Reinforced-Plastic Hulls

Ever since the introduction of fibre-glass, or to give it its more correct name, glass-fibre-reinforced plastic, it has been used for many purposes in the construction of boats, from complete hulls in fibre-glass and resin with no other materials involved at all down to the mere sticking together of various parts of a wooden boat with fibre-glass and resin. One of the more common applications which has been used for a number of years in many classes of dinghy is fixing bulkheads and buoyancy tanks to the skin of the boat. These items are quite difficult to fit accurately, and one way of getting over the trouble is to put a fibre-glass tape and resin fillet on either side which will cover many inaccuracies in fitting. If the job is well done it will be perfectly satisfactory and absolutely watertight (Fig. 8.1).

Some years ago I was able to have a hand in starting the development of a new kind of boat construction using plywood and fibre-glass tape and polyester resin. The idea of building a complete boat out of plywood sheets merely stuck together with fibre-glass tape and resin with no solid timber or fastening at all really started in Norway. I built some boats by this method in my own workshop several years ago, and later other boatbuilders in Britain, Australia, France and Canada, also took up the idea for certain types of dinghies. The method is specially suitable for hard-chine hulls and those which have one or two or more transverse bulkheads at widely spaced points in their hull. Nowadays some hard-chine racing dinghies, and many cruising dinghies also, have bow and stern buoyancy tanks which are sealed off by bulkheads right across the boat. These give tremendous strength and enable the full benefit of this composite construction to be realized.

The first boats that were built by this method were in the O.K. Dinghy Class, which has a hull about 13 ft long and is divided into four compartments by three transverse bulkheads. In normal construction these bulkheads are cut to the exact shape given on the building plans and are set up as frames upside down on a rigid base, so that the planking is formed round them in the way discussed in the previous chapter. In this new composite method of construction we need to make a jig consisting instead of exterior moulds. These are set up on a firm base, so that the hull is built inside it and the right way up. Planking is fitted into the jig and the bulkheads go in last, pressing the planking out against the jig. The photographs will show this more clearly.

First you must make a set of moulds from the building plans, which may entail allowing for the thickness of the planking, so that they will exactly fit outside the finished hull. These are set up on a firm floor or base in the correct relationship to each other, as has been described earlier, and well braced. Battens are

8.1
How an ultra-light plywood bulkhead and plywood bulkhead knee have been taped on to a fibre-glass shell by means of glass tape and resin. Note also the special plastic screw fixings, which avoid the need for wooden reinforcement behind the thin panel. (Keith Paul, Five-o-Five.)

8.2
The stern end of the exterior jig used for building the O.K. Dinghy by the composite plywood and fibre-glass method. The exterior moulds can be seen set up in their correct relationship, and the battens which were let in at the keel and chine to assist in making the plywood conform to the right shape. Note the well-braced subframe. (Rogers, O.K. Dinghy.)

8.3
Extra strutting and reinforcing was necessary at the stem to hold the battens firmly to the correct shape. The stem template can be seen connecting with the first mould, together with jutting out ledges on the upper part to hold the ends of the planks. (Rogers, O.K. Dinghy.)

8.4
The two bottom panels have been placed in the jig and a cramp has been constructed to press them down in the stem area, where there is considerable twisting. Note the additional strut right up in the forefoot to help push the planking downwards against the stem template. (Rogers, O.K. Dinghy.)

8.5
The planking is now assembled in the jig and cramped firmly in place. (Rogers, O.K. Dinghy.)

8.6 ►
The centreboard case and centre bulkhead have been assembled in one unit. A deckbeam holds the two halves of the bulkhead rigidly straight. And the whole assembly is simply dropped into the jig and holds the planking apart and against the moulds. (Rogers, O.K. Dinghy.)

let in about 1 in. each side of the chine and 1 in. each side of the centreline. A stem template is also set up, and you may need some sort of cramp to press down the lower planks in the bow so that they take up the right shape and lie tight against the moulds and battens. In fact, other cramps may be needed in any place where the planking does not lie tight against the moulds and battens (Figs. 8.2, 8.3, 8.4, 8.5, 8.6).

This method of construction is not really economic for one boat. It comes into its own when about three or more boats have to be built, because it then pays to make templates the exact shape of the planking and other parts and to cut them out in bulk. Getting the exact shape of the planking for the first boat is a bit of a fiddle, and takes rather a long time by the method of trial and error. One cuts out the panels, having scarfed up sheets to the full length, and then one gradually trims them down until, when pressed down tight into the jig, they fit exactly. One must reverse each panel and make sure it fits exactly on the other side of the boat. If it does not do so, then the jig has been set up incorrectly and there is some slight error in the positioning of the frames. With this method it does not matter if there is quite a large gap in between the planks where they would normally meet. This can be filled up with fibre-glass and resin or resin putty and will do no harm to the final strength of the boat. However, it is necessary to work as accurately as possible from the start, so that the final errors and gaps are not too enormous. Once you have got the planking fitting well on both sides this first panel can either be used as a template for future hulls or you can mark out its shape on to hardboard or the floor for future use. The planking can now be laid in the jig temporarily.

Meanwhile the various bulkheads and the transom should have been cut out exactly to the right shape, and then deckbeams and any other solid timber needed for reinforcing, such as is found on the inside of the transom to receive the screws from the rudder fastenings, can be glued on to the plywood. If the boat has only fore and aft bulkheads it may be necessary to make a temporary bulkhead or strut to go in the centre to keep the planking pressed against the side of the jig. Similarly, temporary struts may be needed in the bow to help get the plywood to conform to the shape where it bends most. The centreboard case can be made and fitted at this time also. It can be of plain plywood with filler pieces to separate the sides to the required gap. No other bottom framing is needed; put temporary battens inside to keep the box straight and also drill the centreboard pivot hole.

It is essential to be very careful about keeping the edges of the panels completely clean and dry where the fibre-glass tape and resin is going to have to stick. Where possible it is wise to plane a thin sliver off each edge of the panels about 2 in. wide and then to assemble the planking in the jig with rubber gloves so that grease from the hands does not mark the newly cleaned surfaces. It is almost certainly better to plane a clean sliver off the wood than to roughen the surface with a hacksaw blade as has often been recommended. You can now set everything up in the jig and tack or nail the panels, bulkheads and centreboard case into position temporarily. Do not drive tacks or nails fully home, but leave the heads projecting so that they can be removed before the taping is started. When you are sure everything is in the right place, you can start taping.

MATERIALS

(See also Chapter 9, pp.120–38)

We can now consider the materials needed for the taping. There is a list of suppliers of fibre-glass and resin materials at the end of this book, and it will be wise for intending builders to write to them to find out current prices and exact materials available. I used materials that were available at a local boat-yard and later in this section, on page 112 you will find a list of the rough amounts that are needed and an idea of the prices. The O.K. Dinghies which I built are hard-chine hulls about 13 ft 2 in. in length and have three bulk-heads, and therefore there was quite a consider-able length of tape needed to complete the hull. Tape can be used for all the joints, but it is quite expensive, and most builders will find that cloth cut up into strips of the required width will show quite a saving, with the dis-advantage that it is rather messier to use, owing to the frayed ends which continually get in the way and look rather untidy. However, after the resin has set most of these frayed ends can be scraped off quite easily. For parts of the boat which show, tape can be used, and for the parts inside tanks and bulkheads strips of cloth can be used. Pre-impregnated cloth can now be obtained from some glass weavers. This has been soaked in resin and when cut does not fray. It may not be obtainable in quantities less than one roll, though, and it may be hard to find at boatbuilding yards.

It is important to obtain the right sort of tape or cloth. In my opinion one needs cloth or tape of a fairly loose weave which will con-form to double curves well, and which will wet-out easily. I used some 2-in. and 3-in. 12-oz glass tape of a loosish weave, costing from £2·60 to £5·15 per 50 metre roll. The cloth used was 12 oz (400 gr) open weave material which is easy to cut with scissors down the line of the weft or the warp and does not fray quite so easily as close-woven cloth. There are some types of very loosely woven cloth and tape available, but I do not really think that these are suitable. They do not give a high enough glass content to the final job and are therefore not rigid enough. Also the strands of cloth can pull apart under the action of the stippling brush and leave quite large empty holes, with no glass reinforcement at all. For an explanation of the mat and cloth weight system and some conversion tables, see Appendix G on page 217.

It is recommended that you also obtain a small quantity of some material called Format or needled mat. It is thick material, looking rather like a loosely woven felt and is very useful for making a rigid fillet right in the corners of right-angled joints. I suggest that the Format is cut into very narrow strips about $\frac{3}{8}$ in. wide and pressed into the very corners of right-angled joints. This will provide a slight rounding which makes it much easier for the succeeding tape strips to follow. If the tape or cloth is worked into a plain sharp corner, it very often leaves a narrow gap which will be dry and hollow behind after the resin has hardened. The use of a narrow strip of Format in the corner avoids this hollow dry corner. It

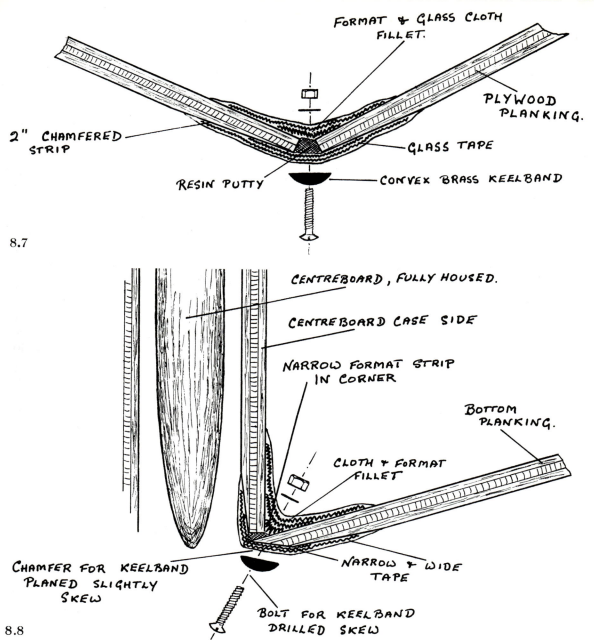

FORMAT & GLASS CLOTH FILLET.

PLYWOOD PLANKING.

2" CHAMFERED STRIP

GLASS TAPE

RESIN PUTTY

CONVEX BRASS KEELBAND

8.7

CENTREBOARD, FULLY HOUSED.

CENTREBOARD CASE SIDE

NARROW FORMAT STRIP IN CORNER

BOTTOM PLANKING.

CLOTH & FORMAT FILLET

CHAMFER FOR KEELBAND PLANED SLIGHTLY SKEW

NARROW & WIDE TAPE

BOLT FOR KEELBAND DRILLED SKEW

8.8

is also useful to put a slightly wider strip of Format down the centreline, as this helps to stop resin running through the gap. It also provides some slight extra reinforcement along the centreline. No other glass materials are needed.

The resin which is used is normally an ordinary polyester impregnating resin; for an O.K. Dinghy you should need from about 5 to 7 kg, and it will cost about £1 per kg. You may also need about 250 gr of polyester priming resin, which is much thinner than ordinary impregnating resin and is used as a first coat on the timber in order to provide a good key. You will also need some catalyst, which is mixed with the resin immediately before being applied and causes it to harden. The amounts of tape and cloth used in the O.K. Dinghy were about 20 yards of 75 mm. tape, about 8 yards of 50 mm. tape, about 1 yard of 600 gr Format and 3 yards of 400 gr knotted-weave cloth costing in all about £6. There are various different sorts of polyester resin available. Avoid one that is too thick, as this will be difficult to use and it takes a long time to wet-out the cloth. Mix up the resin with the required amount of catalyst only immediately before it is needed. It will start to go off at once and will become suddenly solid after a period of time depending on the amount of catalyst used and the temperature of the room. Setting off in about one hour should be aimed at. I use ordinary $\frac{1}{2}$ kilo food tins and have small measures available in which to put the required amount of catalyst so that it is easy to get the exact amount into each mix. One needs 1-in. brushes with about one-third of the bristles cut off to make them a bit stiffer.

Brush on the resin just as if it was a thick and rather sticky varnish. A primer is well brushed in first and can be allowed to harden, but the taping must be continued within twenty-four hours to make a satisfactory bond, and it is best to get the whole job finished as soon as possible. Paint on a strip of resin and then press on the tape or cloth and stipple it thoroughly to get the resin well impregnated into the fibres. Continue with another strip, and then go back to the first and give it another coat of resin to make sure it is well impregnated. If the weather is cold a certain amount of heat may be needed to get the resin to go off properly, and electric blowers or infra-red lamps are quite satisfactory. However, do not apply too much heat or expansion troubles may cause the bond to break on hardening. A temperature of about 50° to 60°F. should be considered ideal. It can be quite difficult to do this sort of job at a temperature much higher than about 70°F., because the resin will set off too quickly.

It is useful to have a proportion of thixotropic filler added to the resin. This helps to stop the resin running out of the glass on vertical or near-vertical surfaces. Always use clear impregnating resin, so that you can see that the bond is properly made and that all air bubbles have been expelled by stippling or rolling.

It is probably only necessary to use a single strip of 400 gr cloth on the inside of chines, though, if required, two thicknesses of a narrow and a wide strip of cloth or tape can be employed here. This also assumes that a narrow strip of Format has been used on the more acute-angled joints. The knack of the whole business is to work smoothly and steadily and not to get flustered. If the resin in the tin starts to go into lumps, empty it out immediately. When working quickly, thoroughly wash out the brushes in acetone about every three tinfuls. If working slowly wash out the brushes each time. This is done by putting a little acetone in a small bowl and squeezing out the brush thoroughly and then knocking and shaking it out immediately. Then put a second small quantity of acetone into the bowl and do the same again. Acetone evaporates very rapidly and so it is wise to do this job as quickly as possible. Barrier cream is a great help in avoiding getting the hands completely stuck up with resin. The hands can be wiped with a rag dipped in acetone and then washed in detergent and warm water (Figs. 8.7, 8.8, 8.9, 8.10, 8.11).

In warm weather the resin will have hardened off sufficiently for the hull to be removed from the jig by the following day. If in any doubt about whether the resin has cured properly, leave it for a further day and apply some heat to bring the temperature up to above 50°F. When the hull is lifted out of the jig it can be turned over and put on trestles for the work to be done on the bottom. The bottom will probably look pretty rough with wide gaps in between the planks and drops of resin sticking through. The first thing is to get a Surform tool and rasp off the exposed resin. Then it is necessary to plane a 2-in.-wide chamfer about ⅛ in. deep at the joint edge and tapering away to nothing 2 in. from the joint, all the way round all the joints at the keel, the chine, the stem and the transom. Then with the Surform round off where necessary along

8.9

Taping has just started in the interior. As it progresses the tacks which are used to hold the bulkheads temporarily in position can be steadily removed. Note the deckbeam on the transom and also the reinforcing piece to enable the screws for the rudder pintles to bite. (Rogers, O.K. Dinghy.)

all the joints. The centreboard slot can be cut out at this time also and cleaned up in the same way.

Next you will need to make up or get hold of resin putty. Resin putty is just the ordinary polyester resin with a proportion of filler added to make it stiff. The fillers normally used include chalk, china clay, talc, or slate powder. Asbestos powder and asbestos fibre are also used, as are chopped fibre-glass and even wood flour and pulverized fabrics. It is important to use one of these recommended fillers, because some materials will affect the setting of the resin and may even cause it never to set at all. Most of the suppliers will be able to offer resin putty already mixed. The resin putty is

8.10
Taping usually starts in the stem. In this case small blocks have been taped in to receive the mast step. The heel of the mast rests on plywood covered in glass tape. Note the strip of tape along the inside of the chine. (Rogers, O.K. Dinghy.)

8.11
No solid timber is needed in the boat at all apart from filler pieces, packing pieces and light deck-beams. A single strip of fibre-glass tape is all that is needed round most of the joints. The keel joint needs two thicknesses. The centreboard case is kept straight by a loose batten inside it during assembly. (Rogers, O.K. Dinghy.)

used in the same way as an ordinary stopper and is knifed into all gaps and imperfections in the joints to make a smooth surface. It has to be mixed with catalyst in the same way as the resin before being applied.

One should use tape as opposed to strips of cloth on the outside of the boat in general, because it produces a much neater finish and causes less trouble in smoothing and fairing up afterwards (Fig. 8.12). First put a coat of primer over the strips to be covered with fibre-glass tape and then carefully put a full coat of resin followed immediately by the tape. Take great care not to get resin beyond the edge of the 2-in.-wide chamfer, because it will

be extremely difficult to clean off later. Two layers of tape will almost certainly be needed along the keel, but usually one layer is sufficient on the chines. Apply some heat at this stage especially along the centreboard case to make the resin go off quickly before it has time to drain out and cause air bubbles. Wait until the first coating of resin and glass has just hardened and then clean it up with the Surform to get the nibs and small projections off. Then apply the second layer, and, as soon as this has hardened, clean it up again with the Surform much more severely. It is necessary to do the cleaning with the Surform as soon as the resin has set. If it is left until the following day, it will be very much harder to remove. Finally give a gel coat of pure resin over the top.

The 2-in.-wide chamfer will accommodate most of the thickness of resin and glass, and if the job has been done carefully it will be found that very little stopper will be needed to make a fair surface, which will be undetectable when the boat is painted. If the job is done very carefully, it is even possible to varnish a hull without the signs of the taping being obvious. If the tape has been thoroughly wetted-out it should be almost invisible.

Using this sytem of construction, ordinary fastenings such as nails and screws are not necessary and, in fact, are undesirable, because they might cause local breakdown of the bond, and allow introduction of moisture which could cause trouble later. Areas can be reinforced where necessary to take the loadings of toestraps, and other such things. Boats built this way can be assembled very quickly and with unskilled labour once the technique of the fibre-glassing process has been mastered. One does not need to be an expert joiner to get a really good and sound finish. Jigs are only in use for about one day, and even less if care is taken and some heat is available. The same methods are applicable to small jobs such as fitting bulkheads into existing boats. Cleanliness is essential, and if heat is to be applied, let it be mild. The O.K. Dinghies which I built were easy to get down to the minimum allowed weight and were absolutely watertight (Figs. 8.13, 8.14).

For dinghies which are to be raced it

8.12
Glass tape can be tailored to fit along the chines and round the stem, having been recessed slightly below the surface by the chamfering of the edges of the joints. After cleaning up with a Surform tool a further coat of resin can be applied. (Rogers, O.K. Dinghy.)

might not be necessary to put on protective keelbands, because great care is usually taken of these boats. But for ordinary general-purpose boats it is essential to use a keelband, because the fibre-glass and resin will get chipped and worn and knocked about on trolleys and concrete hards, and if the tape wears through most of the strength is lost. Keelbands should be bolted using through-bolts and not screwed on, and it is not recommended that self-tapping screws be used. Figs. 8.7 and 8.8 (p 111) show how the keelbands are fastened. The rest of the boat can be completed in the ordinary way. The taping can continue

8.13
After the hull has been removed from the jig notches are cut to receive the inwales at the sheer. It can be seen that a great deal of the interior of the boat can be fitted while it is still in the jig. (Rogers, O.K. Dinghy.)

up to within about an inch of the sheerline, and then a light gunwale can be put through and the decks fixed on top of this. It is not considered to be economical to tape the decks on. I did tape on the deck of one boat, but it is just as simple to fix it on in the ordinary

way, and it was found to be less trouble. The advantage of the composite method of construction is mainly in the chine and keel areas of the boat. The compound curves which need fairly skilled attention from the joiner in ordinary construction are taken care of by the moulding properties of the resin. Costs have worked out to be a little less than those for the normal method of construction.

COMPOSITE DEVELOPMENTS

There have been further developments in this

8.14

The final deckbeams, inwales, and cockpit carlins have now been fitted, and the hull is ready for decking in an extremely short period of time. (Rogers, O.K. Dinghy.)

field and the promotion by a national newspaper and a well-known designer of "do-it-yourself" knock-about boats of rather similar construction shows that the fears of traditional builders and buyers of traditional craft are shown to be groundless. Everyone said when glued, ribless, clinker construction appeared that the boats would fly apart as soon as they hit anything solid—but they didn't. Even earlier, grave fears were expressed over the soundness of cold veneer moulding, and yet it is now acknowledged as being possibly the best method of all for building small boats. In my opinion the composite ply G.R.P. system, if properly used, is at least as satisfactory in use as any other, and is very simple to do.

After many years' experience with light racing boats using the system the only failures were due to factors not attributable to the method itself. During the early period of trial in Britain there was one joint failure out of about seventy boats, traced to dirt or grease on the face of the timber to be bonded—hence the warning on cleanliness.

The first boats were made far too strongly owing to our fears of possible weakness, but this brought trouble from an unexpected quarter. The massive amounts of resin and glass used, especially in acute angles, such as the inside of the stem and the base of the centreboard case, caused excess heating during the cure, which in one case broke the bond between the ply and the resin. After great efforts, the entire stem reinforcement of this hull was broken out complete and remains in the workshop as a warning and a lesson in the matching of strength characteristics when using different materials.

After this we started reducing the glass and resin content of the joint, believing, I think rightly, that a thinner reinforcement which could flex slightly in sympathy with the adjacent panel would give a lasting bond. The glass and resin in the joint was finally reduced to well below what I thought was safe until finally a heavily stressed joint gave way under very severe sailing conditions. However, the skimpiness of the actual reinforcements in this particular joint, and the punishment it received before it finally gave way, were convincing proof of the success of the system.

To sum up, then, the main points to watch out for when making joints are: absolute cleanliness of the timber surfaces; no voids in the sharp angles of the joints (use narrow strips of Format in the corners); do not use cloth or tape of such a loose weave that holes appear when stippling in the resin; do not use a cloth of too dense a weave; one layer of tape on each side is satisfactory except where abrasive wear is expected.

The dinghy sponsored by the national newspaper, the Mirror Dinghy, uses a method to obtain its hull shape which is many thousands of years old. Instead of either bending the hull panels round male moulds or pressing them into a female jig, the edges are simply sewn together with copper wire after the panels have been cut to shape from the plans and drilled to accept the wire. Careful design has enabled the required hull shape to be formed without undue pressure or twisting of the plywood. As soon as the stitching is complete the joints are taped inside and out with the wire still in place.

Another variation is seen in the *Yachts and Yachting* Scowler, which is a clinker-built scow, where the plank edges are not bevelled off. The narrow gap between planks is filled with a resin putty which effectively holds them together. Tape is used for extra reinforcement and at the transom, stem and bulkheads.

All this goes to show that this method and its variations are now established systems of boatbuilding and particularly suitable for amateur use. The old traditional system of boatbuilding, using nails, ribs and stringers, had many disadvantages and was craftsman's work. The new fibre-reinforced plastics moulding methods are a great step forward, but again have disadvantages for amateurs. Many new methods using combinations of wood in strip, veneer, or ply form, together with resins are proving a really exciting new field for the amateur, and this chapter gives food for thought in this direction.

9 *Glassfibre Reinforced Plastic Hulls*

THE tremendous revolution that the use of plastics has brought to the world has extended to the field of boatbuilding, where objects of complicated shape and with compound curves have to be constructed. The traditional methods need much fairly skilled and time-consuming labour, but at their best can give a beautiful and satisfying result both to builder and owner. The use of plastics, however, gives a great opportunity for reduction in man-hours spent on the job. Boats have been built of glass-reinforced plastics only since several years after the last war, and the materials which can be employed are still undergoing rapid and constant development.

The chemical reactions which take place within the resins which are used are highly complicated and quite beyond the comprehension of an amateur like myself, but being placed in the position of the amateur, I ask myself firstly, "Is it feasible for someone without technical knowledge to build a boat out of glass-reinforced plastics?" and secondly "If it is feasible, how does one set about it?"

I have myself dabbled in fibre-glass materials, and have produced results which were adequately strong and satisfactory, and have had no unexplained failures. Thinking about the problems involved in constructing a complete boat in this material, I feel that any enterprising amateur could quite easily build a satisfactory hull shell in this material. In general there is nothing any more difficult in building a shell in glassfibre reinforced plastics (let us call it G.R.P., for short) than there is in building a cold-moulded veneer shell.

When one comes to the deck and interior considerable problems arise, though again a determined amateur will overcome them. The problems really centre on the actual making of the mould on to which the G.R.P. will be laid. The amateur may spend so much time constructing the mould that it might not be an economic proposition.

It is perfectly feasible, and indeed one could make out a good case for it being actually better, to use a G.R.P. hull shell with normal timber decks and interior, and this might be the best way for an amateur to start his acquaintance with the material.

I have been considerably impressed, both from experience and from what I have been told, by the extreme care which is needed in order to make a thoroughly sound article in G.R.P. There are so many technicalities which cannot be understood by the non-scientific amateur that it cannot be too strongly emphasized that, though the process is basically simple and the making of boats or any other object of straightforward shape is well within amateur capabilities, the detailed instructions of the resin manufacturer must be followed absolutely. Deviations or short cuts might be perfectly all right in practice in some conditions, but might just as easily be the cause of ghastly and expensive failures.

There are so many hundreds of different types of resins and reinforcing materials for various applications that the intending builder would be well advised to contact one of the suppliers of resin and to ask for suitable materials for the purpose. Many suppliers issue highly detailed brochures giving all the necessary information on their products, and often suitable resins can be selected from these.

For the amateur who is going to use only a comparatively small amount of material it could prove best to go to one of the many reputable builders of G.R.P. boats or other objects and ask them to supply the materials. Most will be only too happy to do so, and might give valuable advice as well.

You get the glass, by the way, from different firms from those who supply resins. However, if you say what you want it for, they can advise on the best materials to use.

The reader must take any remarks made concerning difficulties or failures experienced with an open mind, and inquire, when ordering materials, whether these remarks are still valid. The materials are constantly being improved, and earlier causes of failures or trouble are gradually being eliminated. For instance, surface crazing is almost a thing of the past now, provided the right types of surface coatings are used. The use of fillers is also better understood, and failures resulting from using too much or the wrong sort are hardly known today.

I hope I have not frightened anyone off trying his hand at G.R.P. work with all these reservations and warnings. I only want to impress on the amateur that the material is a complicated chemical, and, while basically very easy to use, needs extremely careful control if failures are not to result. In other words, if you follow the directions carefully it is simplicity itself. Make a few small trial laminates first, to get the hang of the technique, before embarking on a complete hull shell.

RESINS

The laminate consists of a resin reinforced with layers of some material, in this case fibreglass. Additives can be used to colour the resin or to make it less likely to drain from vertical surfaces, or to stiffen it so that it can be used as a putty.

The resin which we are mainly considering is of the polyester type and is thermosetting—that is, it needs heat for it to change from its treacly state to the rigid solid we finally require. When you get some polyester resin it will probably look just like a fairly clear honey. If you then mix in a very small quantity of a catalyst, which is usually a type of liquid peroxide, and then heat it, a chemical reaction will cause the resin to start to solidify. It is inconvenient to have to heat the laminate to get it to set off in boatwork, and so a very small quantity of an accelerator is added. In its original state the resin is perfectly stable and will not set off unless exposed to bright sunlight or a catalyst, so don't keep your resin in glass jars. When the time comes to use the resin, you pour out a known quantity into a tin and then add and mix in a few drops of catalyst from an eye-dropper bottle. Between 1 and 4 per cent is the usual amount, which works out at around 6 to 24 drops per ounce of resin. The catalyst not only reacts with the resin to put it in a state where it can set, but also reacts with the accelerator to produce the heat needed for the cure to take place.

In cold conditions more accelerator and catalyst will be needed. Adjusting the percentage of catalyst from 1 to 4 per cent in normal variations of temperature will usually be all that is required, but in difficult cases either more or less accelerator can be ordered or alternatively external heat can be applied.

Another point to note is that the thicker the laminate the greater the heat that is generated, and thus thick laminations laid up at one time will set off quicker than thin ones. This point must be watched in order to avoid cracking due to expansion caused by excess heat. It also means that if remaining resin starts to set off in the tin it could generate heat or smoke or even start a fire. Therefore pour out any remaining resin as soon as its starts to go lumpy. It is interesting to note that the heat only appears after the resin has gelled, or started to go solid.

Other things besides the amount of catalyst, accelerator and the thickness can also affect the curing. Moisture can delay the cure and this can be in the form of a damp atmosphere or even damp glass materials that have been lying about. Dry off the workshop and the mould carefully, and store the rolls of glass mat in a dry place. The type and quantity of any filler or colouring material can also affect the cure. Use only the types recommended by the manufacturer and in the right proportions. If the air temperature is too low (say around 40°F. or less), the resin may not cure at all. If

left in this state for too long certain vital constituents will evaporate until there will be too little left to complete the cure at all, even if heat is then applied. Therefore do not use the material unless the room temperature can be kept above 45°F. long enough to effect a complete cure. This time will vary depending on the resin and the amount of catalyst and accelerator, but manufacturers' brochures will give all the information needed to work it out. The ideal temperature for reinforced plastics work using polyester resins is around 60°.

Resins are supplied in several viscosities (or degrees of stickiness). It is easier to wet-out the glass thoroughly with a low-viscosity (or runny) resin, but if vertical surfaces have to be laid up and the temperature is low, the resin may drain out of the glass before it has had time to gel. Addition of a thixotropic paste makes the resin take on a slight tendency towards a grease-like consistency which helps to stop it draining out, and for boatwork it is usual to ask for a small percentage of this filler to be added. The manufacturers will recommend the right proportion.

Another point to note concerning resins is that though they may set to a hard solid within an hour or two the cure is not complete for days or even weeks. It is possible to apply heat to accelerate this ageing process, but if not done, the laminate should be left in the mould for at least a couple of days, and preferably longer. Kinks, dents and warping can result if this advice is not followed.

Manufacturers of resins list many different types under their own code numbers. Mostly these resins are basically the same, but with varying proportions of additives, accelerators and fillers to enable standard mixes to be ordered for varying purposes.

Some of the more obvious differences are as follows:

The normal polyester resin is rather hard and brittle when cured, and so, for surface coatings and when used for taping plywood panels together, or for fixing bulkheads to hull shells, it could be an advantage to mix in a proportion of one of the flexible resins which are stocked by most makers. Special gel-coat resins are also obtainable incorporating a wide range of colour pigments if desired. It is highly desirable to use one of these special resins for gel coats (i.e. the first coat or two of plain resin next to the mould), because they are especially tough and flexible and designed to resist knocks and surface crazing, as well as giving a smooth glossy finish.

The normal impregnating resin dries to a slightly tacky surface. This is caused by the air acting on the surface skin of the setting resin, and the surface will never cure fully. Whilst this is of no importance when further layers are to be put on top, it may be a nuisance for the final coat. Special tack-free resins are marketed, and for the amateur who is only using a small amount it could be economic to find one which could be used for all of the lay-up except the gel coat, rather than obtain a special small quantity just for the inner surface coat.

Resins with varying amounts of thixotropic filler are often sold under different code numbers, and if you tell the manufacturer the sort of conditions you are going to work under, he will advise the right proportions. The usual amateur's building conditions are rather poor for plastic work, being frequently cold and draughty. Thus a low-viscosity resin with rather high proportions of accelerator and thixotropic filler will be the choice.

As an example—the Filabond range of resins are marketed in about thirty types under seven main headings. For the normal cold (or wet) lay-up purposes in which we are interested this narrows the choice down to the "low-reactivity types", of which five are listed, only the first three being of interest to us. These three are the same, but with varying proportions of styrene added to give varying viscosities.

Also listed are various thixotropic pastes, one of which has such a low viscosity that it is recommended for use alone, as an impregnating resin on large boats. However, on studying the catalogue, one sees that this manufacturer, in common with most others, markets a special ready-use mix consisting of a low reactivity, low-viscosity resin, together with just the right amount of thixotropic paste for ordinary workshop conditions, and, assuming there are no special considerations, this will be the one to select.

Beware of being lured into selecting a fast-curing resin for boatwork. Resins of this type are meant for rapid repetition work of small objects, and cure much too fast for our purpose.

The only other resin we shall need is that for the gel coat. Suppliers list a special mix for brush application containing suitable proportions of flexible resins and thixotropic filler for boatwork.

Gel-coat resins for spray application may set off too fast for brushwork.

In all these resins accelerator can be added in about four standard percentages at the works, and catalysts are ordered and supplied separately.

If the accelerator and the catalyst are supplied separately, they must never be mixed together in this neat form. They would react violently and could cause an explosion. Always mix either one or the other thoroughly into the resin first. The resin with the accelerator mixed in is still stable and is frequently stored for several months in dark containers in this condition.

Resin putty can be made or bought and consists of resin with some added filler to make it the desired stiffness. It takes rather a long time to set off hard but there are now available rapid setting fillers which go hard in a few minutes. P38, for example, is a grey paste into which is mixed a very small quantity of hardener. It can be knifed on and is soluble in acetone before setting. It can then be smoothed with a file. There are fillers of various consistency and hardness on the market.

EPOXY RESINS

There is another type of resin which is quite different chemically, called an epoxide. This is not quite so easy to handle or to cure as the polyester type, and is more than twice the price, but is preferred for some specialized applications.

Its main advantage in boatwork is its extremely high adhesive property. Thus one would prefer to use an epoxide if attempting to fix a panel or object to an already cured polyester surface or to a wood or metal surface. One would not normally use an epoxide resin for a complete hull of a boat. The Epophen range made by Borden Chemicals is typical, and if the amateur wishes to use this type, a study of the technical leaflets shows which resin would be the most suitable. A curing agent, of which there are many types, is mixed with the resin to promote the hardening process. You would need a type which is suitable for curing at room temperatures. Accelerators can also be added to speed up the whole cure which would normally take four to seven days. Fillers, including thixotropic and colour pigments can also be added, but use only recommended types. Another point to watch out for is that the "binder" or "surface finish" of the glass reinforcement is compatible with the type of resin and hardener to be used. Check with the glass manufacturer. Pot-life of the mixed resin and hardener is comparable with that for polyester.

Epoxide resin is also the best material for use when sheathing wooden hulls, owing to its superior adhesive powers.

GLASS REINFORCING

Glass materials are obtained from the manufacturers and weavers, some of whom are listed in the Appendix on page 232. Alternatively, the amateur can obtain small quantities from retail firms advertising in the yachting or motoring Press, or from some boatbuilders and chandlers (see also the Appendix). Broadly, the glass is made up into two types of interest to us. The first is glass filament in various forms, and the second is woven material. The woven materials are stronger and easier to handle, but they are more expensive. There are two main subdivisions of this type; woven cloth which looks just like coarse canvas in various weaves, and woven rovings which is very coarse-looking indeed, consisting of bundles of rovings, or filaments, up to $\frac{1}{4}$ in. or so across, woven together.

Mats are made by a machine which chops glass filaments into 2-in. lengths and drops them at random on to a moving conveyor belt. The chopped strands are lightly held together into mat form by a binder. This random mat is very cheap and is largely used for general-purpose work, where extreme strength is not needed. Most boatwork can be undertaken with mat. Its main disadvantage is that it tends to be messy to use, and it does not like conforming to sharp double curvatures much. Bits tend to come adrift and get stuck to everything in sight. However, once the technique is mastered it is quite satisfactory.

Cloth and woven rovings can be tailored to fit, provided a generous overlap is given to joints. It is as well to cut the cloth or mat roughly to shape before starting to mix up the resin. See that everything is ready so that the lay-up can go ahead without delays.

The only other glass materials of interest to the beginner are tapes of varying sizes and thicknesses, and some stuff called needled mat. This latter is just like a thick felt and is useful in narrow strips for filling in sharp-angled corners where cloth or mat would leave a hollow owing to inability to conform (Figs. 9.1, 9.2, 9.3, 9.4, 9.5, 9.6).

Cloths and tapes can be had in many different weights and weaves and something suitable can always be selected.

The weavers treat the glass material in various ways to meet differing requirements.

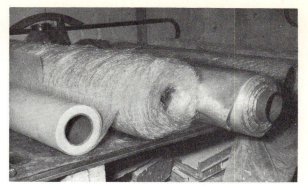

9.1
Glass materials usually come in rolls. On the left can be seen thin surfacing mat. Next is random chopped mat for general lay-up purposes. The next roll is of a heavy cloth. (Souter.)

9.2
The heavy material is woven rovings, which is suitable for strong structures and main laminations in boatwork. The 2-in heavy tape is ideal for use in the taping of bulkheads on to hull shells or in the composite construction described in Chapter 8. (Tape by Marglass.)

In an untreated state, the size which is used in the manufacturing process would cause poor

9.3

This is a very heavy roving indeed. There are only about four weaves to the inch and this would be used in very heavy construction. This 1½-in tape is, in my opinion, almost useless for any purpose in boatwork. Tape or cloth of this density weave has very poor inter-laminar bonding powers. It is not suitable for taping bulkheads or panels together.

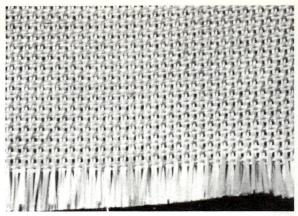

9.4

Twelve-ounce knotted-weave cloth, suitable for cutting into strips and using as tape in the composite construction method. It can also be used for reinforcing in ordinary lay-ups. (Peter Webster.)

bonding and resin impregnation. The material is first cleaned of size by a heat process, but this leaves it considerably weaker. Further treatment with chemicals restores most or all of the strength and also allows it to accept various types of resin. It is important to obtain alkali-free glass with a treatment suitable for polyester resin. A general-purpose silane treatment is a suitable example.

You obtain the following from a glass spinner, such as Fibreglass Ltd: Chopped-strand mat, needled mat, yarn, rovings, surfacing mat. And the following from a weaver: Woven cloth, woven rovings, woven tape, and pre-impregnated material.

The weight of mat is usually measured in ounces per square foot, and woven materials in ounces per square yard, which is rather confusing. Metric conversions are given in Appendix G, page 217.

Glass materials must be stored in a dry clean place.

Surfacing mat is a thin glass tissue which is useful for two purposes. It can be laid immediately after the gel coat and before the main reinforcing to provide a sound basis for the gel coat to help it withstand knocks. It also prevents any showing through of the reinforcing layers. It can also be used as a final layer to make a smooth and efficient-looking finish.

Chopped-strand mat is the most commonly used reinforcing material nowadays, especially since advances in making soluble binders have allowed easier through wetting, easier conformation to curves, and a higher glass ratio in the laminates.

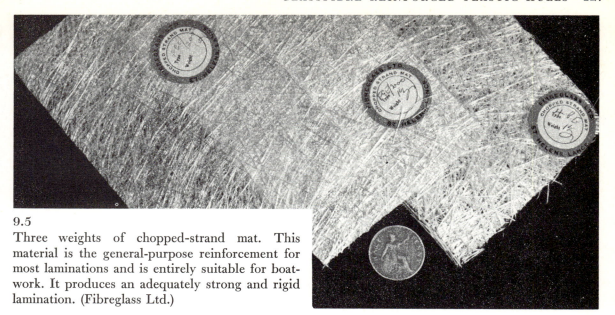

9.5
Three weights of chopped-strand mat. This material is the general-purpose reinforcement for most laminations and is entirely suitable for boat-work. It produces an adequately strong and rigid lamination. (Fibreglass Ltd.)

9.6
On the left is a very light overlay mat. In the middle is a slightly heavier surfacing mat, and on the right is the heavy felt-like needled mat weighing 2 oz per square foot. (Fibreglass Ltd.)

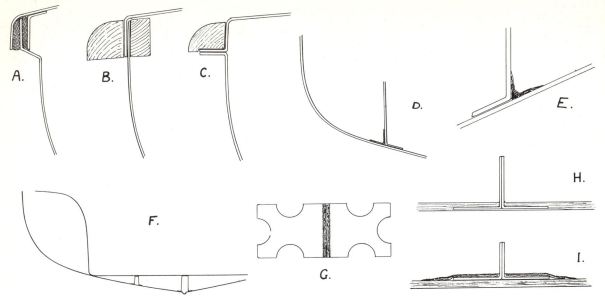

9.7

Drawings A, B and C show three possible methods of fixing a fibre-glass deck to a fibre-glass hull. I prefer method C, as there is protection from the wooden rubbing-band as well as this being easy to fix and replace. Drawings D, E and F show ways of fixing tanks to the hull. (See also Fig. 9.12.) The tanks can be combined with a watertight double bottom as shown in Drawing F. It is rather difficult to make sure that all the edges are properly bonded, and it would need a great deal of planning to get the necessary moulds correct. The floor supports would have to be moulded separately and then bonded in place. Drawings G, H and I show methods of fixing load-bearing brackets. System H is much to be preferred. The brackets ought to be moulded in rather than bonded on afterwards.

Woven rovings are often used where extra strength is needed.

Personally I do not much like using cloth unless it is of the open-weave or knotted-weave variety. The close-weave cloths are hard to impregnate thoroughly and air bubbles do not like coming through, and have to be squeezed to the edges. Inter-lamination bonding is better with the mat and open-weave cloth, too. There is the added difficulty of accurate tailoring of the close-woven cloth to fit the curves. The more open the weave the easier the cloth will be to drape. The chopped-strand mats do not at first seem to be easy to drape, but the resin very soon dissolves the binder and the mat will then fall into place.

The strength of the laminate depends on the skill of the operator. The higher the glass content the stronger. All air bubbles must also be removed, and the glass must be completely wetted out. There must not be excess pools of neat resin in the lower areas; neat resin is brittle and also adds unnecessary weight.

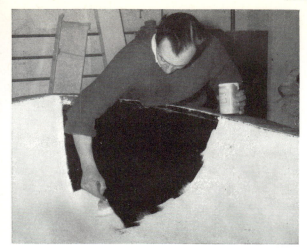

◄   9.8

The gel coat can be painted or sprayed on to the mould after the mould has been very carefully treated with a release agent such as polyvinyl alcohol. It is essential to use a gel coat designed for brushwork if one is using a brush. Do not try to brush on a gel coat designed for spraying. The gel coat should be allowed to get really hard before applying a second gel coat or a normal lay-up. If this is not done, the gel coat may wrinkle. (Souter, Penguin Dinghy.)

A slight disadvantage to great efficiency in laying-up is that the lamination will be thinner, as it will contain less resin. This means that though stronger, it will be less rigid. Bulky fillers can be added to the resin to add stiffness if this is really a problem.

Stringers and other reinforcing may need to be added in some places and often a paper or cardboard tube is all that is needed to make a former. The former is stuck in place and glass and resin laid over it. Wooden blocks can also be moulded in, thus allowing fittings to be fastened to them with ordinary wood screws. Shape the blocks carefully by rounding off the corners and bevelling the sides, so that the glass can conform easily.

Metal brackets and anchorages can also be moulded in, but careful design of the bracket and its surrounding lamination is essential if any strain is to be taken. The drilling of holes and scolloping of the edges of the immersed portion will assist in obtaining a firm fixing (Fig. 9.7 (G), (H) and (I)). Through-fastenings are perfectly satisfactory, provided that metal bushes are fitted to stressed bolts. The resin

9.9

The mat or other reinforcement is tailored as nearly as possible to shape and then a full coat of neat resin is applied. The tailored pieces are then pressed on to the resin and stippled with a stiffish brush to bring the resin up from underneath to permeate the glass. (Souter, Penguin Dinghy.)

would otherwise crush and allow water to enter. Use broad washers under bolt-heads.

THE LAY-UP

The lay-up must be continued at a steady rate. Do not leave longer than about a day between the layers or a doubtful bond may result. Equally do not lay-up more than a couple of layers at a time or the heat generated would cause distortion or cracking. Watch out when putting on gel coats that the first coat is hard before applying a second (Fig. 9.8). Wrinkling of the surface coat is caused by haste here.

The actual sequence of a period of laying-up might be as follows:

Cut out a convenient-sized piece of mat or cloth and roughly trim it to the space to be filled.

Do not deal with too large an area at a time. A square yard or so would be enough for one man.

Then pour out about 8 oz of resin to which accelerator and filler has previously been added in bulk either by you or by the makers.

Measure out the exact amount of catalyst needed. If you are using a standard size of tin you can work out in advance a convenient measure for the amount of catalyst, and this will save a great deal of time.

Mix the catalyst into the resin thoroughly, using a stick.

Then take a paintbrush and start liberally coating the area where the mat is to be placed. One- to two-inch brushes are convenient sizes for dinghies.

As soon as all the area is covered place the mat on to it and trim off the excess. It may be necessary to do some last-minute tailoring. Press the mat into place and start stippling to get the resin to work into the mat (Fig. 9.9).

If the mat starts to come to bits try taking a new brushload of resin and continue stippling.

When the area looks to be pretty well wetted through, start rolling vigorously with a special roller consisting of discs mounted on a spindle. Work all the air out and consolidate the mat (Fig. 9.10).

Add resin to dry areas and pick up excess resin that has drained to the bottom (Fig. 9.11).

Refill the tin as necessary, but after every three tinfuls or so, depending on the speed of the work, you must thoroughly wash out everything in acetone.

You will need quite a large quantity of acetone as well as a fair amount of barrier cream, such as Rozalex No. 9, for the hands. The catalyst is very irritant to the hands and eyes, and it is a very wise precaution to use cream.

The resin will set off at the end of its pot life and nothing you can do will stop it. Therefore it is essential to have this periodic clean-up. If two people are working constantly on the mould there is at least enough work for a third person in keeping them supplied with glass, resin, tools, and cleaning out sets of brushes, rollers and tins.

If the resin starts to go lumpy in the can, stop work immediately, pour out the resin and start cleaning up everything in acetone.

Acetone evaporates very rapidly, and so keep the lid on the can. The way to clean brushes and tins is to get them as clean as possible by brushing out and then to put a small quantity of acetone in the tin. Beat the brush around the bottom of the tin thoroughly, and then immediately, and before the acetone has had time to evaporate leaving neat resin again, both empty the tin and knock out the brush. Then repeat the process again. This should keep you going, but there will inevitably be a slow build-up of resin until at last the tin and brush become unusable.

MOULDS

The actual laying-up and handling of the reinforced-plastics material is not difficult for the amateur as long as care is taken. The part of the business which may well cause problems is in the making of moulds. It is not that the basic principle is difficult, or indeed very different from the making of moulds for other types of boat construction. The problems are really twofold.

Firstly, it is usual, though not absolutely essential, for the outer surface of the boat's hull to be that which touches the mould. It is also normal and indeed highly desirable, for the finish of the mould surface to be perfect enough to give a resulting automatic high finish to the moulding, so that no painting, filling, or polishing are necessary after removal. This is, in fact, one of the major points in favour of this process for the professional boatbuilder; the labour costs for boat finishing are expended only at the start of a pretty long run of hulls. The work done on the mould can be thought of as being spread over fifty or more boats. Therefore the professional takes a great deal of trouble in getting his mould surface both fair and smooth. There is

also to be considered the normal mould-making process, which requires a male mould to be made first, rather in the same way as we have done for a cold-moulded boat. Then we make a reinforced-plastics female mould from this. Finally we make our hull inside the female mould.

This brings us to the second problem for the amateur, who may only be interested in making one hull—that of cost. The time involved, which is closely related, also comes under this heading.

There is no doubt at all that the two-process method of making G.R.P. hull moulds is totally uneconomic for one boat or even for two or three. It may be that the amateur will not consider this aspect of the problem as severely as would a professional, because he traditionally never costs up his time, but, even so, the actual expenditure on materials might still prove daunting. If the amateur can sell or hire out the mould after use, then this may be the answer to the cost problem. If he does decide on this course, and he is intending to build a mould for a class one-design, he would be very well advised to get the mould checked by the class association measurer, and to obtain a certificate of accuracy from him first. Intending purchasers or hirers will not be interested in the least without some guarantee of accuracy.

This still leaves us with the man-hours. The production of an acceptable finish to a mould is certainly a time-consuming, laborious and tedious job. But if one compares it with the time spent on preparing, rubbing down, and applying say six coats of paint on a wood hull, there is not so very much difference.

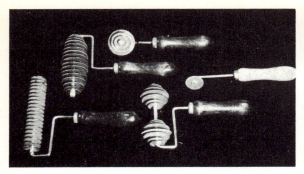

9.10
Various types and shapes of split ring rollers suitable for consolidating glass and persuading the resin to wet it out thoroughly. (Peter Webster.)

9.12
Here the after tank-cum-seat has been moulded separately and bonded in after the shell has been laid up. The insertion of items such as this can be done before removal of the shell if you are using a female mould. In order to mould in a rolled gunwale at the same time as laying up the shell some sort of removable mould section would be needed. It would be impossible to remove the shell otherwise. (Tod, Dinghy.)

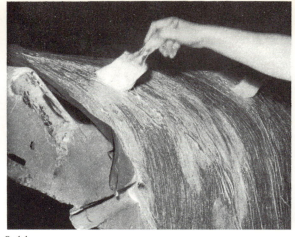

9.11
After the glass has been thoroughly stippled to bring the resin through from underneath, further resin may be needed on top to make a thorough impregnation. (Peter Webster, Elizabethan.)

Nevertheless there still remains the need to make both a male and a female mould before you can start.

There are ways of short-cutting the mould work, but this is mainly of interest to those building boats not needing to pass accurate class measuring rules. However, since these are simpler we shall deal with them first.

DIRECT MOULDING

The simplest way of making a boat hull, and one which needs no expensive mould construction at all, is to mould directly off an existing hull. The procedure is to prepare the hull carefully by filling and repainting where necessary, and removing fittings which are not needed, such as bailers, stembands, bilge rails, transom fittings, and so on. Then make sure there are no places where undercuts would cause removal of the shell to be difficult. Fill in the centreboard-case slot also. After careful polishing, apply a release agent such as polyvinyl alcohol, which can be obtained from suppliers listed in the Appendix on p. 232. Allow the P.V.A. to dry and then start laying-up.

There are several things to think about when preparing to make a hull in this way. There is no real point in obtaining a super finish on the hull which is to be used as a mould so long as it is fair and smooth, but irregularities, scratches, and blemishes, could cause difficulty in the lifting off of the shell owing to sticking, and so these need to be removed. Also the inner finish is obviously going to be superior to that outside. This has to be accepted, but nevertheless a very good result can be obtained by this method. A great deal of cleaning up, rubbing down, filling and painting will be required, and the amount of trouble taken will be reflected in the final finish.

Extra care will have to be taken in the actual lay-up to avoid bulges and humps, and this applies particularly to overlapping layers. It will be easier to get a generally smooth surface if cloth is used in the lay-up. Mat tends to move about and become thicker in some places and thinner in others. On the other hand, mat can be joined in the same layer without overlapping, whereas cloth definitely needs a 1½-in overlap, or more.

Thought will also have to be given to how the deck is to be fastened, as this may mean removing the rubbing-band from the mould boat (Fig. 9.7 (A), (B) and (C)). The centreboard case will almost certainly have to be fitted afterwards (Fig. 9.12).

Nevertheless in spite of the difficulties and the fact that the finished hull will be fractionally larger than the original, this is the cheapest way for an amateur to build a G.R.P. hull.

MIRROR-IMAGE MOULDING

To obtain an exact replica of a hull shape it is necessary to make a female mould. The next cheapest way of doing this is to make it from an accurate example of the existing hull shape in rather the same way as we have described above. However, since the new shell is to be made inside the female mould, which is itself to be made from the existing hull, we must be particularly careful in obtaining the finest possible finish on the latter at the start.

Fillers such as plaster of Paris can be used to raise hollow areas, and remove undercuts. Items such as bilge rails, rubbing-bands, and keel- and stembands can be left on if they are to appear in the replica reproduced in plastic. Otherwise they must be removed, and in any case, all screw-heads should be filled and faired up smooth and a really high gloss obtained on all parts.

The centreboard slot will have to be filled, but a tapered wooden mould can be fixed to the female mould later if it is desired to mould this in at the same time as the hull shell.

This is the obvious method for the amateur to use, provided he can persuade the owner of a really accurate boat to allow it to be used as a model. Even so, the material cost for the female mould will be higher than that for a hull shell, since it will need to be more substantial and well braced, and reinforced with flanges, cross-struts, and bearers, moulded in place (Fig. 9.13). But as long as the original model is accurate and certified by the class measurer, then there should not be much difficulty in selling or hiring out the mould afterwards.

MAKING A MALE MOULD

Finally, we have the "start from scratch" method for those building to a new design for the first time. In this case the original male mould is usually made on a plywood mock-up filled in with plaster of Paris.

A possible method is as follows: Mark out and cut out a complete set of templates from plywood for each section of the body plan. They will need to be the actual finished exterior size with no allowance for hull thickness. Set them up in exactly the same way as we have described in Chapter 1. They can be fixed to the floor, or to a subframe, whichever is convenient, and they must be braced so that they cannot move. The frames and bracing can be quite light, since there will be no strain on the mould other than the well-distributed weight of itself and that of the female mould when laid up (Fig. 9.14). Before setting up the frames on the base, drill a row of small holes about an inch apart and half-an-inch from the edge round each (Fig. 9.15). Having set up the frames, wire is threaded fore and aft through the holes to form a framework to support the plaster. Cover the wire framing with sacking and then you can start daubing on plaster of Paris; the idea is to

9.13
It is no use making a mould too lightly. Moulds will always be flexible when removed and must be braced rigidly to stop them twisting. Otherwise the boat when built will also be twisted. (Souter, Penguin Dinghy.)

build up the plaster in successive layers until it is slightly proud of the frame edge.

Allow to dry and then start scraping down the plaster until the main humps are removed. Skarsten scrapers can be used for this work. To get the surface fair it is necessary to cut a springy metal lath long enough to span three

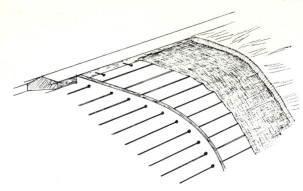

9.14

A possible method of constructing a plaster male mould for making an original female mould. Plywood templates are made for each station the exact full-size shape, including the skin thickness. Holes are drilled round the edge and wires passed through from end to end. Then hessian is laid over the wires and the spaces in between the templates filled up with layers of plaster of Paris.

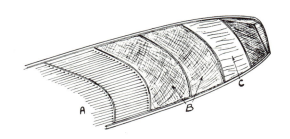

9.15

This drawing shows, A, the wires in place; B, the hessian laid in between the templates; and C, an area filled in with plaster of Paris and faired up.

frames. By holding this on edge and bending it, it should be possible to see the high spots and scrape them down either with the lath itself or with the scraper. By patient scraping and filling using thinner mixtures of plaster it will be possible to arrive at a fairly good surface. Be careful not to damage the edges of the frames, which will become exposed as the scraping progresses.

The next stage is very dusty and consists of sanding, using a long cork block and coarse sandpaper. Finally when you are satisfied with the fairness of the surface, it must be painted and cut down to give a highly polished smooth and dense facing to receive the G.R.P. lay-up.

The whole process is basically quite simple, but as is the case with everything to do with boatbuilding, extreme care and patience are needed.

PRE-TREATMENT AND REMOVAL

The mould surface, when finished to a high enough degree to satisfy the builder, must be treated with a release agent to avoid the resin sticking to it. This job must be done extremely thoroughly, as one small patch missed could mean that the hull would be impossible to remove without damage to the mould or hull.

It is recommended that two separate coatings are made to the mould surface to ensure a perfect release. The first is an ordinary wax polish which should be liberally applied and then polished off to a high gloss. It is better not to use a silicone polish, as it is extremely difficult to remove traces of the silicone, which would cause trouble if painting was contemplated later. Secondly, a solution of polyvinyl alcohol is carefully sprayed or painted on.

The finish of the hull surface depends on the care with which this coating is applied. Do not start laying-up until the P.V.A. is quite hard.

Removal of the hull can cause some trouble, especially when moulding directly off another hull. Normally the procedure is to prise the shell and mould apart all round the sheer and then to pour some water in between and continue prising round. The water should gradually work in between the shell and the mould and finally the two will part cleanly. This can only be done if the moulding is the normal way up, of course.

DESIGN HINTS

I hope that intending builders will have by now gathered enough basic information to go ahead and start building. Do ask the technical advice of the resin suppliers on any special problems. The glass weavers and spinners will also send samples so that you can choose suitable materials.

If you are building to a set of racing-class rules you will need to have an accurate idea of the finished weight of the boat. The weight of a lamination per unit area varies considerably depending on the type and density of reinforcement and number of layers. The skill of the builder also affects the weight and one should aim at as high a glass ratio as possible. The glass weavers and spinners should be able to give approximate laminate weights, using varying weights of reinforcement, and you can use this as a guide. By careful weighing of both glass and resin as the lay-up proceeds, you can see whether you are running above or below the estimate. Don't forget to weigh up and substract the offcuts of glass and wasted resin. Unless you keep a very accurate check you may easily find that the finished boat is many pounds overweight and it is almost impossible to lighten an already completed plastic boat. You cannot prune it as is often possible with wooden construction. An overweight racing boat is useless both for racing and for resale, and so take great care!

The thickness of the laminate for a boat hull is difficult to specify exactly. If full advantage is to be taken of the material the hull shell will be thicker in some places, such as the floor, and the turn of the bilge, where stamping of heavy feet occurs, whereas on the side it might well be thinner. Extra layers can be added where extra strength is needed, and stringers or timber reinforcements can be moulded in where stiffness is required.

A rough average guide would be about $4\frac{1}{2}$ oz of glass per square foot for a 14-ft racing boat, and 6 oz for a heavier boat. Not counting surfacing mat or gel coats, this ought to be divided into about four layers. A cheap but perfectly adequate lay-up would consist of an average of four layers of 1-oz mat, or three layers of $1\frac{1}{2}$-oz mat. Cloth or woven rovings could be substituted for one or more layers for extra strength. A very strong laminate could consist of two layers of 12-oz cloth with a $1\frac{1}{2}$ oz mat sandwiched in between. The cloth bonds better to the mat than to another cloth layer, and the extra bulk of the mat gives extra rigidity.

A rough guide for thickness is that each $1\frac{1}{2}$-oz mat will give about 1 mm. of finished thickness. Twelve-ounce cloth will finish rather thinner. Another rough guide when

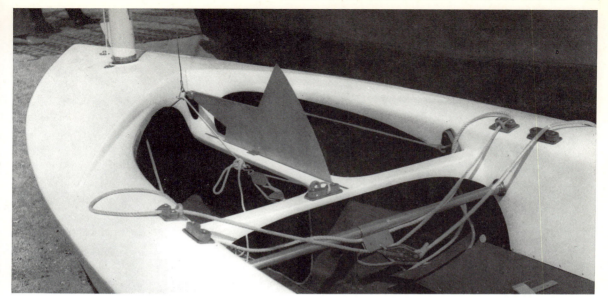

designing a laminate is to think of the plywood counterpart thickness and then work on slightly more than one-third of this in plastic. Thus a racing boat such as an International Fourteen or a Firefly, which has a skin thickness in wood of 6 mm., would need 2 mm. in plastics. Actually you might find that the skin could be too flexible if only 2 mm. thick. Extra rigidity can be obtained by using all mat in the lay-up or by using a light filler in the resin to give greater bulk or by building in hollow stringers. International Finns use 9–10 mm. wooden skins, and thus $3-3\frac{1}{2}$ mm. in plastics will be highly satisfactory both for strength and rigidity. An International Five-O-Five uses 6-mm. wood and is an excellent subject for plastics, owing to the strength given by the double curvature of the sections. This enables full use to be made of thin cloth laminates.

The International Flying Dutchman is

9.16
Complicated and beautiful shapes can be made in a moulding material such as reinforced plastics. This type of construction would be far too heavy if made in wood, and would take a great deal of time. (Elvstrom, Finn.)

nearly 20 ft long and very flat, and uses a 6-mm. wooden skin. Reducing this to only 2 mm. in plastics presents serious problems for the amateur, and this boat is probably right outside the amateur's scope. The design problems would be too acute for any but a real expert to have a hope of producing a strong boat which is also on the minimum weight.

General-purpose boats are, of course, no problem, and when not tied down by tight building rules to control distribution of weight, you can do whatever you like in the way of

reinforcement. Always bear in mind though, that unnecessary strength has to be paid for pretty severely both in cash for the expensive materials, and also in weight, to hump around on shore. Keep at the back of your mind the rough guide $\frac{1}{8}$-in. G.R.P. equals $\frac{3}{8}$ in. of wood.

9.17

This boat has been made in two main mouldings connected together along the gunwale. To conceal the join advantage has been taken of placing a wooden rubbing-strip to receive the first knocks. Fibre-glass is not very satisfactory at withstanding abrasion, and it is a good plan to protect corners with wood.

I PROPOSE to let the photos and drawings explain a great deal of the subject-matter of this chapter. There is nothing very difficult or technical about finishing off a hull in wood. It is mainly straightforward joinery and any handyman should be able to cope easily. You may have to take extra care if you are building to class rules, because some are very strict about the size and position of such parts as deckbeams and thwarts. In other classes you are free to design your own cockpit shapes within limitations. Frequently the amount of camber on the foredeck is controlled, and almost always such things as the width and depth of gunwale rubbing-strips and the shape of centreboards are specified.

INWALES

The first items to be fitted into the interior of a hull shell are almost always the inwales. This will not usually apply to chine boats, since the inwales will be part of the framework to which the hull panels are fastened, but in all other systems the hull will be very floppy and flexible on removal from the moulds, and it is essential to make some sort of jig or chocking arrangement to hold it into the correct shape whilst the inwales, deck-beams, and supports are being fitted. If this part of the work is neglected or skimped, a twisted or otherwise wrongly shaped boat might result. Even $\frac{1}{2}$ in. of error on the keel profile could result in a racing boat which will not balance correctly when under sail. This could affect its racing

performance considerably, and I mention this from several first-hand experiences. It is in my opinion more important to get the keel profile absolutely correct than the shape of the sections. In cold-moulding work the hull will tend to spring wider on removal from the mould, as the sharp curve of the bilge tries to straighten. This is more likely to be troublesome in two-skin hulls than those with more layers of glue to resist the timber forces. Some builders deliberately make the moulds narrower at the gunwales and with a more acute curve at the bilge to compensate for this slight spreading, but it is a tricky thing to decide how much to allow without putting some other part of the hull wrong. It is best to build exactly to the lines and then to force the shell to the right shape while fitting in the interior struts. All of these will help to maintain the correct shape (Fig. 10.1).

If the beam is allowed to spread, then the ends of the boat will rise and thus make a big error in the keel profile. One should set up at least three exterior moulds at the correct heights and then to pull in the beam with cross-ties until the keel-rocker drops into the correct curve, and touches at all points. If the sections are still not exactly to plan and you cannot force them to conform more closely without altering the keel profile, then I suggest you leave them, unless they are still outside the measurement tolerances for your particular class (Figs. 4.21, 4.22, 4.24, pp. 67–70).

The inwales can now be fitted. The tops of these will be at sheer height less the deck

10.1
When the boat is complete it may finally have to pass the measurer. This may involve fitting metal templates at specified points over the hull, like this, to see that the shape is correct. Apart from the accuracy of the original mould the next most important factor governing the shape is the care with which the shell is supported whilst the interior joinery is being fitted. (Rogers, Finn.)

in place and tap it to the correct position. Then scribe a line round the top so that you can replace it quickly, drill for nails or screws and then fasten in place with glue.

You can also fit a breasthook at the stem and perhaps quarter-knees at the transom if required (Fig. 10.3). Remember to fit them to stand a little proud to allow for fairing into the deck camber.

If there is to be a glued deck, the knees can be just simple blocks of wood glued in. If they are exposed as in an International Fourteen you may be moved to make a fancy lamination out of wood of contrasting colours.

It is also important to take very much greater care with the fitting of the breasthook and quarter-knees in an undecked boat because the rigidity of the hull depends largely on how firmly these angles can be kept constant. A glued deck holds the angles absolutely rigid and makes an extremely strong hull.

The next step is to cut off the surplus hull skin above the sheer. This is where a jig-saw comes into its own again.

thickness. If you have made outside moulds into which the shell has been dropped, then you can mark the sheer heights on these. These, with the transom and stem, will give you five points each side through which to sight a fair curve for the inwales. If you have not got mould marks you will have to measure up from keel level using a straight-edge across the underneath of the boat. The measurement from keel level to sheer at each station can be got from the plans and this can be transferred to the shell. Then you can cramp your inwale

CENTREBOARD CASE

The only unusual job in the interior which might cause trouble is the centreboard case and backbone assembly. A daggerboard case or a short case like that for the Finn is really no trouble at all to fit (Figs. 10.4, 10.5, 10.6), but some boats have a very long case and spine all tied in together, and sometimes this assembly stretches from the stem to the transom. These can indeed be quite a fiddle to fit

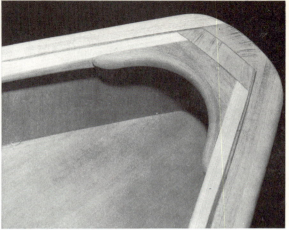

10.3

A beautifully finished laminated breasthook, and the component parts of the gunwale assembly can also be seen. Starting from the outside the wide gunwale has been assembled in three laminations. Then comes the thin skin of the boat in three veneers, and then the inwale. Starting from the bow we have the outer stem, the inner stem, the main moulding of the breasthook, and then the outer lamination of the breasthook. (Souter, 14-ft International.)

10.2

A light inwale butting up against the inner stem. (Souter, 14-ft International.)

◄   **10.4**

An easy centreboard case to fit because of its short length is that in the International Finn. Here a taut line from the point of the stem to the centre of the transom is being used to assist in checking that the case is vertical. (Rogers, Finn.)

accurately, as they usually have to be assembled on the bench and then dropped in and screwed and glued down.

It is almost essential to make a full-size template either out of hardboard or of a skeleton nature out of batten nailed into a lattice girder. It is quite a help to make your template to include the upper profile of the whole assembly as well as the critical curve along the hog.

The simplest centreboard case is made out of two sheets of wood screwed together along two edges with spacing pieces in between. Only very small boats or those using dagger-boards have quite such simple cases. Usually the centreboard case ties in with a spine aft (Fig. 10.7), and with an extension forward carrying the mast step (Fig. 10.8). The top may also form a seat (Fig. 10.9), and there may be a built-in anchorage for a central main-sheet. Often the whole spine, centreboard case, mast-step assembly, provides the backbone of the boat when screwed and glued to the hog (Fig. 5.28, p. 83).

Some classes call for solid timber sides of the case, each perhaps an inch in thickness. The spacing between the sides varies depending on the type of centreboard. If this is to be of galvanized steel or aluminium alloy, then about $\frac{1}{2}$ in. (12 mm.) is all that is needed. Wooden centreboards vary from $\frac{3}{4}$ in. (19 mm.) to $1\frac{1}{4}$ in. (30 mm.), and the gap may therefore be as much as $1\frac{1}{2}$ in. (38 mm.). The spacers are often pieces of solid timber only about $1\frac{1}{2}$ in. wide, but sometimes the backbone or spine is inserted to form the spacer itself.

Such massive and heavy constructions are not in the least necessary for strength, and a

10.5
The method of fixing the case down on the hog. A capping piece has been fitted along the after edge to protect the end-grain of the plywood sides. (Rogers, Finn.)

great saving in weight can be made by using plywood case sides and plywood web spines. The plywood usually has to be reinforced at the edges with square section batten, but with a little thought, neat, light and strong constructions can result. Suitable arrangements are shown in Figs. 10.10, 10.11.

Solid cases will have to be screwed from underneath, and this is easier if the keel has not yet been fixed. However, if the case ever has to be removed again, you will want to get at the screws, and so remember this point when deciding where to drill.

Before fixing the case you must mark and cut out the slot in the keel. Drill a hole at each

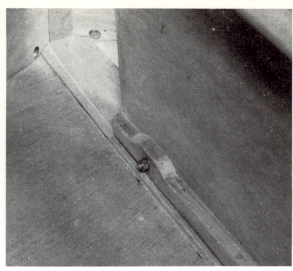

10.6
The bottom rail of the centreboard case has had to be thickened where the bolt passes through, because this is a little higher than the top of the rail. (Rogers, Finn.)

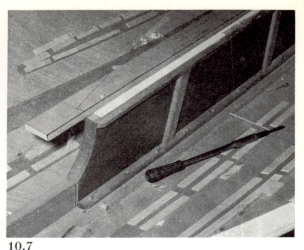

10.7
The after end of this built-up plywood centreboard case ties into the spine, which stiffens the after half of the boat. The capping forming a seat along the case is being fitted. (Souter, 14-ft International.)

end of the slot and the same width. If you have a jigsaw, you may now be able to cut the slot out in one operation. If not, drill some more holes close together, and chop out with a chisel. You should then be able to introduce a panel saw and continue cutting.

It is well worth while using bronze screws for a boat that is to last or one that is to remain on a mooring. They are more expensive than brass, but brass loses its zinc content when in contact with sea water and quite soon crystallizes.

Solid timber cases are more troublesome to fit than those made of plywood, since it is almost essential to screw from the outside

10.8
At the forward end of this centreboard case the spine continues and forms the mast-step and locks in with the forward bulkhead. (Souter, 14-ft International.)

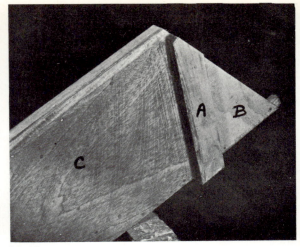

10.9
Beautiful joinery on the centreboard case of this 14-ft International which also forms a comfortable seat for the helmsman or crew in light weather. (Souter.)

10.10
The interior construction of a fabricated plywood centreboard case. A is the filler or spacer piece, which controls the width of the gap in the case. B is a projection which will be used to tie into the spine projecting forward. C is the inside of the case side and is here covered in fibre-glass. (Chippendale, 14-ft Merlin/Rocket.)

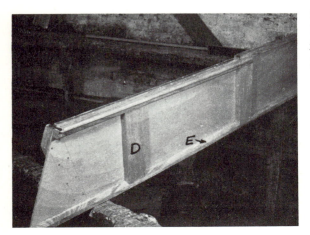

10.11
The exterior of the same case. D is a vertical stiffening strut, and E is the bottom rail. (Chippendale, 14-ft Merlin/Rocket.)

10.12
Solid timber centreboard cases are massive and heavy, but some classes demand them. This case will have to be fixed by screwing through from underneath into the sides. (Chippendale, 14-ft Merlin/Rocket.)

10.13
It is usual to fit a ledge on the inside of the planking to rest the main thwart on. This can also carry the side-deck load, as in this case. (Rogers, Finn.)

(Fig. 10.12). This means that the hull will have to be turned on its side for the operation, which in its turn means that it must be held rigidly to the correct shape. Since the centre-board case and backbone form one of the main girders which assist in controlling the shape, this is not all that easy to arrange. In fact, you will have first to fit some deckbeams and some rigidly screwed temporary beam ties to hold everything steady. You must also do all the fitting for the joint at the hog whilst the hull is still resting in its jig, and only turn it on its side for the final fixing operation.

Plywood cases will have ledges screwed and glued along the bottom edges and the fixing screws can therefore be driven down through these from the inside (Fig. 7.8, p. 95).

Cases are made up in two halves and the inside is painted before final assembly. The curve of the keel is transferred to the case side and cut as near as possible. Then screw and glue the sides together and try it in the boat. You will be able to trim the bottom curve to a fairly good fit with the plane, but an accurate joint needs a trick with some chalk. Rub chalk over one face to be joined and then put the case in place. Tap it down, and then remove it again. Only the high spots will transfer chalk to the other side and so you can easily trim these off. Make sure you plane square to the sides or you will find the case will be out of the vertical when fixed.

If you are sure you have made a very close joint you can glue the case to the hog. For boats such as the International Fourteen, which has a complete backbone assembly, it will be almost essential to use glue to make a satisfactory job, but for simple isolated centre-board cases it is just as good to screw them down on to sealing strip. Sylglas tape or Prestik are often used for this joint, whilst traditional builders use white lead and boat-cotton. The modern materials are better, since they always remain plastic and hence can accommodate slight movements without leaking.

If you have to screw from the outside it will be necessary to hold the case in place from the inside whilst the boring and screwing is going on. Struts across under the inwales and bracing the top of the case with wedges are often sufficient to hold it down. Temporary ties to hold it in position sideways can also be fitted.

Make absolutely sure that the case is straight before boring for screws. A taut line and a spirit level can assist in this (Fig. 10.4). If the case is comparatively flimsy with ply sides, it is as well to put a loose piece of wood inside of the same thickness as the end spacers to keep it straight. It can be knocked out when the case is finally fixed.

Remember to bore the pivot-hole before screwing the case down, for it is very difficult to do this job neatly afterwards (Fig. 10.6). Brass tube is often sufficient for a wooden board. Galvanized steel or alloy plates will need a piece of stainless steel rod as a pivot. There is no need to use proper bolts and nuts.

10.14
The light framing for the bulkhead can sometimes be more easily installed by fixing it to the hull first, and finally screwing the plywood panel to the laminated rail. In this case the framing has been made straight from thicker plywood. (Rogers, Finn.)

The pivot can finish flush at each side and be covered with a small plywood pad bedded in sealing compound to stop leaks. An even easier method is to cut the rod off short and to plug the ends of the holes with small corks.

The cross-thwart, if any, usually goes in next, and it can be screwed to a small ledge fastened through the skin at the sides and notched into the centreboard case (Fig. 10.13).

BULKHEADS

You may want to fit bulkheads, and if these were not built into the jig in the first place

10.15
The plywood panel for the bulkhead has been fitted by spiling, in the first instance. (Rogers, Finn.)

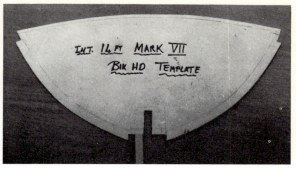

10.16
If you are lucky you may be given the shape of templates for bulkheads on the plans. (Souter, 14-ft International.)

it is best if they go in before the deck beams. Athwartships bulkheads will often have beams screwed to their top edges and may have hatches in them, but fit the curve of the ply panel first. Start by marking where the bulkhead is to go and then laminate a rail to which one can fasten it. This can be made *in situ* out of thin strips of veneer or ply tacked and glued down (Fig. 10.14). The face to be glued to the bulkhead can be cleaned up with the rebate plane later, provided surplus glue has been scraped off. Remember to leave drainholes at the bottom.

Bulkheads are frequently made out of very thin ply and may need backing strips to keep them straight. Cut out a piece of ply oversize, but as near as you can judge. Fit the curve of the bottom by spiling as explained in Chapter 3, p. 44 (Fig. 10.15). When a good match has been obtained you can fit and fix any deckbeams, hatches, and bracing and then glue and screw in place. Any slight inaccuracies at the edges can be filled with paint filler or with clear resin if the area is to be varnished. You can also start by making a template out of card or hardboard (Fig. 10.16).

Bulkheads can be fitted much more quickly and perfectly satisfactorily with glass tape and resin, as described in Chapter 8, and the fit of the panel need not be nearly so accurate.

Fore and aft bulkheads can be dealt with in two main ways. Either you can build the framing as for the International Fourteen and fix the ply last (Fig. 10.17), or you can make up the panel complete with its framing, and then finally fit it to the hull as in the Fireball (Fig. 10.18). In the latter case you must trim the ply to shape first, and then fix the framing to it. Finally, plane the bevel on the bottom rail by trial and error. Again, the joint at the bottom can more easily be made with glass tape and resin.

FLOORS AND STRINGERS

These are perfectly straightforward and the plans will usually give shapes for floors, but if not, then resort to the ever-useful hardboard or card template method, and transfer the shapes found. Battens can be used to check that all the floors are at the right height (Figs. 10.19, 10.20, 10.21).

Stringers and floor stiffeners can either be riveted through the skin or screwed from the outside. Again, no problems here. Remember to leave generous limber-holes for bilge water in all floors. Screw floors in place and do not rely on glue alone, because there is too much flexing in this area and the joint would soon be destroyed without some backing up by through-fastenings (Figs. 10.22, 10.23).

DECKBEAMS

The easiest way of fitting deckbeams to the inwales is with a simple notched joint (Fig. 10.24). In days gone by all good-quality work was done with dovetailed joints, but the advent of good plywood and marine glue has made such jointing entirely unnecessary. The deck ply will hold the whole assembly together even though the framing might seem very flimsy. Use a bevelled notch in the inwale and a matching bevel on the end of the beam (Fig. 10.25).

Cut the beams oversize and to the correct camber as shown on the plans, for they will have to faired-in finally later. If the foredeck ply will not cover the whole width you

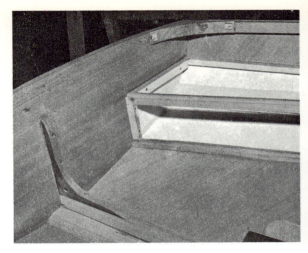

10.17

A built-up buoyancy side-tank with framing installed first, and then covered with ply sheeting. Remember to paint the inside of the tank before you assemble the last panel. Bottom rails should be screwed and glued through very carefully. Note also the spine connecting with the transom via a laminated knee. (Souter, 14-ft International.)

may want a joint down the middle. You can deal with this by notching in a king plank along the centreline flush with the deckbeams, and then the ply is glued down on to this (Figs. 10.26, 10.27, 10.28). A rather more fancy finish is given by a rebated king plank, the top of which will be exposed and planed flush with the deck finally. Still another method is to glue a capping strip over the joint in the centreline afterwards, and this can look very neat if done carefully (Fig. 10.29).

Fair off the tops of the deck beams by using battens parallel to the centreline. If the deck is cambered, the fore-and-aft direction

10.18

Another form of side-tank construction where the panel, complete with its framing, is assembled first, and then fitted into the boat. (Chippendale, Fireball.)

10.19

The International Finn has raised floorboards and the plywood panel is supported on these fitted floors. (Rogers, Finn.)

10.20

The fully fitted floors form a very strong and rigid structure for the bottom part of the hull. (Rogers, Finn.)

10.21

Another type of floor is the one used to support the mast-step. In the case of the Finn it has to carry considerable sideways loadings, and must be very firmly secured. (Rogers, Finn.)

10.22
Stringers glued to the side of the hull support the thwart, and also form a fixing for the top of buoyancy tanks. Note the laminated strengthening strip to carry jib fairleads. (Souter, International Fourteen.)

10.23
It is usual to fit light battens along the floor, where there is considerable stamping from the feet. It is often best to leave the timber unvarnished to provide a better grip. (Chippendale, 14-ft Merlin/-Rocket.)

10.24
The very light and simple deckbeam-gunwale joint looks too fragile, but when the plywood is glued to both the whole assembly becomes very strong and rigid. (Rogers, Finn.)

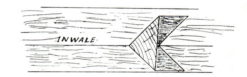

10.25
The easiest and most satisfactory way of fitting deckbeams to the inwale when using glued plywood decks.

10.26
The light king plank is notched into the stem with no breasthook. The taut line is used to line up the deckbeams. (Rogers, Finn.)

10.27
The king plank is notched into the inner stem and is later faired off to match in with the stem capping and the gunwale. (Chippendale, 14-ft Merlin/-Rocket.)

10.28
Most modern racing dinghies in the 14-ft sizes are now too wide across the foredeck for a single 4-ft wide sheet to be used. It is therefore extremely common to see the foredeck plywood jointed down the centre and glued on to a king plank. (Rogers, Finn.)

10.29
Three different methods of arranging for the foredeck plywood to be split down the centreline. The first two are normal king planks and the second is really a capping piece.

10.30
An impression of a cambered deck can be obtained much more easily by making the two sides of the foredeck quite flat, but angled up towards a high point in the centre. This Fireball foredeck construction shows the easy cutting and planing needed. Note also the massive but light central web beam. (Chippendale, Fireball.)

will be a straight line and the ply will only be bent in the direction of the beams (Figs. 10.30, 10.31).

All the deckbeams and carlins will have to be fitted before any plywood is glued down. Cut out the carlins and fit them in position with temporary struts to hold them. They can be notched into the foremost afterdeck beam, or into the transom if the side deck is to run right aft (Fig. 10.32). The photos show a possible method of laminating a curved front to the cockpit which fairs into the carlin (Figs. 10.33, 10.34). Side-deck beams can be

notched into the carlin and inwale, and there will normally have to be two or three knees or other supports each side. Fig. 10.35 shows how the thwart can carry the side-deck load if suitably placed. Other knees can be fitted to the planking or alternatively struts can be taken vertically downwards (Fig. 10.36). Remember when fitting side-deck supports that the boat is frequently carried when on shore by people holding the carlin, and so make sure your supports will stand an upward pull as well as heavy bodies thumping down on to them (Fig. 10.37).

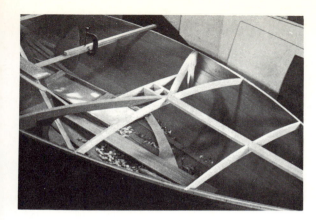

◄ 10.31

A more conventional foredeck arrangement with two angled beams to take the compression loading from the shrouds. Note the mast gate assembly. (Chippendale, 14-ft Merlin/Rocket.)

10.32

An angled carlin assembly which is notched into the bulkhead of the after deck. The shape is controlled by the cross-ties. (Rogers, Finn.)

10.33

Some of the best-looking cockpits have rounded ends and corners. Here is a simple way of obtaining a rounded front for the cockpit by laminating a carlin up out of four thicknesses of plywood. A is the normal carlin. B is the laminated carlin which merges into it on either side quite smoothly. (Rogers, Finn.)

10.34
The support for the fore-end of the laminated carlin looks very flimsy, but the whole structure becomes quite solid when the plywood is glued down on to it. (Rogers, Finn.)

10.35
The main thwart rests on a glued-in ledge and the loading of the side deck can be carried on top of the thwart by means of a block such as in this photograph. (Rogers, Finn.)

PLYWOOD DECKS

There is no difficulty in the fitting of decks, but plan out the shapes of the panels for the most economical use of the ply. If you are keen on obtaining a really good match for grain and colour, this may not be so easy. For one thing not only will one side of the ply sheet be better finished than the other, but also the grain and colour may be very different. Thus an economical cut necessitating the reversal of the sheet for the two halves of the foredeck may produce odd-looking results. Usually however, the odd shorter length for the sidedecks and afterdecks can be shuffled round so that there is not too much wastage.

Arrange for joints to come on the centre of a deck beam, or fit double beams at this point and make sure that the jointing edges of the first panel are quite straight, since this makes it easier to fit the adjacent one. The foredeck panels are usually no trouble to join, since the second one can be trimmed gradually and tried as many times as one likes (Fig. 10.38).

It is best to fit the after-deck next, and finally the side-decks in one or two pieces each. Leave the shortest piece to the last and fit one end by trial and error. Then gradually trim down the final edge, slightly undercutting it with the plane. At last the undercut edge will start to drop over the edge of the fixed panel and you can see exactly how much

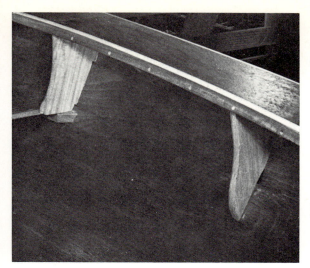

10.36 ▲

Knees or other struts will almost certainly be needed to carry side-deck loads. Remember that there may be a considerable upward pull at times. (Chippendale, 14-ft Merlin/Rocket.)

10.37 ▼

The simple halved joint for the carlin into a deck beam is not entirely suitable, because if a heavy load is applied at F, the carlin will be likely to split along A. It is better to use the bevelled joint.

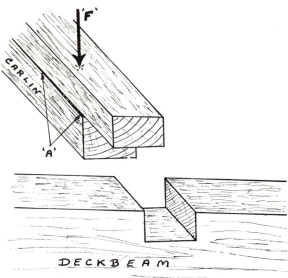

10.38 ◄

It is tricky to deal with an after deck where the plywood will not quite reach across. It is usual to run the grain of the ply fore and aft and therefore an additional corner piece will be needed very often. It will need careful matching of the grain to make sure that this sort of thing is not unsightly. (Rogers, Finn.)

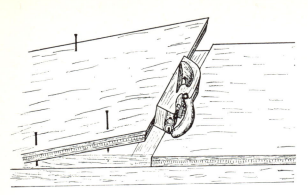

farther you have to go. A few final careful shavings and you will get a fit so tight as to be almost invisible (Figs. 10.39, 10.40).

It is wise to arrange matters so that all ply edges are covered. Not only does this look neater, but it prevents the vulnerable veneer from sustaining damage which would be both unsightly and also allow water to enter.

The transom deck edge can be dealt with

10.39, 10.40
A really close join between plywood deck panels looks very professional and impressive. The easiest way of doing this is to fasten down and fit one end of the panel, and finally trim off the other edge by undercutting it slightly. The bottom corner will drop over the edge first, and then you have a guide for how much more to take off.

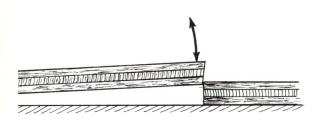

10.41
It is best to finish off the corner of the transom and deck by planing a flat and gluing a small piece of beading. Otherwise you will surely split the top veneer of deck off at the transom in time and water will be able to enter.

10.42
In this case the actual carlin is quite a light piece of timber, and the main strain is taken by the decorative capping which is set at an angle of about 45 degrees. (Rogers, Finn.)

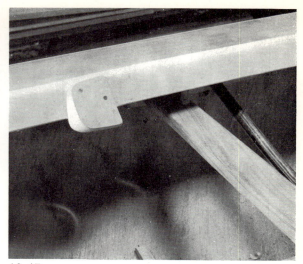

10.43
This capping in sycamore looks really good. The small wooden block is to carry the centreboard hoist cleat. (Rogers, Finn.)

either by planing a flat at 45 degrees to the deck to receive a strip of batten faired in, or alternatively, if you do not mind a small projection, a strip of half-round moulding can be glued over the exposed edge (Fig. 10.41). A capping can be glued over the inside of the carlin and frequently this is quite substantial and is designed to take the major loadings on the cockpit edge, the actual carlin being quite light. It is often set at 45 degrees to the vertical to provide a flat surface for the backs of the legs to rest against when racing crews are hanging out on the toe-straps (Figs. 10.42, 10.43).

If there is much curve to the cockpit edge the capping may need to be made out of two thinner strips glued on top of each other. Screws can often be driven from underneath so that they do not show, but another way is to nail the capping in place. If the heads are punched below the surface and the holes stopped with a matching filler they will not be noticeable.

Gunwale rubbing-strips seem to get wider and wider these days. If they are over $\frac{3}{4}$ in. (19 mm.) in width they will almost certainly have to be fixed in two layers. Get them cut out with as much of the bevel planed off as possible, so that they are easier to bend. You can finish planing and fairing the top and outer sides after fixing. Fix the strips so that they stand proud of the deck surface and then plane them down flush later. Straight-grained rock-elm is the best timber for rubbing-strips. It is hard and tough and shows no discolorization when knocked. Mahogany is too brittle and promptly goes black round screw-holes

10.44
It is usual to screw the rubbing-bands and glue them as well. Screws should be countersunk well below the surface, and the holes dowelled. If the rubbing-band is wider than about $\frac{3}{4}$ in. it may have to be fitted in two laminations. (Rogers, Finn.)

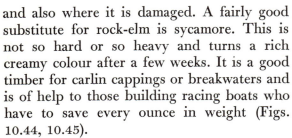

and also where it is damaged. A fairly good substitute for rock-elm is sycamore. This is not so hard or so heavy and turns a rich creamy colour after a few weeks. It is a good timber for carlin cappings or breakwaters and is of help to those building racing boats who have to save every ounce in weight (Figs. 10.44, 10.45).

Breakwaters are usually fixed by screwing through the deck from underneath. The curve for the bottom edge to fit deck camber is found by spiling (see p. 44) (Fig. 10.46).

Remember to countersink all exposed screw-heads sufficiently for filler to get a good hold. Use matching filler, or better still, dowel the hole (see p. 54).

10.47
The deck reinforcement for an International Finn mast can be arranged very simply in the manner shown. The solid plywood block takes the place of any struts in between the deckbeams. The king plank carries the load forward and the two side struts carry the load back to the carlin and thence to the side of the boat. (Rogers, Finn.)

◄ 10.45

This neat assembly stiffens up an otherwise very flexible fibre-glass shell. The inwale and the gunwale are riveted together. (Souter, Penguin Dinghy.)

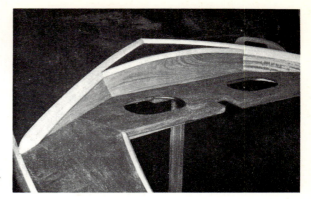

10.46 ►

This breakwater is more decorative than practical. It is hardly high enough to keep any water out of the boat. On cambered foredecks breakwaters usually have to be fitted by spiling. They are then screwed through from underneath. (Chippendale, 14-ft Merlin/Rocket.)

10.48

Many racing dinghies have drain flaps in the transom to remove the main part of the water after a capsize. The otherwise simple after bulkhead method of securing buoyancy has the disadvantage that it is difficult to fit drain flaps, but in this case the problem was overcome by running a 4-in diameter plastic tube through both bulkhead and transom. (Rogers, Finn.)

10.49

Fibre-glass dinghies can be built in this simple way and then have strengthening reinforcements screwed straight on to the panelling. In this way it is simple to fix fittings and to move them if necessary. (Souter, Penguin Dinghy.)

10.50
The wooden version of the Penguin Dinghy shows first-class joinery. Notice the laminated quarter-knee and the light stringer on which the thwart is supported. Note also the laminated floor strips. (Souter.)

10.51
The light stringer carries the centre thwart, which is also secured by laminated knees braced to the inwale. (Souter, Penguin.)

ANCHORAGE FOR FITTINGS

The dividing line between interior joinery and fitting out is rather vague in some instances. At all events, a good deal of thought will have to be given at this stage to the fittings. Some of them carry great strains and the part of the boat to which they are fixed may need to be reinforced by a block of wood or a strut. Other fittings may need to be mounted on small blocks in order to lead ropes exactly at the right angle. You may also want a central mainsheet which may have to run on a track mounted at the aft end of the centreboard case. All these things must be thought of at this stage, so that any reinforcements can be painted at the same time as the rest of the hull. It is a waste of time scraping off areas of paint later so that blocks of wood can be glued on (Figs. 10.47, 10.48, 10.49, 10.50, 10.51, 10.52).

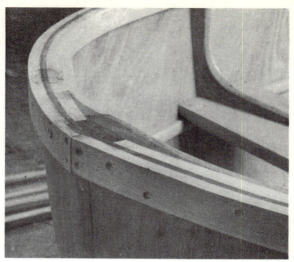

10.52
This light and strong assembly of inwale and gunwale has been developed over the years and is entirely trouble-free and strong. A moulded rubber buffer strip is screwed to the outside of the gunwale. (Souter, Penguin Dinghy.)

11 *Masts, Spars and Rigging*

A GREAT deal of the subject-matter of this chapter is considered too specialized for a general book of this sort. In particular, making satisfactory sails, while not beyond the powers of a knowledgeable amateur, is so large a subject that whole books have been written about it alone. The modern synthetic materials are not nearly so kind in concealing minor errors as was the Egyptian cotton on which I was brought up. Terylene (or Dacron, or Tergal) is also not so easy to sew smoothly or so easy to handle. I make no apology therefore, for not dealing with sail-making from scratch, but confine myself to the parts of the rig that can easily be made by amateurs.

Metal masts are virtually universal on professionally built boats today but are very sophisticated and hence expensive to buy. It is felt to be beyond the scope of this book to go into the technical subject of metal mast-making beyond a few general remarks. Nevertheless a wooden mast is still by far the cheapest proposition for the amateur who is prepared to start from scratch or even from a roughed-out blank. We shall therefore deal with wooden spar-making in fair detail.

Rigging, likewise, has become a specialized field, and the ordinary wire-splice is hardly ever seen nowadays. I last battled with spike, pliers and vice, in making up my own standing rigging many years ago now. Although I had the advantage of having been taught wire and ropework at Dartmouth Naval College, it did not seem to reduce either the inordinate time spent on wire splicing nor on the blood spilt from pricked fingers. Perhaps it was this which prompted me to use high-tensile galvanized single-strand wire, on a 12-ft National in 1952. The ends were merely bent round a thimble, and lasted not only through a really tough racing season, but were seen to be still intact and untouched ten years later. Then, abandoning wire altogether, I remained faithto the unstayed cantilever Finn rig until 1961, when the rigging of a small "X" Class keelboat was called for. Funking re-acquaintance with wire splicing, I resorted to the Talurit clamping system, which is so satisfactory, cheap, and above all quick and painless, that it seems to be the obvious answer nowadays. Wire and rope splicing is exhaustively covered in many manuals, and nowhere better than in the little booklet *Knots and Splices* by Cyrus Day (Adlard Coles Ltd). Rope splicing is extremely simple and I am astonished at the number of boat-owners who do not know how to do it (Figs. 11.1, 11.2, 11.3, 11.4, 11.5). But perhaps even this faculty will not be needed soon. The use of plaited and braided lines is fast becoming universal even for halyards, and other methods of making eyes have to be used on them. A wire terminal fitting which has the advantages of the Talurit or swaging systems, but can be done by anyone at home, is the Norseman swageless wire rope terminal (Fig. 11.6).

MASTS

The masts and sails have to be considered together when you are building a racing boat.

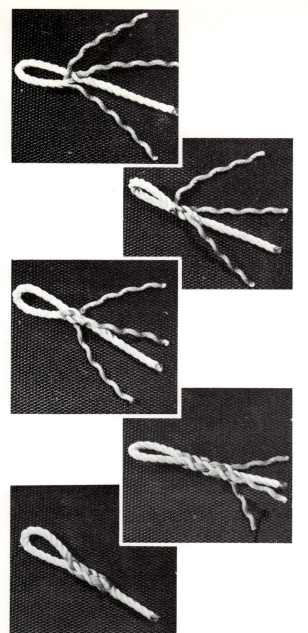

11.1, 11.2, 11.3, 11.4, 11.5

How to splice a rope. First carefully unwind about 8 in. of rope for the size shown in the photo, which is ¾-in. terylene. Seize or whip the ends, or in this case heat-seal them with a match. Spread out the three strands into a fan shape and lay them across the rope as shown. Holding the rope firmly on either side of this position, untwist the rope so that a loop is formed, whereupon you can push the centre strand through. Turning to the second picture, then tuck the lower strand by going back and upwards in the same direction as the first. Finally tuck the third strand on the far side. This is your first tuck. Continue evenly one strand at a time until you have done three complete tucks, as shown in the fourth photograph. Cut the ends off about ¼ in. from the rope and seal with a match, pressing down with a metal object to spread the end out slightly. Then roll the splice to and fro firmly in your hand to bed it down, and the job is done.

Mast bend and flexibility are so important to boat speed that one cannot just build a mast to a plan and leave it at that. If you are building to a racing class it is essential for you to find out the lastest trends in mast design for your class. The use of the wrong mast or rigging would be fatal to the performance of your boat in top competition.

For the cruising owner all this is not important and the need is merely for a strong, trouble-free spar on which to hang the sails—quite a different requirement.

For a cruising or general-purpose boat building a mast will be quite simple, as the plan will show the dimensions, wall thickness, and amount of hollowing if any. It will merely be necessary to note whether the piece of wood which you are proposing to use is particularly open grained. If so, then take out less hollow and leave the walls thicker to resist compression.

If the boat is to race seriously, the matter of wood density, wall thickness and hollowing as well as the actual cross-section of the mast may have to be allowed for. All this is really a matter of design, but building plans cannot tell you the finer points of adjustment which will have come to light under racing development. This is a matter between you and the top owners of the class. Pick their brains and see how their masts are shaped and stayed. The best timbers to use are the spruces, either Sitka or silver. Other timbers are sometimes used, but are not recommended owing to wavy grain, warping (or winding) or splitting. Spruce varies in density, and a rough guide can be obtained by counting the number of rings per inch on the end grain. It is not easy to count them on a plain sawn end, but a little chiselling or planing will reveal them. Seven rings per inch would be a light or open sample, whereas twenty would be a dense or heavy timber. Try to obtain a medium sample, though this is not easy, owing to the shortage of good spruce and the variation often seen between the inner and outer rings of one tree.

One of the main anxieties for the amateur is whether the timber is going to wind or warp as soon as it is sawn through. One does not want to have to buy timber, convert it into strips of the right shape for hollowing, and then find that it has twisted. There are several things that can be done to minimize the risk. Firstly, buy your timber from well-seasoned stock from a well-known merchant, or preferably if you can, from a reputable shipyard who may have had it in their shed for some time.

The sample of timber must have straight grain which runs parallel the whole way down the timber baulk without running out at the side. The main danger is that the moisture content may not be low enough. In any event when you get your timber do not convert it immediately. Store it in a dry shed for at least a month to acclimatize, preferably in the place where you are going to work on it. Support it evenly on battens and keep it straight with air all round it. The timber yard might store it for you and then you can mark it and get them to convert and plane it on their machines.

Assuming all goes well and it remains straight when sawn, mark which were the newly cut faces and take the timber to the workshop. It is unlikely that a full-length gluing bed will be available, so you will have to make one up by packing tables and trestles in line all of the same height. They must be arranged so that the mast can be cramped down on to them straight (Fig. 11.7).

When working out the sizes of timber needed, and marking out the saw-cuts, remember that it is desirable to reverse the two pieces end for end and turn one round 180 degrees also. Any warping tendency should then cancel out.

The next thing to do is to borrow a large number of suitable cramps—about one per foot should do. If you cannot borrow screw "G" cramps there are various types one can make out of scrap ply and wedges, but they are rather fiddly to use and not often so powerful (Fig. 3.14, p. 52).

Now you have to work out how much hollowing to allow, and also roughly prepare slots for winches and halyard sheave-boxes. It

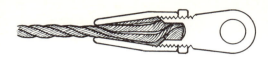

11.6
The Norseman "Swageless" Terminal. You can buy these with either an eye end, as shown, a forked end to receive an eye-splice, or a stud end to screw into a bottle-screw. The ends are interchangeable, as is the centre cone round which the wire is formed and which jams against the outer shell under tension. The big advantage of this system is that the wire can be shortened by very small amounts, which is impossible with any other splicing system. Also the terminals are interchangeable and can be changed very quickly. (Norseman Ltd.)

is usual to split masts fore and aft down the centre, and therefore there will usually be some taper on the fore side, which can be cut and planed to within about $\frac{1}{8}$ in. of size at this stage.

The marking for the tapered hollow to follow the external taper can be made with the aid of a gauge (Fig. 11.8). The mast is left solid at the hounds, and where the spreaders

---

11.7
This rack has been made by a professional spar-maker in order to glue up spars quickly. All the little shelves are at the same height, and the uprights are in exact line with each other. The spars are simply cramped up with long packing-pieces on either side to spread pressure. (Collar.)

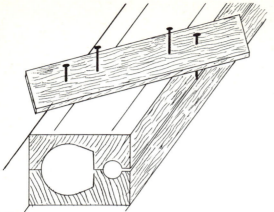

11.8
A simple marking-gauge can be made up out of a scrap of ply and four nails. If the two outer nails are kept pressed against the mast the taper will automatically be scribed parallel to the edge, either for marking how far to hollow, or, as in this sketch, where to limit the knocking off of the corners.

11.9
The nearest piece of timber is half of a mast which has been hollowed out. The gouge is resting on the solid which has been left for the spreaders to pass through. The narrow hole for the halyard to pass through the solid can also be seen. (Collar.)

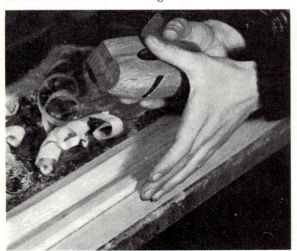

11.10
Moulding planes with convex bottoms and cutters can be used for cleaning out the hollows when this is done by hand. (Collar.)

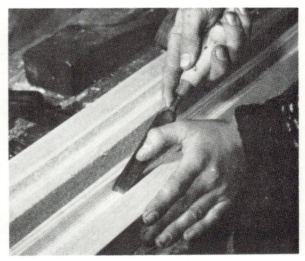

11.11
Gouges are also used for cleaning out the hollow, but be careful that you do not go too deep. It is not easy to keep straight. (Collar.)

come, except for a small hole for the halyard (Fig. 11.9). The photos show methods of hollowing and one-half of the lower part of a deck-stepped Enterprise mast (Figs. 11.10, 11.11, 11.12, 11.13). This example was prepared from a broken spar and thus the exterior is completely rounded off, whereas our mast is still in the squared blank stage, of course.

Before starting to scoop you must make some templates out of cardboard of the final hollow. These will be used to try the hollowing to help you avoid going too far. Secondly, you must be very careful to note the lie of the grain. It will never be absolutely true all the way and it could be fatal to chisel away against the grain and find you had gone too deep. Small round moulding planes are very useful for cleaning up the hollow. Make sure that there are no snags to catch internal halyards and that there are smooth entries to the channels through the solids.

The hollowing is perfectly straightforward and only needs great care with chisel, gouge, and moulding plane. When it is to your satisfaction, fasten a guide block to the side of a suitable moulding plane to run out the luff rope groove (Fig. 11.12). Half an inch or 13 mm. is the usual diameter for this, and one leaves about 4 mm. of wood between the hollow and the aft edge of the mast. When the groove is complete, the slot sides must be planed down so that the thickness of the sail tabling can pass (Fig. 11.14). Three millimetres is usually left here for the usual dinghy sail, which means 1½ mm. for each half. Try the amount planed off by laying a straight-edge across the face. A small bullnose or rebating plane is used for this job.

11.12
A section through half of a completed mast. It shows half of the D-shaped hollow with parallel-sided walls. It also shows half of the luff rope groove. (Collar, Enterprise.)

The actual entry for the luff-rope can be cut after assembly; just run the groove down to a point just above the gooseneck or the top of its sliding track (Fig. 11.15).

Cut out the slots for winches and sheave boxes (Fig. 11.13). These are best finally trimmed after assembly.

Now comes the gluing operation; it is essential to do a dummy run and highly desirable to have helpers. The main thing is to get the two parts into exactly the right position and to stay in that position whilst cramping up. Cramp up dry and then run a couple of screws through the top and bottom, where they will not matter. This will stop up and down move-

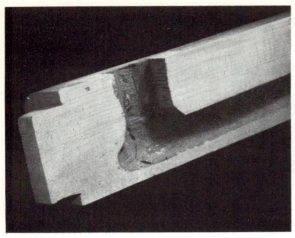

11.13
Half of the base of a completed mast with the slot for the sheave cage for the halyard and the channel where the halyard passes. The tenon to locate the heel of the mast in the boat can also be seen. (Collar, Enterprise.)

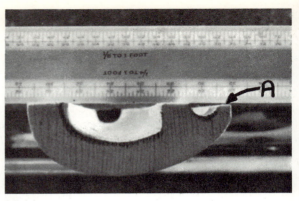

11.14
This shows at point A how the outer edge of the luff groove is planed down to enable the sail tabling to pass. (Collar, Enterprise.)

ment. Sideways sliding can be dealt with by putting a couple of cramps at right-angles to the others with packing blocks under their heads and feet. Do not be afraid to pin the parts together with small nails.

Dismantle everything and leave all the cramps and packing close by. As quickly as possible spread a thin coating of glue on both faces. Make sure that all areas to be glued are wetted but not spread too thickly, and ensure that a thin line is laid inside one half of the mast so that you can pull the halyard through later (Fig. 11.16).

Without delay place the two faces together and put in the guide screws at head and heel.

Then start cramping as fast as possible. Do not cramp too tight to start with, but when all are in place and you are sure the faces are in proper contact and in the right positions, go along and screw them up to a light even pressure. Then go along again and give them a half-turn. Finally when the glue has gelled give them another half-turn if they need it. Do not overtighten for fear of distorting the section and putting the faces out of contact in their outer edges.

The exterior of the glued and squared blank is then marked for "eight-squaring". This means taking the corners off so that the section is roughly octagonal. A scribing gauge is used similar to that for marking the limits of the hollow and the wood can be trimmed off with a band-saw; it's a long job by hand! (Fig. 11.8).

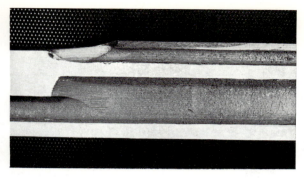

11.15
This shows a very good treatment for the entry for the luff groove. A strip of hardwood has been scarfed in at the entrance to take the brunt of the wear caused by the sail roping rubbing at the entrance. (Collar, Enterprise.)

11.16
Before you cramp up the two halves of the mast make sure that there is a line down the centre so that you can haul the halyard through afterwards. (Collar.)

Using these marking lines and the glue lines as guides, you can then complete the shaping quite simply, though it is a time-consuming job (Fig. 11.17).

If the hollow is not uniform you should make notes of its dimensions using the aft face of the mast as datum. You can then plane away the outside, checking diameters with callipers every so often.

You may find it easiest to chop out any slots for halyard sheave-boxes or winches before gluing, but if you do so you should make them undersize to allow for possible inaccuracies.

RIGGING

There are various ingenious ways of connecting the rigging to a mast, but the simplest is the tang and bolt method shown (Fig. 11.18). It is not a good plan to connect rigging direct to a fitting, because the slight flexing that always takes place would soon break the wire at the fitting. Similarly at the deck there should always be a certain amount of free play between wire and rigging-screw and between rigging-screw and chainplate. Bent rigging-screws are dangerously weakened and the same goes for bent chainplates (see also Figs. 11.30, 11.31, p. 175).

The usual shackle for providing the necessary free movement is considered by many to be too bulky, especially at the mast end, and the small stainless steel rigging links are not a great deal better (Fig. 11.19).

A double tang and clevis pin is the best simple answer (Fig. 11.20), though with the greater use of swaging it is possible that we might see a ball and keyhole plate on the

11.17
The first main part of the shaping can be done with a draw-knife. This takes off a great deal of wood at one go, and can save a lot of time. (Collar.)

11.18
This shows a very strong way of fastening the shrouds to the mast. There is a double tang with a clevis pin passing through the end of both with the main shroud eye in between. A strap carries the strain from the top of the bolt farther up the mast to another bolt, thus spreading the load.

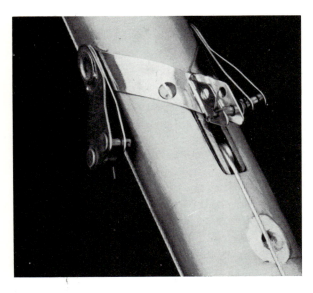

◄   **11.20**
A very neat and comprehensive set of mast fittings on a metal mast. There is a combined hounds fitting comprising two pairs of double-hole tangs suitable for carrying the main shroud and diamond bracing. The forestay can also be carried on this strop. The fore halyard sheave can be seen in the mast and also a lead hole for the spinnaker halyard. (Ian Proctor Metal Masts Ltd.)

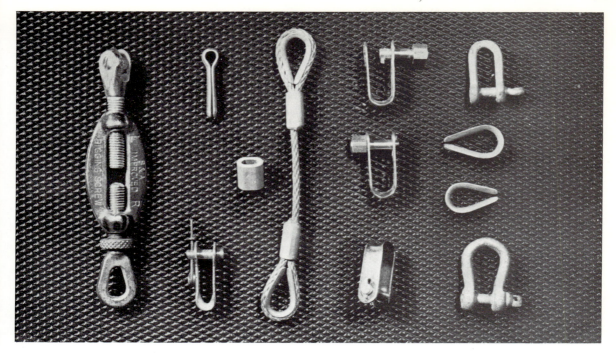

11.19
A selection of rigging fittings. On the left is a good type of rigging-screw with a locknut on the eye end. The forked end has a flush-fitting screw which will not catch in anything. Next to the top is a stainless steel split pin whilst below it is a stainless rigging-link with a clevis pin held by a wire Terry clip. The next item is a piece of wire with Talurit clamps and stainless steel thimbles. The Talurit sleeve shown just to the left in the centre, is oval before being inserted into the clamping device, whence it is compressed into the round shape seen on the wire. The next row shows a very useful type of stainless shackle with a captive pin. More normal "D" and bow shackles are shown in the last row with stainless steel thimbles in the centre.

market soon (Fig. 11.21). At the lower end there is really nothing better for simplicity, cheapness, and free movement than an eye and a few turns of terylene line (Fig. 11.22). This is not so retrograde as it sounds, and more and more people are realizing the potentialities of the small braided terylene lines now available. I have used this system for three hard seasons on a keelboat with no sign of wear.

Failing this it is neatest to pass the shroud through a reinforced hole in the deck and on to a channel plate underneath drilled for various positions of a clevis pin. The final adjustment is then made on the forestay at the stemhead either with rigging-screw or line.

Additional mast staying can be provided if necessary in many ways. Jumper struts or even

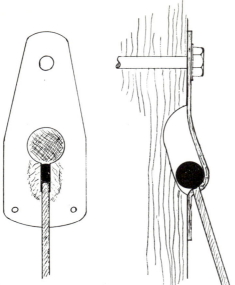

11.21

A suggested way of fitting a shroud on to a mast with absolute minimum windage. This assumes that you can find someone who can swage a ball on to the very end of your shroud wire.

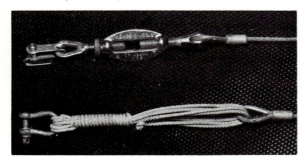

11.22

In olden days rigging was always set up by means of line. Hemp line used to stretch, shrink and rot, but the new terylene lines have none of these failings. In the two examples shown above the rigging-screw assembly might cost as many shillings as the other would cost pence.

topmast forestays can be used to control the part above the hounds. Diamond bracing (Fig. 11.23), lower shrouds, or swept spreaders (Fig. 11.24), are used to limit bending of the lower part. Minor rigging wires for jumpers and diamond bracing are usually made from stainless piano wire or galvanized 110-ton steel wire. The latter is very cheap and can frequently be obtained in small quantities from manufacturers such as Bruntons of Musselburgh, Scotland. Use not thinner than 16 s.w.g. for sail areas up to 100 sq. ft. Minor rigging for larger boats should be 15 or 14 s.w.g. You can use this material for main shrouds in 12 s.w.g. for 12-ft Nationals or similar, and 10 s.w.g. for larger boats, though it is difficult to bend the latter satisfactorily. It is quite sufficient to bend the wire round a stainless thimble (Fig. 11.25), push it through a ferrule and then bend the end back. The ferrule can be copper or brass tube in the smaller sizes and stainless tube for the larger. An alternative and simple way of making a ferrule is to wind a short tight coil of 16 s.w.g. wire round a suitable-sized drill.

The actual spreader or strut is usually made from alloy tube and there are numerous mast fittings on the market designed to cope with any staying problem.

Swinging spreaders connecting to the main shrouds have to be slotted and pinned securely at their ends, since they frequently are in tension and not always in compression. The length of these spreaders is usually critical, though a rough guide is to make them an inch longer than the distance between mast and shroud when the mast is standing straight. The exact length depends on the type of boat

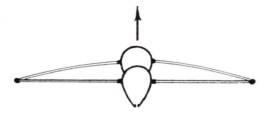

11.23
Diamond rigging cannot be used on a mast which bends considerably. The centre of the mast being displaced forwards throws the diamond wires out of line and would cause the spreaders to collapse.

11.24
A type of swept-back spreader socket fitting. Stainless steel tubes fit into the sockets, and are held by split pins. (Ian Proctor Metal Masts Ltd.)

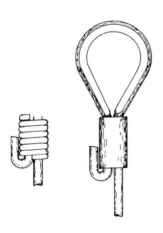

11.25
An eye can be made in solid wire by bending it round a thimble, passing it through a brass or copper tube and bending the end back. A tube can be made by winding a spiral of piano wire also.

11.26
Shrouds should be held to the ends of spreaders by slots cut in the ends and split pins outside the wire. Then wrap a good solid pudding of insulation tape round the wire and the spreader end.

11.27
There are now on the market very neat cast aluminium sheave boxes such as this one which are simple to fit into slots cut into the mast. Alternatively sheave boxes can be made out of a piece of bent brass strip. It is not wise to fit a sheave without a sheave box. Wire halyards can easily jump off the sheave and jam between the side of this and the mast. (Collar.)

11.29
The correct method of wiring a rigging-screw. The best material is tinned copper wire of about 18 s.w.g. The other rigging-screw is of a special open type with split pins through the ends of the studs for locking.

11.28
This photo taken at random shows a common failing of the ordinary locknut method of stopping rigging screws slackening off.

and mast, and how much you want the mast to bend. Consult top owners in your class for advice.

Always wrap a good pudding of adhesive tape round all spreader ends to avoid the sails catching in projections and getting torn (Fig. 11.26).

Fixed wire bracing can be tensioned by small rigging-screws at the lower ends or by nuts and machine screws slipped into the spreader ends, but do not despise the ubiquitous terylene line for this job. There is nothing better for the main rigging than stainless wire of 1×19 construction. This cannot be spliced by hand and is usually swaged or Talurit clamped (Fig. 11.19), by a rigging specialist or boatyard. However, there is now a range of special end-fittings made by Norseman Ropes which can easily be fitted to the ends of 1×19 wire and the system is approved by Lloyd's

(Fig. 11.6). The arrangement has the advantage that the end-fitting can be changed for one of a different type in a few moments, and also the wire can be shortened by a small amount if required.

Wire for running rigging must be of the special flexible construction which usually has a hemp heart, but a new type using a p.v.c. heart is just becoming available. Sheaves for wire rope must be of the largest diameter possible and fitted into sheave boxes with the minimum possible clearance between sheave and sides, though remember that Tufnol expands 30 thousandths per inch and can jam if this is not allowed for. It is very easy for small halyard wires to get jammed between the sheave and the side of the cage, if there is any slackness here (Fig. 11.27).

Rigging-screws will undo themselves if steps are not taken to prevent it. Many models have locknuts fitted to the studs which can be screwed down hard against the barrel to prevent the screw slackening off. This arrangement is not entirely reliable and the nuts sometimes slacken off in some mysterious way (Fig. 11.28). It is better to secure the barrel with copper wire passed through the tommy-bar hole (Fig. 11.29).

If a gooseneck track is to be fitted to the mast, make sure that it is well secured, because there is a considerable force tending to wrench it off when the boom is squared off. If you recess the track tightly into a slot cut in the aft face of the mast, this will help to hold it firm.

If spreader tubes pass right through the mast you should bush the hole with a large tube first and this should project from the

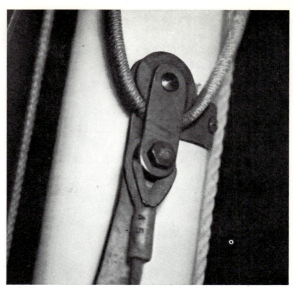

11.30

A good way of supporting the forestay, and in some cases the jib halyard as well, is by running a sheave carrying these two items on a strop held by the main hounds bolt.

mast enough to enable a split pin to be put through both it and the spreader. This is a simple method but the new and properly designed spreader fittings are better and stronger (Fig. 11.24).

The forestay can be carried by a sheave running on a short wire strop. The eyes at the end of the strop are slipped over the same bolts which carry the shroud tangs (Fig. 11.30). Another way is to pass a single 10 s.w.g. tang through a slot in the foreside of the mast. The hounds bolt passes through a hole in the top of the tang whilst the forestay is shackled to the lower end (Figs. 11.31, 11.32, 11.33, 11.34, 11.35, 11.36).

◄   11.31, 11.32   ▲

Both these methods would give just enough play in the end fitting to avoid bending and fracture.

◄   11.33, 11.34   ▲

Fitting halyard winches is bound to weaken the mast in that area. Nevertheless, here is a very popular type of winch and the way to fit it. (Lewmar & Collar.)

11.35, 11.36
Some boats use a single mast jack at the heel instead of rigging-screws of all the shrouds. These photos show how to fit such a jack. (Collar.)

12 *Painting and Varnishing*

Now we come to the protection of the woodwork of a boat. To all intents and purposes this boils down to considering the various paints and varnishes and how to apply them. There are other methods of finishing boats such as waxing, linseed-oiling, cellulose-spraying and so on, but the practical home boat-builder has no need to worry about such things. Ordinary synthetic marine finishes and the newer polyurethane finishes are the two materials which best cover all the needs of the boat-owner.

The purpose of paint and varnish is twofold. Firstly it is intended to protect the timber and to produce a hard, tough, smooth surface. Secondly it is intended to decorate the article. One can be confident that all paints and varnishes sold under the main well-known brand names will perform equally well for their type. It is wise, therefore, to stick to a well-known brand unless you have a particular reason not to do so. The differences between brands are significant only in lesser respects.

For the person who is going to apply the material some of these lesser factors may weigh towards making his choice. For instance, some brands might have a more pleasing colour range. Some may have a higher pigment content and therefore be capable of better covering power. Some may dry quicker. Some may have an undercoat that is easier to rub down or flows better without showing brushmarks. And so on.

Due to the use of different solvents in manufacture it is also wise not to mix brands on the same job, though it is perfectly all right to use one brand of synthetic paint on top of an already fully hard surface of a different brand. This does not necessarily apply when attempting to put a polyurethane material on top of a normal synthetic paint. It is wise in this case to try a small patch first to see that the bottom coat shows no signs of pickling. However, it is not advisable to put a polyurethane paint on top of a normal one, for other reasons which will be explained.

SYNTHETIC PAINT

The procedure for painting with ordinary synthetic marine paint is as follows. Firstly a wood primer is required. This is a quick-drying, matt-surfaced paint which penetrates the pores of the wood and serves the double purpose of stopping suction from the timber and of making a firm ground to which succeeding layers of paint can adhere. Secondly, one needs a stopper or filler which usually comes in the form of a paste which can be knifed into depressions in the surface with a broad-bladed and flexible tool. In top-class work the whole surface to be painted is knifed over immediately after the priming coat. When dry it is rubbed down smooth. The undercoats come next and are used to build up a solid background of colour. They are not intended as fillers to enable the surface to be got smooth, though they are often used as such by amateurs because the rather tedious operation of knifing the whole surface makes it seem the harder operation. I must confess that personally I very rarely knife the whole area, and in fact I have always found it easier to use the undercoats as fillers. Hence I usually go for a brand of paint that has a quick-drying undercoat of a chalky consistency that is easy to cut down with the sandpaper.

The bare wood surface should have been well prepared by sanding carefully and must be clean and dry. Usually one coat of primer is sufficient. However, if the surface has not been rubbed down and scraped thoroughly it will be necessary to go quickly over it after the primer has dried, with dry sandpaper to remove the "nibs" and whiskers. These will be stiffened with paint and easy to remove. It will then be necessary to apply a further thin coat of primer to cover the patches bared by the sandpaper. If the surface has been knifed it will probably be found easiest to rub this down dry also. However, when it comes to the turn of the undercoats to be smoothed it will be much more satisfactory to use wet-or-dry paper and water.

Wet-or-dry paper is much more expensive than the ordinary glasspaper, but it lasts a great deal longer and so one usually finds that it is more economical to use in the long run. The best way to use it is to cut the sheet down its centre longways and then to fold each strip thus formed into three. Each section can then be used alternately and the pad will hold itself together quite well in face of the rubbing action of the palm of the hand (Fig. 12.1). The palm and fingers are used to apply pressure to the pad of paper. The pad is dipped into a bucket of water frequently and rubbed with a

12.1
A good way of folding wet-or-dry abrasive paper for rubbing down a hull. The standard-size sheet should be folded down the centre of the long direction and divided in two. Then the narrow strip thus formed should be folded in three as shown and held in the palm of the hand.

circular motion on to the surface. It will be found that the paper hardly clogs at all and can easily be cleaned by dipping into the water. Once the system has been used for a few times you will find that an extremely sensitive touch can be developed, enabling the operator to detect minor irregularities remarkably precisely. There is no doubt that this hand method of wet rubbing down will provide the very finest finish obtainable. About 320 grade paper will be satisfactory for the undercoats and a finer grade (higher number) for the final coat.

For all dry rubbing down I can recommend the reddish-brown garnet paper as being greatly superior to the ordinary sandpaper. It lasts longer and does not clog easily, though it is a little more expensive.

Dry off the surface carefully after wet rubbing down and make sure there is no damp remaining in cracks and hollows before applying a new coat.

Rub down the undercoats thoroughly and do not mind if you go through to the bare wood in places. It will be easy to see how smooth the surface of the next coat will be because, if you look along the rubbed-down surface against the light, the low patches will show up as shinier areas. Theoretically the final coat will not be absolutely smooth until there are no low areas at all. In practice this ideal state is almost never realized.

I normally put on two top coats of enamel. One is all that is strictly necessary, but I feel that the extra thickness of tough enamel withstands the rough and tumble of launching and trailing better. The surface should be very carefully rubbed down and cleaned. Then at the last minute rub a linen cloth damped thoroughly in white spirit all over the surface. This will pick up remaining particles of dust and be the best insurance of a mar-free final finish. Knock out the brush to be used to free dust from the bristles. The brush should be the best you can afford and be as wide as you can manage. A 3-in. brush is about ideal. The better quality the brush the better the finish and the easier it is to apply the paint. It really is worth getting a good brush and taking great care of it.

Apply the paint evenly in strips from keel to gunwale about 18 in. wide. Work as quickly as possible but make sure that the brushloads are evenly smoothed out so that "runs" and "weeps" are avoided. You can feel when the paint has been applied to a patch too thickly because the brush will give the impression of "skidding" over that patch. Watch out for "holidays" which are areas missed. It is not easy to see if you have missed a tiny area, but a wandering light set up beyond the end of the hull so that you can squint along the surface towards it helps a lot.

Keep everyone out of the workshop and try to create as little dust as possible by your movements. Do not wear whiskery sweaters. A boiler suit is best. There is no need to worry about flies settling on the surface. They can be removed after the paint has dried with almost no mark to show for it.

Do not touch the surface for at least twenty-four and preferably for more than forty-eight hours. If the boat can be left untouched for a week or more there will be even less likelihood of damage and the paint will have a chance to harden. Paint does not get fully hard for a month or more, and the longer it can be left between coats the better.

Varnish is essentially the same material as enamel but it has no colouring pigment in it. A really smooth surface in a varnished finish is more difficult to obtain, because one is unable to use the various fillers, stoppers, and undercoats as one can with pigmented paint which conceals their presence. Therefore you must take very great care with the preparation of the original wood surface. The rubbing-down action will only be able to cure the very shallowest of depressions. One can fill major holes or cracks with a filler coloured to the shade of the timber. Make sure that the shade used is the same as the timber will be when wetted with varnish. This is normally a good deal darker than the dry colour in the case of most timbers such as mahogany. Because there is no primer that can be used with a varnish finish, one uses a thinned-down coat of varnish as the first coat. Most varnishes can be thinned with turps or white spirit. I prefer to use genuine turpentine for the thinning of this priming coat. About 10–40 per cent of thinners can be used and the mixture should be very well brushed in. Succeeding coats can be unthinned varnish.

Brushes can be left with their bristles immersed in cold water for short periods. For instance, if you are varnishing a hull and going to take a week over it, it would be satisfactory to leave the brush in water overnight each day until the job was finished. Shake out the water each time and brush out several brushloads on to a rough piece of timber before starting the actual work. However, after a few days the brush should be thoroughly cleaned in white spirit. The way I do this is as follows. Put some white spirit in a basin and thoroughly squidge the brush into it for a minute or two or until there seems to be only well-thinned-down paint emerging from the roots of the bristles. Then throw away the white spirit, or if you are economical or have time on your hands, leave it for the paint to settle out so that most of the spirit can be used again. Then put some more spirit into the basin and squidge again. Leave the bristles with their tips in the spirit overnight. Squidge yet again

in the morning and then knock and shake out the brush until no more spirit comes out of the bristles. Unless this operation is well and truly done you will find that paint will start to harden up in the bristle roots and gradually the brush will become more and more solid and finally useless.

Synthetic paints can be thinned with turps or white spirit if required, but they should not normally need it.

The warmer and drier the atmosphere the better for painting. If conditions are poor it may be necessary to leave two or three days between coats. In really cold weather one can sometimes get away with satisfactory painting by warming the tin before and during use. Stopper takes a long time to harden when used in large holes and cracks, and it often pays to use plastic wood in them.

A note about stripping paintwork when the time comes to renew it: if the paintwork is so damaged or blistered that it does not seem to be feasible merely to put on a couple more coats, it is well worth while stripping. On a large area it is probably easiest to use a blowlamp, but the modern paint strippers are now remarkably effective and quick. I have always used a brand called Nitromors, and when it is soft I remove it with one of the many shapes of Skarsten scrapers which have removable and replaceable blades and which are very easy to sharpen every few minutes as the work progresses with a few strokes with a file (Figs. 12.2, 12.3). After using stripper, thoroughly swab down the work with a rag soaked in petrol, turps or white spirit which cleans off the waxy suspension.

POLYURETHANE PAINT

Polyurethane is the name for catalysed poly-ester, and paints marketed under either of these headings are of the same type. The use and treatment of the paints is quite different from that for the normal synthetic paints. The normal paint dries by the oxidizing of the active ingredients and forms a skin on the surface first and gradually solidifies from the outside inwards. Thus one has to be careful handling a newly dried paint surface in case the lower regions are still tacky whereupon the surface skin could slide over them like a ripe pear skin.

True polyurethane finishes come in two parts, which are often of roughly equal bulk, though this varies with different makes, but there are now types of polyurethane paints that come in only one part. However, my experience is that the one-part types are not so durable or as hard as the two-part mixes. One part is the paint and has the colour pigment in it. The other part is a colourless liquid called the hardener. When the two are mixed together in the correct proportions a chemical reaction starts and after a set period the mixture gels and then sets hard. It sets simultaneously all through the mixture and does not skin on the surface first. The time of setting is delayed a good deal by being in bulk rather than spread thinly, but it will harden in the tin nevertheless. Temperature has an effect on the time of setting as indeed it has with ordinary paint, and one should not apply polyurethane paint in a lower temperature than about 45 degrees. Equally it may be impossible to apply polyurethane paint in a high temperature, because it would start

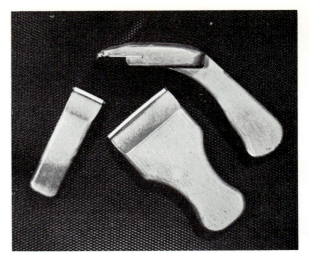

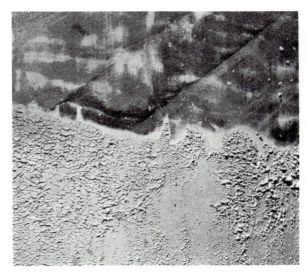

12.3
Paint remover does not always pickle the surface as shown in this photograph. Particularly on polyurethane paints there may be no sign at all that the paint has been softened.

◄ 12.2

A selection of Skarsten scrapers. These can be obtained in all shapes and sizes and have replaceable cutting hooks. The hook can be sharpened with a file very easily every few minutes, and a carefully sharpened wide scraper can even be used for finishing plywood veneer surfaces before painting.

12.4

The effect of damp and frost on paint finishes is as shown in the photograph at A. There is no remedy for this other than scraping the area and repainting.

to set off so rapidly that one would not have time to spread it out before it started to gel. A temperature of about 60 to 65°F. can be considered ideal.

Another point to watch with polyurethane paints stems from the fact that the catalyst will react with water in preference to its intended opposite number. It will even react with the moisture in the air and so if the tin is left open it will harden. Catalyst smeared round the mouth of the tin will set off overnight and the lid will be difficult to open next time unless one wipes the mouth with a rag damped in the correct matching thinners. This fact also means that one has to be particularly careful to eliminate the traces of moisture on the surface and also to avoid the wetting of the coating for at least a day and preferably three days after applying. The cure is not fully completed for several weeks, but to all intents three days is sufficient.

You will see that more care is needed in handling these paints, and this is also true of the actual mixing, the application, and cleaning the brushes. However, there are also a number of advantages to the material. To start with, the surface dries hard enough to handle in a few hours, and the fact that the cure takes place uniformly throughout the coating means that there is no danger of "skinning" the surface like a ripe pear, and also it means that it is possible to rub down or cut out runs, wrinkles, and drips almost immediately without danger of making a mess.

Another advantage is that the surface of the cured coating is very hard and scratch-resistant and retains its gloss for a very great length of time. The coating is also very much more waterproof than ordinary paint, though this latter fact means that it is more important than ever to see that the timber is really dry before application and that both inner and outer surfaces of the timber are protected. Otherwise damp cannot escape except by lifting off the paint (Fig. 12.4). There is a further group of advantages which results from the quick hardening and the gelling characteristics. Succeeding coats of paint bond extremely well to previous layers if the latter have not completely cured. Thus there is no need to rub down to provide a key if the next coat is applied within twenty-four hours. In fact, it is possible to apply four coats in one day in warm weather. As soon as the first coat is tacky the second can be applied and so on. This can be a great time-saver, especially in the case of interiors, spars, gear and other such things that do not need an especially smooth surface. Another point is that, due to the immediate hardness, it is possible to rub down with dry sandpaper almost immediately and the rubbing off of runs or other blemishes is very easy.

It is probably better to use dry sandpaper rather than wet-or-dry and water if this is to be done within twenty-four hours of application, but after this time the rubbing down can be wet and lubricated either with water or white spirit. I again use garnet paper for the dry rubbing and find it very satisfactory.

It is important to remember that polyurethane paint needs special thinners which are sold with it. Turps or white spirit should not be used unless the instructions specifically say so. Brushes should be cleaned in the special thinners also.

There is one further point which needs to be watched, and this is that one must try and estimate in advance the exact quantity of paint needed, because any left in the pot will have to be thrown away. This can be modified to a certain extent in that the pot life of the mixed paint can be up to twenty-four hours and can be extended slightly by the addition of thin-

ners. One can also mix a small quantity left over in this way with a new batch mixed within the following twenty-four hours. Thinners can also ease brushing difficulties in warm weather.

Some brands of polyurethane paint are quite thick in consistency and others are extremely thin. It is obviously more economical in time to use a thicker type, as fewer coats will be needed.

When applying the paint or varnish it is essential to work as fast as possible with the widest brush which can conveniently be handled. The paint should be spread rapidly. After a few seconds it will start to "pull", and shortly after this you will not be able to join up the new with the previous brushload without horrible puckering and lumps. If you stop trying to brush out these imperfections immediately they start to appear you will find that in a few minutes they will have disappeared, but if you persist in trying to smooth them down you will surely make a mess.

There is normally no primer for this type of finish and so the first important keying coat should always be of thinned-down polyurethane varnish. After this, continue with coat on coat of the desired colour unthinned. Rub down as directed to obtain the desired smoothness of surface.

Note carefully that the polyurethane finishes differ completely from the ordinary synthetic paints in their action in drying and whereas the synthetic need the maximum possible time between coats the exact reverse is true for the former.

Polyurethane paints cost rather more than the ordinary synthetic paints and therefore they should be used only when one is sure that their advantages are going to be fully realized. With the present materials available it seems to be certain that if water is allowed to get behind them it will cause the film to be lifted off in the same way as it does with ordinary paints. This means that the material will prove uneconomic on boats that are kept in the water and whose seams open and close in varying temperature conditions. The dry-sailed dinghy is an ideal subject for the application of polyurethane paint and it can also be successfully used on moulded keelboats. It will be perfect and extremely long lasting on interior surfaces and it will also be effective on masts, spars and other small gear. It can also be used on polyester-reinforced-glass boats (fibre-glass) and indeed should be used as a finish in the method of reinforced-plastics building explained in Chapter 9.

A few years ago it was usual to mix pigments with the resin when making a reinforced-plastics boat, but in the top-class work nowadays this is not normally done, owing to the difficulty of seeing how well the "lay-up" is progressing. After this it was usual to use pigment only in the gel, or surface, coat, but trouble was often experienced with surface crazing owing to the hardness of the resin used. Nowadays flexible resins are on the market which are designed especially for gel coats and have the pigments included. They are, in fact, almost identical to our polyurethane paints and can be used in their place. It is, however, easier to get a really good smooth surface used as a gel coat than to paint it on afterwards with the attendant risks of dust and brushmarks showing later.

As far as the question of putting polyure-

12.5

If you leave the brush too long in polyurethane paint, this is what happens. It is impossible to recondition the brush in this case.

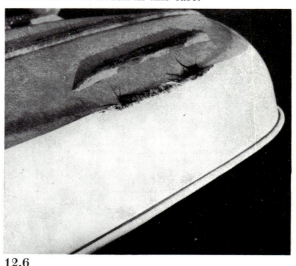

12.6

Plastic boats should be anti-fouled in the same way as ordinary boats. In this case the anti-fouling did not quite cover the area touched by the water, and during the season weed grew on the bare plastics and not on the anti-fouled area.

thane paint on top of ordinary paint goes, a test section must first be tried to see that the action of the polyurethane does not pickle the other. However, even if this is satisfactory, it is still not really advisable to continue, because the ordinary paint will be the weak link in the chain of coatings and thus the whole coating may start lifting off before the polyurethane component has served more than a part of its useful life.

The thing that ruins paint, woodwork and gluing more quickly than anything else is frost. Frost does not act on the paint directly, but must have water to enable it to perform its costly work.

All painting should be directed towards denying entry of water. Subsequent care of the boat should also be aimed at keeping water out of it and to keeping the boat out of water. Long wet grass in the dinghy park can do a great deal of damage through its continual wetting effect. When painting make sure that the interior and the undersides of decks are thoroughly covered. Fill cracks and shakes with mastic and sealing compound and do not miss old screw-holes where fittings have been removed.

It is only too easy for timber, especially plywood, to become soaked with water. If a frost occurs when the timber is in a condition of high moisture content the water may freeze. This action causes the ice to expand and this is frequently sufficient to cause cracking, glued-joint failures and, most frequently, paint lifting.

Therefore make sure that the boat is thoroughly covered with paint from the start and thereafter keep moisture away from it except when actually sailing.

ANTI-FOULING

If your boat is to be kept on a mooring it will have to be protected from the waterline down with an anti-fouling composition. The best of these usually have a very rough finish, but there are special racing anti-foulings which can be burnished. They are not usually so effective and for racing purposes you will still need to scrub fortnightly in the summer.

Cruising owners can often get away with only one or two scrubs per season. The photo shows a fibre-glass yacht's tender, the bottom of which was coated with Detel Marina. Owing to inaccuracy a small area of the bare plastic was immersed and grew weed, whereas the rest of the bottom was covered with anti-fouling and remained perfectly clean even though no scrubbing took place during the whole season. So much for the myth that plastic does not foul! (Fig. 12.6).

13 *Fitting Out*

THE selection of fittings and providing for their anchorage, together with all the fiddling and adjustment associated with fitting out, can take as much time as building the hull. It can also be proportionately the most expensive part of boatbuilding. If you are handy with drill, hacksaw and vice, you can actually make almost all the fittings needed for a sailing boat, but most people spend many pounds buying splendid glossy blocks and cleats in Tufnol and polished stainless steel, and I have no doubt that many of my readers will do the same. I used to make almost all my own fittings, including blocks, cam cleats, claw rings, and metalwork such as chainplates, rudder, mast and boom fittings. Nowadays time seems to be shorter, and I only make special fittings which are either for some particular and unusual purpose, or are unobtainable in standard form. You can get a good deal of satisfaction from making fittings, and at the same time save a substantial amount of money.

Tufnol, stainless steel, aluminium alloy, brass and copper in sheet, rod and tube form can be obtained in the comparatively small quantities needed from one of the fittings manufacturers, or from some boatyards. Larger quantities can be bought from metal merchants or from Tufnol Ltd.

The most useful sizes are listed below:

$\frac{1}{8}$-in. Tufnol sheet for blocks and various small jobs around the hull and spars. It can be bonded to timber with glue.

$\frac{1}{4}$-in. Tufnol sheet in two or more layers for claw rings, sliding mast-steps, cam cleats.

16 s.w.g. sheet stainless steel (E.N.58J), brass (half-hard), and marine-grade alloy for block cheeks, tangs, boom and mast fittings, halyard and line guides, angle plates, toe-strap fixing plates, webbing plates for buoyancy bags, kicking-strap anchorages, and many other purposes.

10–12 s.w.g. stainless steel and brass sheet for chainplates, heavy anchorage plates and tangs.

$\frac{1}{8}$-in., $\frac{3}{16}$-in., and $\frac{1}{4}$-in. copper rod for rivets.

$\frac{1}{8}$-in. stainless steel and brass brazing rod for rivets and pins, and also racing-flag staffs.

$\frac{3}{16}$-in. and $\frac{1}{4}$-in. stainless steel and brass rod for bolts and sheave pins.

$\frac{3}{16}$-in. inside diameter $\frac{1}{4}$-in. outside diameter, and $\frac{1}{4}$-in. inside diameter $\frac{5}{16}$-in. outside diameter brass, stainless steel, and aluminium alloy tube for bushes in blocks and spacers, and also for struts and spreaders.

$\frac{3}{8}$-in. and $\frac{5}{16}$-in. rod in scrap lengths for centreboard pivots and mast hounds anchorages, also rudder pintles.

16 and 12 s.w.g. stainless wire for springs, racing flag frames, and rigging.

You will find it very useful to have $\frac{3}{16}$-in. and $\frac{1}{4}$-in Whitworth thread dies so that you can run a thread on to brass or stainless rod (Fig. 13.2). Frequently you may also want to run an existing thread down farther and

unless you have these dies you will have to waste time going along to the local garage. It is worth remembering that if you are faced with a B.S.F. thread and only have Whitworth nuts, you can run a Whitworth die on to it and an adequate thread will result. But you cannot do the reverse.

Similarly $\frac{3}{16}$-in. and $\frac{1}{4}$-in. taps are useful, but are not needed nearly so often as the dies. The reason is that one nearly always has the nuts, but wants to make a bolt of a non-standard length. Bolt-heads are made by running a nut hard on to a short length of thread and riveting the end over. Do not use a spanner on these

13.1
A selection of non-ferrous materials. From the left at the bottom are three sizes of convex brass strip. The smallest is suitable for the leading edges of rudders and centreboards. Next is flat brass strip, then brass rod, then brass tube, and finally small rod suitable for flag-making. At the top on the left is copper tube for making ferrules on the ends of spreaders or tiller extensions. On the right is aluminium spreader tube. The curved piece is a section of brass protective strip ready to be fixed to a rudder blade.

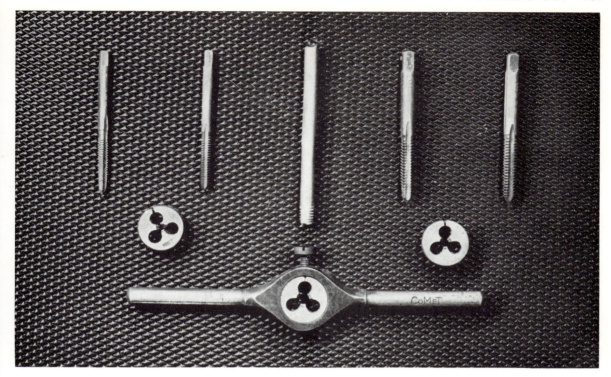

13.2
Useful sizes of Whitworth taps and dies. These are $\frac{3}{16}$ in. on the left and $\frac{1}{4}$ in. on the right.

makeshift boltheads, or they will come off, but they are perfectly satisfactory for most boat-fitting applications. Most grades of Tufnol will take a thread quite satisfactorily.

CUTTING AND DRILLING METAL

To cut stainless steel one must use high-speed hacksaw blades—they are the ones usually painted blue. When drilling stainless steel use the greatest pressure possible and the slowest speed. Ordinary handyman electric drills are no use on this material, since the speed causes too much heat to be generated and this blunts the drill straight away.

This points to the big advantage of the vertical bench drill where speed and pressure can be accurately controlled (Fig. 0.4 p. 14). You must use high-speed steel drills correctly ground, and if all is in order you ought to be able to drill stainless steel of the grade used for boat fittings (E.N.58J) almost as easily as soft brass.

There are detachable epicyclic reduction gears available for electric drills, but to my mind a simple bench drill is far more accurate and trouble-free (Fig. 13.3). Remember when using any drill that the pressure we are talking about is that per unit area of the hole. So don't press too hard when drilling $\frac{1}{16}$-in. holes for pins in rudder protecting strips, or you will quickly break the drill. Conversely, $\frac{1}{2}$-in. holes will call for a great deal of pressure. You must always start holes in metal from a centre-punch mark. It will be impossible to make the hole accurately without this starting-mark.

It is a good plan to use some lubrication when drilling stainless steel. I usually use ordinary thin oil, but almost any liquid will do and there is an easily obtainable cutting compound called Rocol R.T.D. The main thing is to get the heat to dissipate as quickly as possible to avoid taking the temper out of the drill. There is really no difficulty in working stainless steel if you remember these points, which apply equally to drilling, hacksawing, threading and filing—work slowly, and use as much pressure as possible.

BENDING METAL SHEET

Bending metal sheet can cause a lot of bother in the absence of proper tools. You can only make one right-angled bend in the normal vice, because the vice itself is too wide. One often wants to make a double bend for sheave cages, or for boom-end fittings. I now use a simple jig which I made out of two short pieces of square-section bar bolted together at the ends. The bars are held in the vice as well and are small enough to enable the "U" bend to clear them (Figs. 13.4, 13.5).

FIXING FITTINGS

A point to remember when choosing fixings is that of compatibility of metals. Only use alloy, chrome plated or stainless steel screws, when fixing alloy fittings. It is not wise to use stainless-steel bolts if they are a tight fit, because they will have a slight reaction with the alloy which can cause the latter to split. Combinations of dissimilar metals which do not include aluminium cause no particular problems.

We have considered some of the more common problems in making boat fittings, but we are more concerned here with fixing them down so that they work properly and do not come off, and I have rather strong views on this subject. It is not a bit of use taking a lot of trouble building the hull only to use fittings of inadequate strength, insecurely fastened. I never fail to be astonished at some of the fitting-out work on modern dinghies, and it is not only some home-builders who are guilty of incompetence. Even many professional builders seem to have no idea at all how a sailing dinghy works, nor how much strain each part has to stand. One can only think they never sail their own boats or, more important, race them.

The sort of things I am thinking about are good solid jib fairleads merely screwed to the gunwale, main rigging held by bronze shackles, transom rudder-fittings held on with short screws, and so on.

Fittings that are to take any sort of reasonable strain should always be through-bolted, even if it means piercing the hull skin. It is asking for trouble to use short screws on toe-strap anchorages, jib fairleads, and other fittings which carry heavy strains. Think of it as if you were hanging by the fitting and at the same time being thrown about. Would the fitting remain secure? That is the question you must ask yourself.

It may not be possible to use bolts in some positions, and if this is the case, you should use several really long and fat screws with holes properly prepared. An absolute minimum for fixing a toe-strap anchorage to hardwood would be four size 8 screws, with an inch of screw-thread in the wood. Remember that ordinary brass crystallizes and so these screws ought to be changed yearly.

Transom rudder fittings are rather a problem, since the effects of grounding are severe. If a knock-up rudder is used you can bolt the fittings on, but if you use bolts with fixed rudders, the result of running aground might be a large hole or split in the transom. The best answer is to use very long screws passing right through the transom, and screwed into a loose block of wood held pressed against the inside. In the event of severe grounding the thread will then strip out of the block without damage.

For simplicity I usually use ordinary machine screws for all through-bolting of fittings, and then the surplus thread can be cut straight off. Whitworth machine screws are not entirely satisfactory, since, in my opinion, the thread is too deep and too much strength is lost. Therefore, if B.S.F. threads are unobtainable it is necessary to use $\frac{1}{4}$-in. Whitworth machine screws for heavy loadings, and $\frac{3}{16}$-in. only for more lightly stressed parts. Similar sized wood-screws are in theory

13.3
This Masonmaster two-speed reduction gear for an ordinary twist drill enables an electric high-speed drill to be used on stainless steel or masonry. It also means that a drill rated at $\frac{1}{4}$ in. can take bits up to $\frac{1}{2}$ in. diameter, and that it can be used for buffing.

just as strong, but continual sudden yanking stresses very soon loosen them, and they always pull out at the most awkward moments.

Always use the correct-sized washers under the nuts, and always use two locked nuts on bolts which are to remain loose. Battering the end of the thread on loose bolts is not sufficient and the nut usually seems to work itself off.

Don't forget the value of using spacing tubes or bushes. Soft spruce and fibre-glass do not appreciate heavy bolting pressures. It is better where possible to clamp the bolt tight on to a spacing tube, rather than crush the fibres. This type of fixing is particularly useful for fitting tangs for centre mainsheet blocks to booms. All that is needed is a single bushed hole in the centre of the boom section for each block. If you use more than one hole

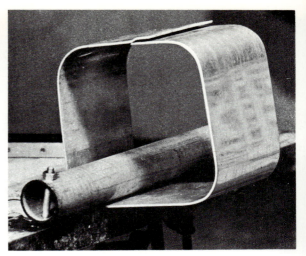

🔨 13.4, 13.5 🔨
Simple jigs for bending sheet metal into complicated shapes. The small size of square-section bar enables U-bends of anything down to its own width to be made. Smaller bars can be used for smaller U-bends. A round bar is needed for bending curves.

there will be racking strains on the fitting and its fastenings as the load angle varies on different points of sailing. The single bolt must go through the centre of the section, since there is negligible longitudinal loading on the timber at this point. When the boom is sheeted down hard the top half of the boom will be in compression, and the lower half will be in tension (Fig. 13.6).

For this same reason I do not much like the usual keyhole kicking-strap plate on the boom. There are too many fastenings for one thing, and the plate itself is usually made too light. For racing purposes one may want to put really heavy strains on this item of gear and the fittings should be designed to suit. Two possible improvements are sketched in Figs.

13.6
These tangs were specially made for the International Finn, where the boom comes extremely low, and unless every half-inch of space is saved, the blocks will come together. It is only necessary to put a single bolt through the centre of the boom.

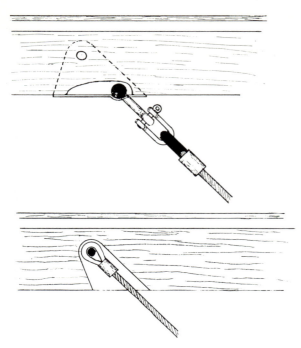

13.8
The normal keyhole kicking-strap plate is generally made too light and has too many fastenings which may weaken the boom dangerously.

13.7
The upper sketch shows a kicking strap keyhole-plate which has only one fixing point. It is not necessary to have any more fastenings than this. In the lower drawing a very strong fixing is provided by recessing the boom and passing a pin right through. This can only be done if the boom is of adequate width.

13.7. Similarly, at the lower end the normal fittings are neither strong enough nor satisfactory mechanically. On one boat I used a very successful lower anchorage consisting of a small block running on a short wire strop round the mast and fixed to a bolt on the leading edge as low as possible. There was

then no tendency to twist the mast and the anchorage was absolutely secure. A simple eye-plate can be used, but it must be bolted right through. Better still is a sheet-metal strap passing under the mast heel.

TOE-STRAPS

Toe-straps must be sited to the convenience of each crew. Often they are fastened at each end of the centreboard case and spread sideways by being held to the underside of the thwart. A more refined arrangement uses sliding lugs on the floor (Fig. 13.9). Use non-stretch webbing. The usual material sold as toe-strap webbing is, in my opinion, nothing like heavy enough. Even the terylene webbing stretches appreciably, and also folds itself up into a sort of giant bootlace which cuts the instep. The best stuff that I have been able to find recently

13.9
Toe-straps can be anchored to sliding plates screwed to a rigid floor or frame. This fitting allows lateral adjustment of the toe-strap anchorage to suit crews with different lengths of legs. (Rogers, Finn.)

13.10
For those who prefer the stiff upright loop system of toe-strap this fitting is nearly ideal. The heavy-gauge machine belting passes through the two slots and is held rigidly, but can easily be adjusted for length. Athwartships travel can be obtained by sliding the bracket and screwing down the knurled knob. The only disadvantage is that the bracket is rather sharp to sit upon. (Elvstrom, Finn.)

was nylon parachute harness from a surplus store—it was 2 in. wide and very thick.

Fasten this webbing as follows: Cut out a plate from Tufnol about $2\frac{1}{2}$ in. $\times$ $\frac{3}{4}$ in. and then put two hefty screws, or better still, $\frac{1}{4}$ in. machine screws through both plate, webbing, and a solid piece of the hull. If you have some odd lengths of sail track you can cut this into $2\frac{1}{2}$-in. lengths, and use these pieces instead, with the track side to the webbing. Whatever you do it is essential to round off all corners and edges. There is a good deal of strain on toe-straps, and wear from sharp edges has a habit of making itself felt very suddenly and wetly.

Some people prefer the type of toe-strap which stands up off the floor in a loop (Fig. 13.10). These are made out of machine belting and are usually fastened to the vertical facings of the frames or floors. Shock cord is useful for holding toe-straps up from the floor so that feet can find them quickly and safely (Fig. 13.11).

TRACK AND SLIDES

Now a word about track and slides. In the pursuit of lightness many owners fit alloy track for mainsheet travellers, often with plastic slides. I would never have this type of material in any boat of mine except possibly if it was to be used solely on fresh water. The alloy gradually accumulates a slight coating of salts and this effectively acts as a brake to the slide. The coefficient of friction between alloy track and alloy, or even nylon slides, is never very good and is not good enough for a traveller which, above all, needs to slide surely and easily.

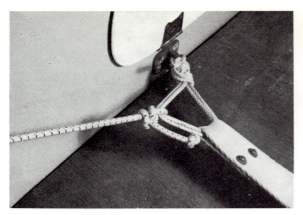

13.11
Shock cord, as on the left, is very useful in racing dinghies, and here is being used to hold a toe-strap off the floor. This toe-strap is of the other type to that in the previous illustration, and is adjusted by terylene line at each end.

13.12
It is simple and cheap to make this type of toe-strap fitting. These toe-straps are long and are held down to the hull at one or two points by terylene line. Notice the eye-plate bolted right through the skin with four bolts.

The best available material for easy sliding is brass against brass. A carefully fitted brass slide on a good smooth hard brass track is difficult to beat, but there is no denying that it will be heavy.

Stainless steel slides on stainless track do not seem to be so good (Fig. 13.13), but a brass slide on stainless track is about the best compromise, and the combination is fairly light.

If slides stick never use grease to try to improve matters. Every particle of grit around will stick to the grease, and in a short time will form a fine abrasive mixture.

The latest trend is towards central mainsheets with very free running travellers, which are continually adjusted whilst under load. This calls for ball or roller bearings, and

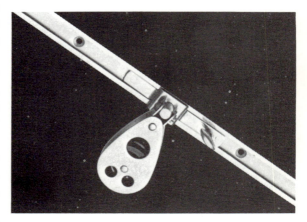

13.13
A special stainless steel slide carrying the main sheet block on stainless steel track. (R.W.O.)

while one enterprising manufacturer has marketed a beautifully made unit using recirculating ballraces (Figs. 13.14, 13.15), a nearly comparable result can be had much more simply and cheaply. The materials needed are a length of galvanized $\frac{1}{2}$-in. water pipe and a special block. Stainless steel tube can be used if you want to be fancy and have some cash to spare. Using sheet steel, brass or Tufnol and a couple of sheaves obtainable from any boat-fittings maker and some chandlers, one can easily make up a roller traveller to run on the pipe (Fig. 13.16). The pipe can be clamped under the carlins, if suitable, using ordinary pipe clips bent out of brass. Otherwise simple brackets can be made up to hold it in the best position.

In all these systems one needs control lines to be led to small cleats on each side so that the travel of the slide can be limited.

13.14
This special mainsheet traveller is designed to run absolutely freely under very heavy vertical loadings. The slider runs on a specially hardened aluminium track, via stainless steel ball-races. Notice the fittings for small sheaves so that the limit of travel can be controlled. (Ian Proctor Metal Masts Ltd.)

13.15 ►
A good mainsheet arrangement for a racing boat. Note that the track must be held down in the centre-line—here, by an aluminium tube bracket. Note also the control line cleats on the traveller and the variable angle of the wire strops to the boom giving more or less push to the gooseneck.

CLEATS

Cam cleats have completely revolutionized racing since the war. Sheets can be held absolutely at the right position for as long as required and yet be freed instantly. They are simple and virtually foolproof, but there are a few points to watch out for when selecting and fitting.

Firstly, make sure that the springs are strong enough and that the teeth are prominent. The fewer teeth there are and the larger each is, the better. Small teeth get blunt quickly and then the rope slips. Tufnol teeth can be sharpened *in situ* by paring the edges vertically with a sharp wood chisel. Another point to look out for is that the tops of the cams at the toothed side are bevelled. This

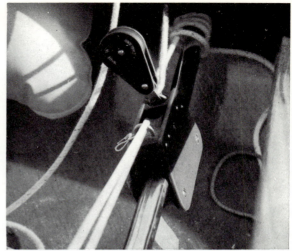

13.16
A simpler and cheaper arrangement than the Proctor Mainsheet Traveller is this roller sheave on a stainless steel tube. The object and effect are nearly the same. (Lewmar Mainsheet Traveller.)

13.17
Two forms of cleat. The cam cleat should be mounted on a small block as shown and should be arranged to point directly away from the lead of the rope. The small cleat on the left is merely a tapered hole cut in a piece of Tufnol. (Rogers, Finn.)

13.18

The clam cleat, in its various forms, has become the standard type for lightly loaded lines. Not very good with spirally laid rope.

13.19

A very useful little cleat for small Terylene lines.

can easily be done in a few seconds with a file and makes all the difference to the ease with which the rope can be jammed. Don't make the teeth too sharp or the rope will be cut.

The next point is that only plaited or braided rope can be used satisfactorily in cam cleats. A heavy load will cause three-strand rope to twist out of the cleat. Finally, make sure that the cleat is set at exactly the right angle, so that the rope can be pulled into it and flicked out from your normal sitting position. It will almost certainly have to be mounted on a small block (Fig. 13.17).

Apart from cam cleats the next most useful for dinghy use are clam cleats (Fig. 13.18). These are available in various sizes and forms and are extremely simple and foolproof. However, due to their design they are only suitable for comparatively light loadings, otherwise they are difficult to release. On the other hand they do not cut the rope and are not so critical of rope diameter as the other main type—the tubular cleat—whose main advantage is that it keeps the rope in a known and fixed position. The design of standard patterns of this style has not been too satisfactory in the past; either the rope slips or the cleat jaws cut the line. It is important to get a cleat of exactly the right size for the rope to be used, and do take along a piece to the chandlery so that you can try it. Sometimes the jaw can be adjusted with a file, but often the metal is too thin at this point and rapid rope fraying or cutting cannot be avoided. It is essential to use braided or plaited rope with most of these cleats unless the metal of the jaw is particularly deep and the rope lightly loaded. Plastic versions have not proved satisfactory owing to rapid wear of the jaw, but once you have found a tubular cleat which holds securely without cutting the rope, this design can be extremely useful for holding lines that are comparatively lightly loaded. Examples are centreboard hoists and traveller control lines (Fig. 13.19). Do not use them on heavily loaded lines, because the higher the tension, the less easy they are to free. Use cam cleats for these applications.

Other types of cleats are available such as the swivelling cam which can be invaluable with central mainsheet leads (Fig. 13.15). Not strictly a cleat, though doing partly the same job is the Novex ratchet block (Fig. 13.21). This allows a rope under heavy tension to be held with only finger-light pressure on the hauling part. It frees instantly the moment the rope is dropped and is thus a very easy way of controlling the sheet.

ROPES

Unless you are really hard pressed for immediate cash, there is absolutely no point in using anything except synthetic fibre for all ropes on board. The advantages over cotton, hemp, sisal, and manila are enormous and easily outweigh the extra initial cost. The synthetic rope used to be criticized on the score of slipperiness, but modern methods have developed ropes with every type of outer surface and you just take your pick.

One of the main synthetic materials is nylon, which is extremely strong and has the advantage for towing warps and painters of having a very high elastic stretch. It cannot be used satisfactorily for halyards owing to this very stretchiness, and also it has a tendency to rot eventually after constant exposure to sunlight, and in some uncommon atmospheric conditions.

Terylene (or dacron) is not quite so strong, but still far stronger than any natural fibre. It does not rot and has far less stretch. It can be used for main halyards in its pre-stretched form, and is very satisfactory for burgee and spinnaker halyards and all other purposes (Fig. 13.22).

Polypropylene is strong but very light and is thus useful for warps and painters and, especially in a racing dinghy where weight is at a premium, for anchor lines. Its disadvantage is that it is susceptible to abrasion and so must not be allowed to rub anywhere.

All these synthetic fibres are made up in various ways and with varying surface finishes. Halyards and painters should be of three-strand twisted rope. Everything else, including burgee halyards, should be in plaited or braided rope, and any rope which is to be used in cam or tubular cleats must be of this construction. There is no need to whip these synthetic ropes; just melt the ends with a match and squeeze with pliers.

Suitable sizes are as follows (circumference in inches)—For a 14-ft boat: Main halyard $\frac{7}{8}$ in. pre-stretched; flag halyard $\frac{1}{2}$ in. plaited or less; main and jib sheets $1\frac{1}{8}$ in. to $1\frac{1}{2}$ in. plaited; spinnaker halyard, sheets and guys $\frac{3}{4}$ in. plaited. The jib halyard is usually of wire with a rope tail, since the stretch in this item must be at an absolute minimum.

BUOYANCY

There is a lot which can be said for and against both main types of surplus buoyancy arrangements.

Built-in tanks form part of the structure of the boat and it is frequently difficult to get into the interior afterwards. Hatches can be built into these tanks, but this is an added complication for the builder, and it is hard to make them watertight. Even the best built-in tanks seem to let in water somehow, and one must always remember not only to remove drain plugs after each sail, but to replace them again afterwards. The presence of the tanks also complicates any hull repair or maintenance in that area. Also a further point, not always realized, is that built-in tanks frequently provide too much buoyancy for general-purpose boats, making them float too high out of the water. The effect of this is to make a capsized boat difficult to get hold of when the crew is in the water, turn upside down too easily, and blow off rapidly downwind if the crew is separated from it. However, the big advantage, provided that hatches are secure, is that the surplus buoyancy is always there and needs no blowing up.

The other main system is to use plastic air-bags. These can be entirely adequate if care is taken both in fixing and maintenance. They can easily be fixed in any sort of boat in any quantity and are not expensive. They do need careful fixing and careful inspection to see that there are no leaks. They also require blowing up and checking every time one goes out sailing and they can be punctured, though this does not seem to be any more likely in practice

13.20
Small clam cleats can be used for lines that are quite heavily loaded but make sure they are mounted at exactly the correct angle by fitting angled blocks under them.

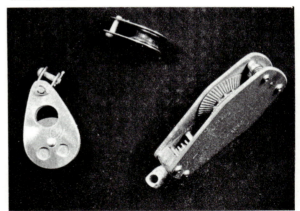

13.21
The Novex ratchet block is being increasingly used not only on mainsheets but also as a genoa fairlead on large dinghies. The tension at which it releases can be adjusted by screwing the knob at the base. The other blocks are very small and light, made in stainless steel with lightening holes cut in them. (Lewmar and R.W.O.)

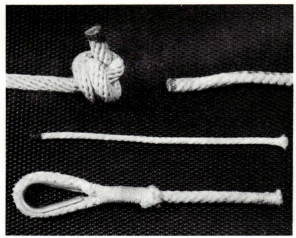

13.22

Various samples of braided line. The stopper-knot shown is much the best one to use, especially for the ends of jib-sheets. These terylene lines can be secured at their ends by heating with a match and clamping with a pair of pliers. Eyes have to be made by very careful and thorough seizing.

13.23

Instead of a swivel cleat, a ratchet block on a swivel can be used for the final block in a mainsheet system. It should be mounted on the hog. This type has an on/off switch on the side and a split sheave which is adjustable to suit various ropes.

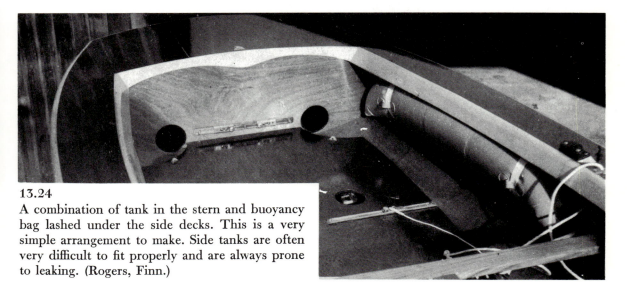

13.24

A combination of tank in the stern and buoyancy bag lashed under the side decks. This is a very simple arrangement to make. Side tanks are often very difficult to fit properly and are always prone to leaking. (Rogers, Finn.)

than is the kicking-in of a built-in tank panel. (Fig. 13.24).

A compromise system sometimes seen is to fix roughly shaped blocks of expanded foam plastic. These are more trouble to instal, since they have to be covered with cloth to hold them together, but they need no maintenance at all thereafter.

Bags should be held in place with webbing straps firmly secured to some substantial part of the boat. Few people seem to realize the forces acting on a bag and its fastenings when submerged, especially if two people are sitting on the upturned hull. As a guide you should think of your own weight hanging by each strap and ask yourself if the fixing would hold you safely.

Webbing should be doubled at each end and secured with stout screws or bolts and pressure plates (Fig. 13.25). At least two straps are needed for each short tubular bag and they should pass through the loops provided in order to stop the bag sliding out sideways. Cold water will contract the air in the bag and it could then escape through a gap previously thought to be far too small. There is nothing more demoralizing than seeing one's bags disappearing at a brisk rate over the horizon.

RUDDERS, TILLERS AND CENTREBOARDS

Let us take centreboards first, because some of this subject also relates to rudder-blades.

Centreboards are made usually out of galvanized steel, aluminium alloy, or wood. There are also variations including hollow foam-filled fibre-glass, but this is a rather technical method, and the only one which calls for much discussion here is that using wood. The metal centreboards are merely shaped pieces of plate with rounded or bevelled edges. Firstly, a centreboard needs to be as stiff as possible for maximum performance of a racing boat. Most class rules limit the thickness of the board, and in some cases this is so small that extreme steps have to be taken in the construction in order to secure adequate stiffness. This can take the shape of multi-laminations of very hard timber such as teak, and even the building-in of metal struts. A great deal of strength is taken out of a board by the careful fairing of the cross-section and this does not help to reduce flexing and consequent twisting of the tip.

For ordinary purposes a hard plywood is adequate. I do not advise using single planks of hardwood, since most are prone to warping and even a slight curve could be extremely detrimental to speed and handling.

If you use ordinary plywood it must be cut out in such a way that *all* the plies run at as great an angle as possible to the waterline when the board is down. This is unfortunately seldom done even by professionals either through ignorance or attempts to economize on plywood. The result is all too often a board snapped off at the level where it emerges from the keel. Some plywood manufacturers make a special anti-fracture type which has the veneers running at an acute angle to each other, instead of the normal right-angle. This, though rather more expensive, is excellent material for both centreboard and rudder-blades (Fig. 13.26).

The actual fairing of the cross-section is a

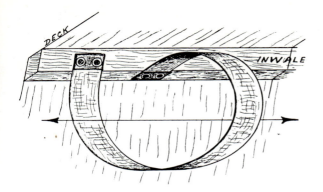

13.25
A method of securing the straps for holding buoyancy bags.

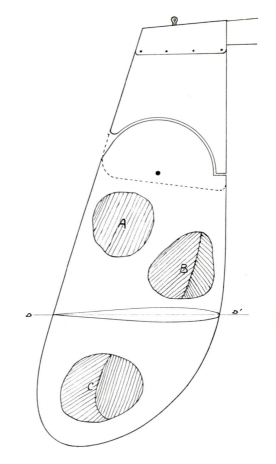

13.26
This sketch shows a number of points. The blade for a rudder can be cut as shown and if it is required to be a lifting rudder then a keyhole saw can be cut round the arc in the upper centre. Then cheek pieces should be glued on to both sides of the upper part projecting down along the dotted line and a bolt passed through the centre of the arc. If the blade is made of solid timber, then the grain should run in the direction indicated in Panel A. If normal plywood with veneer at right-angles is used, then the grain should run as shown in B. If antifracture plywood with grain running at smaller angles than 90 degrees is used then the grain should run as shown in Panel C. The cross-section of the blade should be faired smoothly as shown in Section D-D.

matter of personal preference. For a general-purpose boat there is no need to do more than sharpen the edges back for about three inches or so. Racing owners will want to get the most perfect hydrofoil possible, and the generally accepted standard today is a section having the greatest thickness about one-third the way aft, the leading edge rounded to about $\frac{1}{8}$ in. radius, and the trailing edge as sharp as possible. The followers of the laminar-flow theory, however, go for a section which is almost exactly the opposite way round to this. The only trouble about this in practice is that the slightest blemish or inaccuracy on the

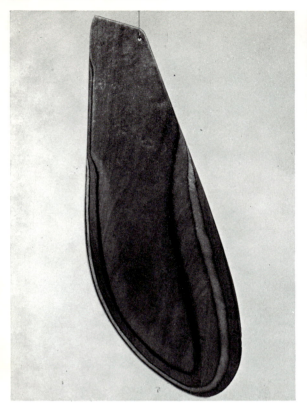

13.27
If you use plywood for your rudder blade it is quite easy to see that you have got the fairing even on both sides. This blade was made from anti-fracture plywood. The difference in width between the glue lines is explained by the difference in thickness of the layers of veneer.

leading half of the board will be likely to destroy laminar flow.

A helpful advantage of the former shape is that standard $\frac{1}{4}$ in. $\times$ $\frac{1}{8}$ in. half-round brass can be tacked to the leading edge of the blade to protect it (see later in this chapter). An

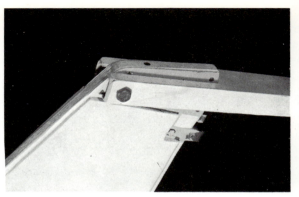

13.28
This rudder was made originally from a single thickness of anti-fracture plywood, but was found to be too flexible and so check pieces were glued on the side. The tiller was made to fork over the rudder head and is only held by one bolt at the after end. It can thus lift.

advantage of using plywood is that you have a series of guide lines to assist you in getting equal fairing on each side (Fig. 13.27).

Rudders can be either fixed or lifting; the former is the simplest type to make and can frequently be just a single piece of wood. If the head is rather narrow, or if the blade is large, you may have to glue on cheek pieces to thicken it, and thus stop too much twist (Fig. 13.28). Tillers can be connected in a number of ways of which the main types are the hooded rudder head and the forked tiller. In the former the tiller is made the same width as the rudder head, and slips into a metal hood bent to an inverted "U" section, rigidly riveted to the rudder (Fig. 13.29). In the second case, which is especially suitable for simple rudders, the tiller is made with a forked end which straddles the projecting top of the rudder head (Fig. 13.28).

It is useful for a tiller to be able to lift a few degrees and the forked type can be made to do this very simply if secured by a single bolt at the after end (Fig. 13.28). One way of arranging for a hooded tiller to lift is shown in Fig. 13.29. Hooded rudders are a lot heavier than the others, because the metal forming the hood needs to be pretty substantial.

Lifting rudder blades can be very simply arranged as in the sketch. They are well worth making for general-purpose boats, but I do not like them on a racing dinghy (Fig. 13.30). The reason is that with them there always seems to be too much twist and slop in the steering arrangements and delicate "feel" is lost. There is also the problem of arranging them to knock up upon striking the ground, but to remain absolutely firm under the very high drag pressure of fast planing. If you rely on shockcord to keep the blade down it will certainly allow some aft movement of the blade at high speed. Similarly a line leading to a cleat on the tiller can still allow a small amount of movement, and even a shift of a few degrees aft can make a boat very hard to control under severe conditions.

Tillers should be carefully made from straight-grained material. Rock-elm is really the only absolutely reliable timber for racing dinghies, where lightness and strength are paramount. I have had an entirely trouble-free and excellent tiller for nine years made out of Tufnol tube and I have seen very satisfactory alloy tillers also.

You will almost certainly need a tiller extension in all but the most staid of small boats.

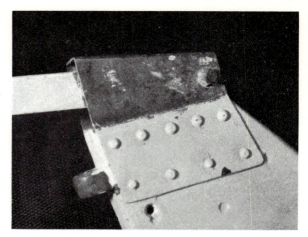

13.29

How a metal hood is fitted over the rudder head to take an ordinary slotted tiller. In this case it has been shaped in such a way that if the tiller is bolted at the after end only, then it can lift a few degrees.

The choice of material for this is not so important, since it is only in compression or tension, and does not have to resist bending loads. Make it fairly substantial, though, because it has a habit of getting sat on fairly frequently.

It is well worth while giving a good deal of attention to the way the extension is connected to the tiller. Many capsizes have been caused by the extension parting company at critical moments of stress, and often the damage is caused by it being lifted out of the horizontal plane. I can wholeheartedly recommend that you use a universal joint on the swivel arranged so that it can be lifted to the vertical in any direction, but will not drop below the

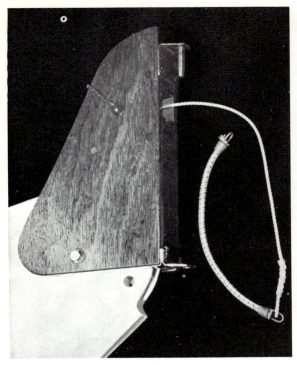

13.30
An example of a lifting rudder-blade. The line passes down round the sheave and on to the leading edge of the rudder. The shock cord hooks on to the fore end of the tiller. Thus the blade can knock up when it strikes the bottom. (Small Craft.)

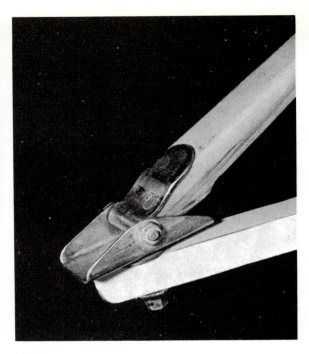

13.31
A universal joint between the tiller extension and the tiller itself made by the author, in stainless steel. The extension cannot drop below the horizontal.

horizontal (Fig. 13.31). It is astonishing to find that no fittings manufacturers make a good swivel at the present time, but they can very simply be made at home if required. One can then steer from any position, even standing up, without having to worry about breaking the joint.

I also think that the traditional T-shaped fingergrip on the end of the extension is a menace and invariably catches in some part of one's clothing, or even goes into a pocket, refusing to come out. I once had to retire from an important Olympic trial race because of a collision caused by this very situation. Since then I have always screwed a small Tufnol revolving disc about an inch diameter to the end of my extension and found this both comfortable and foolproof.

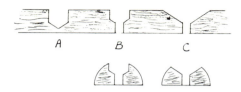

13.32
The holes for fixing screws for half-round brass keelbands should be made as at A and B, and not as at C. The initial countersinking for the screw-head should be done with a twist drill to avoid taking out too much metal. Do not use a counter-sink bit as at C or the band will be weakened too much at that point.

STEM AND KEELBANDS

Most dinghies need metal protective strip along the keel and stem, and it is also very useful to protect the leading edges of rudders and centreboards in this way.

Unless there is a particular weight problem brass is the best material to use, though galvanized iron is very hard-wearing for knock-about boats. For extreme lightness, aluminium alloy is the usual choice, and this must be fixed, as before, with alloy, chrome plated or stainless screws. You can buy all these materials in half-round, convex or flat strip, and the choice is yours. For the weight-conscious the International Finn Rules call for a minimum section of $\frac{1}{2}$ in. $\times$ $\frac{1}{4}$ in. (12 $\times$ 6 mm.) half-round, and in brass this will weigh 9 lb for the 20 ft or so needed.

Whatever material is used it is absolutely essential to bend it to any necessary curve

before drilling any holes. Then drill and countersink for the fixing screws as follows: first make a centre-punch mark in the required position and then drill half-way, using a bit the size of the screw head. This forms the counter-sunk part. Then change to a smaller bit for the hole for the shank. If you drill the shank hole straight away and then use an ordinary rose countersink you will take away far too much metal and the band will be too weak (Fig. 13.32). One inch, size 6, is a suitable screw to use for $\frac{1}{2}$ in. $\times$ $\frac{1}{4}$ in. half-round. If you are using flat strip you can, of course, counter-sink in the ordinary way.

Rudder protective strip is usually $\frac{1}{4}$ in. $\times$ $\frac{1}{8}$ in. (6 $\times$ 3 mm.) half-round, and you fix it by drilling $\frac{1}{16}$-in. holes through it and then nail-ing with 1 in. $\times$ 15 s.w.g. brass panel pins (Fig. 13.1). No countersinking is needed— merely file off the heads flush to finish off. The holes should be drilled at alternate slight angles to provide a tight-gripping dovetail effect.

You will find it extremely difficult to drill accurate holes into half-round material, be-cause the bit tends to wander one way or the other. This is one case when the electric hand-drill scores over the vertical bench drill, for you can correct wander easily with the former, but not with the latter. It helps if you file a small flat before punching and starting to drill.

SLOT RUBBER

Many racing helmsmen insist on fixing rubber flaps across their centreboard slots to prevent turbulence and hence increased drag. Slot

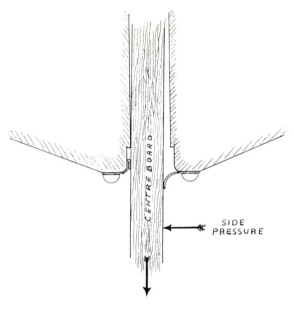

rubbers are a perfect nuisance in every way except for their alleged purpose, and unless extreme care is taken, torn rubber or sticking centreboards will plague you for evermore. I have evolved a fairly trouble-free method of dealing with the problem, but whatever you do, really wide slots are always difficult.

For narrow slots I use either $\frac{1}{16}$-in. thick Neoprene strip or alternatively, and probably better, motor cycle rim-tape, which is about 2 in. wide, and tapers in thickness at the edges. Wider slots need thicker material up to around $\frac{1}{8}$ in. and it may be best to fit this so that it overlaps rather more. Narrow slots seem to need almost no overlap.

13.33
How the slot rubber should be fitted. There should be a recess at the bottom inside corner of the slot to accommodate the rubber and prevent it from jamming the board.

13.34, 13.35, 13.36
Various stages in the fitting of slot rubber. The rubber should be stuck down with a rubber-based adhesive. Then the brass strip is screwed on top, but not too tightly. Finally the surplus rubber on the outside is trimmed off with a knife.

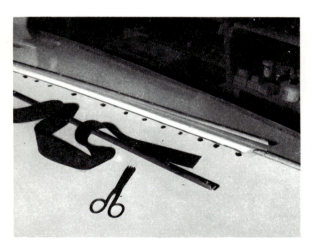

Do not use sheet which has a fabric moulded into it, because this will shrink and cause the rubber to wrinkle. Do not stretch the material when fitting it either.

My system has several vital requirements. Firstly, the difference between the width of the slot and the thickness of the board must be at least four times the thickness of the rubber. This is to accommodate two folds in the rubber as the board starts to raise or lower (Fig. 13.33). If there is not enough gap, then it is necessary to cut a recess alongside the slot to bring this part up to the required width. Secondly, the corner of the slot must be rounded smoothly. Thirdly, the rubber must be held down by the keelband on either side of the slot and this must be set back from the edge a little. Fourthly, unless a very close spacing is given the fixing screws in the keelband, the rubber must first be stuck in place using an impact adhesive (Figs. 13.34, 13.35, 13.36).

13.37
The "wedge" type of bailer is very effective. The speed causes low pressure to develop around the exit hole. The flap then opens and the water runs out. The base plate should be flush with the skin of the boat.

If you follow all these hints, you should not have much trouble with your slot rubber.

BAILERS

These fittings are now standard equipment in most light dinghies and some variation of the wedge type is now almost universal.

A bailer works by creating a hollow, or lowered pressure, in the region of the exit hole, thus allowing water in the bailer to drain out. There is no true venturi, or suction, effect with the wedge bailer.

The main problems are controlling the backflow when the boat slows down (which is usually done by a non-return flap) and water-

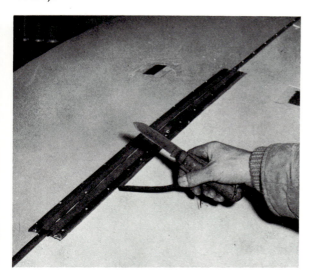

13.38

This type of bailer is mounted into a plain rectangular hole from the inside of the hull. Packing washers under the flange adjust the level of the outside until it is flush.

13.39

A popular type of snubbing winch for holding the genoa sheets on a dinghy. It must be fitted at the correct angle so that the lead from the sheet and to the hand is in a straight line and perpendicular to the axis of the winch. In this case the angle is not right and a riding turn has resulted. (Gibb.)

tightness when closed, which is not so easy to achieve.

Good sealing starts with correct fitting so that the frame is not distorted. Fit the bailer in a flat part of the hull and make sure that the seating is faired up. The steel bailers, though heavier, are more rigid than plastic ones and less likely to give trouble from leaking, either through twisting or through abrasion of the faces in sandy water.

If the seals are in good condition check also that the sealing surfaces are flat and clean and also that the locking mechanism is exerting enough tension.

All bailers should be bedded down in sealing compound and all cut-away ply edges should be carefully sealed.

Unless the boat sails normally at an angle of heel the best place for bailers is level with the aft end of the centreboard case and as close to the centreline as possible. If they can be sited under a thwart they will get some protection from thumping feet.

A bailer's efficiency depends on (a) the speed and (b) the depth of the exit hole. As a guide, a two-man racing dinghy of about 14 feet will bail to windward *when being raced*. Off the wind about $4\frac{1}{2}$ knots will be required for the bailer to start operating. Heavy boats will need more speed.

WINCHES

Some racing dinghies use snubbing winches to hold the foresail sheets. The siting and angle of mounting of these must be very carefully

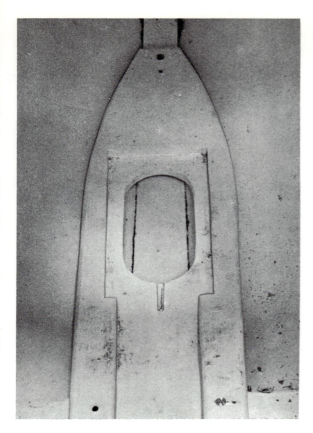

◄   13.40, 13.41 ▲
Details of the construction of a sliding mast-step for an International Finn. The wooden base receives a Tufnol square with a round hole cut in it. This latter is the bearing for the heel of the mast. Travel is limited by the rigging-screw, which is firmly anchored to the base.

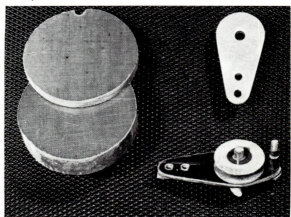

13.42
On the left are two thicknesses of Tufnol. This material which is woven fabric impregnated with a resin, is extremely useful for making blocks and other fittings. On the right is shown the construction of a small block.

thought out, since it is essential that the lead to and from the winch is in the same plane and is itself perpendicular to the axis of the winch (Fig. 13.39). If this is not so, either the sheet will run off the top of the winch, or you will get riding turns at the bottom. The winch will almost certainly have to be mounted on a pillar and also tilted so that the lead to the crew's hand is in the right plane.

One could, of course, go on and on for ever describing and illustrating fittings and gadgets of various types. New fittings appear on the

13.43
A simple way of making a rudder gudgeon. This is made from stainless strip bent and bolted to the rudder. A Tufnol spacing piece is riveted through to act as a bearing surface for the pintle.

13.44
A strong and neat form of rudder pintle, with four fixing screws. The terylene line and split pin are essential for boats which have no horse or other slot in the transom which would prevent the rudder coming adrift in a capsize. (R.W.O.)

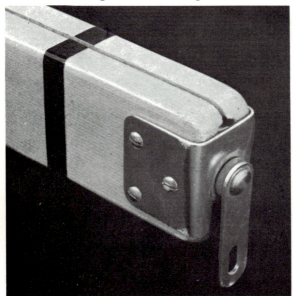

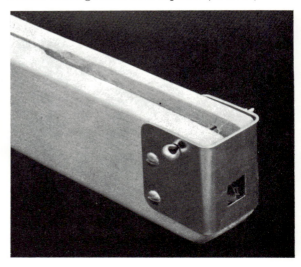

13.45 ▲   13.46 ►
Simple boom-end fittings made in stainless steel. The construction is quite clear from the photograph. The square hole fits over the squared shank of the universally-jointed gooseneck pin. (Small Craft.)

13.48
A laminated lifting handle is useful on the stem of any dinghy and can also do duty for securing the painter. Note the stemband. (Rogers, Finn.)

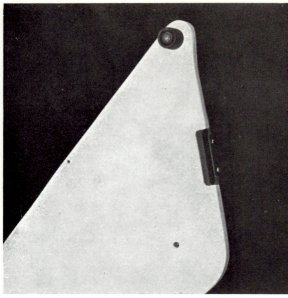

13.47
A simple method of controlling the position of a wooden centreboard is by a friction pad made out of rubber tube and tensioned by screws which can be got at with a long screwdriver whilst the board is in position. Screwing up the screws squeezes the rubber tube which presses more firmly against the sides of the case. (Small Craft.)

market continually. Some are first class, some are developments of earlier ideas, some are cheap imitations, and many are quite worthless. As I have said before, it is no good having a perfectly constructed hull with shoddy and inadequate fittings, or even with first-class fittings insecurely fastened.

Do find out what the top boats in the toughest sailing area use. Faulty fittings could not only cost a race, but also a life.

I hope that you will build the boat of your choice, by the method of your choice, with timber, fastenings, decoration and fittings to your own desires. If this book has helped in the easier understanding of home-boat-building processes, and enabled more people to know the satisfaction of launching and sailing for the first time their very own boat, then I will be satisfied.

I leave you trundling the boat into the water for her maiden sail—and don't forget to put in the bungs!

A Inches to Metric

in.	mm.	in.	mm.	in.	mm.
⅛	3	4⅜	111	8⅝	219
¼	6	4½	114	8¾	222
⅜	9	4⅝	118	8⅞	225
½	12	4¾	121	9	229
⅝	16	4⅞	124	9⅛	232
¾	19	5	127	9¼	235
⅞	22	5⅛	130	9⅜	238
1	25	5¼	133	9½	241
1⅛	29	5⅜	137	9⅝	245
1¼	32	5½	140	9¾	248
1⅜	35	5⅝	143	9⅞	251
1½	38	5¾	146	10	254
1⅝	41	5⅞	149	10⅛	257
1¾	44	6	152	10¼	260
1⅞	48	6⅛	156	10⅜	264
2	51	6¼	159	10½	267
2⅛	54	6⅜	162	10⅝	270
2¼	57	6½	165	10¾	273
2⅜	60	6⅝	168	10⅞	276
2½	64	6¾	171	11	279
2⅝	67	6⅞	175	11⅛	283
2¾	70	7	178	11¼	286
2⅞	73	7⅛	181	11⅜	289
3	76	7¼	184	11½	292
3⅛	79	7⅜	187	11⅝	295
3¼	83	7½	190	11¾	299
3⅜	86	7⅝	194	11⅞	302
3½	89	7¾	197	12	305
3⅝	92	7⅞	200		
3¾	95	8	203		
3⅞	98	8⅛	206		
4	102	8¼	210		
4⅛	105	8⅜	213		
4¼	108	8½	216		

B Feet and Inches to Metric

ft	in.	mm.	ft	in.	mm.	ft	in.	mm.
1	1	330	3	8	1117	9	0	2744
1	2	356	3	9	1143	10	0	3048
1	3	381	3	10	1168	11	0	3353
1	4	406	3	11	1194	12	0	3658
1	5	432	4	0	1219	13	0	3963
1	6	457	4	1	1244	14	0	4267
1	7	482	4	2	1270	15	0	4572
1	8	508	4	3	1295	16	0	4877
1	9	533	4	4	1321	17	0	5182
1	10	559	4	5	1346	18	0	5486
1	11	584	4	6	1371	19	0	5792
2	0	609	4	7	1397	20	0	6096
2	1	635	4	8	1422	21	0	6401
2	2	660	4	9	1448	22	0	6706
2	3	686	4	10	1473	23	0	7011
2	4	711	4	11	1498	24	0	7316
2	5	736	5	0	1524	25	0	7621
2	6	762	5	1	1549	26	0	7926
2	7	787	5	2	1575	27	0	8231
2	8	813	5	3	1600	28	0	8535
2	9	838	5	4	1625	29	0	8840
2	10	863	5	5	1651	30	0	9145
2	11	889	5	6	1676			
3	0	914	5	7	1702			
3	1	940	5	8	1727			
3	2	965	5	9	1752			
3	3	991	5	10	1778			
3	4	1016	5	11	1803			
3	5	1041	6	0	1829			
3	6	1067	7	0	2134			
3	7	1092	8	0	2439			

C Metric to Inches

mm.	in.	mm.	in.
1 :	$\frac{1}{25}$	135 :	$5\frac{5}{16}$
2 :	$\frac{1}{12}$	140 :	$5\frac{1}{2}$
3 :	$\frac{1}{8}$	145 :	$5\frac{11}{16}$
4 :	$\frac{1}{6}$	150 :	$5\frac{7}{8}$
5 :	$\frac{1}{5}$	155 :	$6\frac{1}{8}$
6 :	$\frac{1}{4}$	160 :	$6\frac{5}{16}$
7 :	$\frac{5}{16}-$	165 :	$6\frac{1}{2}$
8 :	$\frac{5}{16}+$	170 :	$6\frac{11}{16}$
9 :	$\frac{3}{8}$	175 :	$6\frac{7}{8}$
10 :	$\frac{3}{8}+$	180 :	$7\frac{1}{16}$
15 :	$\frac{5}{8}$	185 :	$7\frac{1}{4}$
20 :	$\frac{13}{16}$	190 :	$7\frac{1}{2}$
25 :	1	195 :	$7\frac{11}{16}$
30 :	$1\frac{3}{16}$	200 :	$7\frac{7}{8}$
35 :	$1\frac{3}{8}$	205 :	$8\frac{1}{16}$
40 :	$1\frac{9}{16}$	210 :	$8\frac{1}{4}$
45 :	$1\frac{3}{4}$	215 :	$8\frac{7}{16}$
50 :	$2\frac{1}{16}$	220 :	$8\frac{11}{16}$
55 :	$2\frac{3}{16}$	225 :	$8\frac{7}{8}$
60 :	$2\frac{3}{8}$	230 :	$9\frac{1}{16}$
65 :	$2\frac{9}{16}$	235 :	$9\frac{1}{4}$
70 :	$2\frac{3}{4}$	240 :	$9\frac{7}{16}$
75 :	3	245 :	$9\frac{5}{8}$
80 :	$3\frac{1}{8}$	250 :	$9\frac{13}{16}$
85 :	$3\frac{3}{8}$	255 :	$10\frac{1}{16}$
90 :	$3\frac{9}{16}$	260 :	$10\frac{1}{4}$
95 :	$3\frac{3}{4}$	265 :	$10\frac{7}{16}$
100 :	$3\frac{15}{16}$	270 :	$10\frac{5}{8}$
105 :	$4\frac{1}{8}$	275 :	$10\frac{13}{16}$
110 :	$4\frac{5}{16}$	280 :	11
115 :	$4\frac{9}{16}$	285 :	$11\frac{1}{4}$
120 :	$4\frac{3}{4}$	290 :	$11\frac{7}{16}$
125 :	$4\frac{15}{16}$	295 :	$11\frac{5}{8}$
130 :	$5\frac{1}{8}$	300 :	$11\frac{13}{16}$

D Metric to Feet and Inches

mm.	ft	in.	mm.	ft	in.
400 :	1	$3\frac{3}{4}$	5750 :	18	$10\frac{3}{8}$
500 :	1	$7\frac{11}{16}$	6000 :	19	$8\frac{1}{4}$
600 :	1	$11\frac{5}{8}$	6250 :	20	$6\frac{1}{16}$
700 :	2	$3\frac{9}{16}$	6500 :	21	$3\frac{7}{8}$
800 :	2	$7\frac{1}{2}$	6750 :	22	$1\frac{3}{4}$
900 :	2	$11\frac{7}{16}$	7000 :	22	$11\frac{5}{8}$
1000 :	3	$3\frac{3}{8}$	7250 :	23	$9\frac{1}{2}$
1100 :	3	$7\frac{5}{16}$	7500 :	24	$7\frac{5}{16}$
1200 :	3	$11\frac{1}{4}$	7750 :	25	$5\frac{5}{16}$
1300 :	4	$3\frac{3}{16}$	8000 :	26	3
1400 :	4	$7\frac{1}{8}$	8250 :	27	$0\frac{7}{8}$
1500 :	4	$11\frac{1}{16}$	8500 :	27	$10\frac{11}{16}$
1600 :	5	3	8750 :	28	$8\frac{1}{2}$
1700 :	5	$6\frac{15}{16}$	9000 :	29	$6\frac{3}{8}$
1800 :	5	$10\frac{7}{8}$	9250 :	30	$4\frac{1}{4}$
1900 :	6	$2\frac{13}{16}$	9500 :	31	$2\frac{1}{16}$
2000 :	6	$6\frac{3}{4}$	9750 :	31	$11\frac{7}{8}$
2250 :	7	$4\frac{5}{8}$	10,000 :	32	$9\frac{3}{4}$
2500 :	8	$2\frac{7}{16}$			
2750 :	9	$0\frac{5}{16}$			
3000 :	9	$10\frac{1}{8}$			
3250 :	10	$7\frac{15}{16}$			
3500 :	11	$5\frac{13}{16}$			
3750 :	12	$3\frac{11}{16}$			
4000 :	13	$1\frac{1}{2}$			
4250 :	13	$11\frac{3}{8}$			
4500 :	14	$9\frac{3}{16}$			
4750 :	15	$7\frac{1}{16}$			
5000 :	16	$4\frac{7}{8}$			
5250 :	17	$2\frac{3}{4}$			
5500 :	18	$0\frac{9}{16}$			

CONVERSION TABLES

E *Square Feet to Square Metres*

one sq. ft is .092903 sq. m.

sq. ft	sq. m.	sq. ft	sq. m.
2 :	.186	230 :	21.4
3 :	.279	240 :	22.3
4 :	.372	250 :	23.3
5 :	.465	260 :	24.2
6 :	.558	270 :	25.1
7 :	.651	280 :	26.0
8 :	.744	290 :	27.0
9 :	.837	300 :	27.9
10 :	.929	310 :	28.8
20 :	1.86	320 :	29.8
30 :	2.79	330 :	30.7
40 :	3.72	340 :	31.6
50 :	4.65	350 :	32.5
60 :	5.58	360 :	33.5
70 :	6.51	370 :	34.4
80 :	7.44	380 :	35.3
90 :	8.37	390 :	36.3
100 :	9.29	400 :	37.2
110 :	10.2	410 :	38.1
120 :	11.2	420 :	39.1
130 :	12.1	430 :	40.0
140 :	13.0	440 :	40.9
150 :	13.9	450 :	41.8
160 :	14.9	460 :	42.8
170 :	15.8	470 :	43.7
180 :	16.7	480 :	44.6
190 :	17.7	490 :	45.6
200 :	18.6	500 :	46.5
210 :	19.5	1000 :	92.9
220 :	20.5		

F *Square Metres to Square Feet*

sq. m.	sq. ft	sq. m.	sq. ft
.25 :	2.69	8.0 :	86.1
.5 :	5.38	8.25 :	88.8
.75 :	8.07	8.5 :	91.5
1.0 :	10.76	8.75 :	94.2
1.25 :	13.45	9.0 :	96.8
1.5 :	16.14	9.25 :	99.5
1.75 :	18.84	9.5 :	102.1
2.0 :	21.5	9.75 :	104.8
2.25 :	24.2	10.0 :	107.6
2.5 :	26.9	11.0 :	118.4
2.75 :	29.6	12.0 :	129.1
3.0 :	32.3	13.0 :	139.8
3.25 :	35.0	14.0 :	150.7
3.5 :	37.7	15.0 :	161.4
3.75 :	40.4	16.0 :	172.1
4.0 :	43.1	17.0 :	183.0
4.25 :	45.7	18.0 :	193.7
4.5 :	48.4	19.0 :	204.5
4.75 :	51.1	20.0 :	215.2
5.0 :	53.8	21.0 :	226.0
5.25 :	56.5	22.0 :	237.0
5.5 :	59.2	23.0 :	247.5
5.75 :	61.8	24.0 :	258.0
6.0 :	64.6	25.0 :	269.0
6.25 :	67.3	26.0 :	280.0
6.5 :	69.9	27.0 :	291.0
6.75 :	72.7	28.0 :	301.0
7.0 :	75.3	29.0 :	312.0
7.25 :	78.0	30.0 :	323.0
7.5 :	80.7	50.0 :	538.0
7.75 :	83.4	100.0 :	1076.0

G *Approximate conversions*

TIMBER—cubic measure/density.
1 cubic metre nearly equals 35 cubic feet.
1 cubic metre nearly equals 1.3 cubic yards.
1 lb/ft³ = approximately 16 kg/m³
Therefore:
25 lb/ft³ = approx. 400 kg/m³
30	=	480
35	=	560
40	=	640
45	=	720
50	=	800
55	=	880
60	=	960
65	=	1040

GLASS REINFORCEMENT—Square measure/weight.
Chopped strand mat is measured in square feet and square metres.
Woven cloth is measured in square yards and square metres.
Approximate conversions:
1 sq ft = 0.09 m² = 1/9 sq yd
$10\frac{3}{4}$ sq ft = 1 m² = 1.2 sq yd
1 oz = 28.4 grams
1 lb = 16 oz = 0.454 kg
2.2lb = 35.2 oz = 1 kg
Therefore:
$\frac{1}{3}$ oz/sq ft = 3 oz/sq yd = 100 gr/m²
$\frac{1}{2}$ = $4\frac{1}{2}$ = 150
1 = 9 = 300
$1\frac{1}{2}$ = $13\frac{1}{2}$ = 450
2 = 18 = 600
$2\frac{1}{2}$ = $22\frac{1}{2}$ = 750
3 = 27 = 900

⊞ *Principal Types of Plywood*

(based on information supplied by The Timber Research.and Development Association.)

GLUES

Plywood for boatbuilding should conform to the adhesive standard BS 1203: 1963 and in addition should be graded BR (Boil resistant) or WBP (weather and boil proof). Moisture resistant adhesive (MR) is not suitable except for interior joinery.

Plywood for marine use should also conform to BS 1088: 1966 or BS 4079: 1966.

Do not accept "resin bonded plywood" unqualified by other information or standards, since it may be bonded with "extended resin" and hence not be sufficiently durable for marine use.

SIZES

When sizes are quoted as, for example, 3050 × 1525, the first figure is the dimension along the grain of the outer veneer.

Standard dimensions are normally one of the following: 3660, 3050, 2745, 2440, 2135, 1830, 1525, 1220, 915 mm. by:

1830, 1525, 1270, 1220, 915 mm.

THICKNESS AND CONSTRUCTION

Plywood normally has an odd number of veneers of which the face veneers are thinner. One face is usually of higher quality than the other.

Veneers are normally laid at right angles though there is a special type of anti-fracture plywood which is used for centreboards and rudders with the veneers running at smaller angles than 90°.

Plywood is also available with hard face veneers and lightweight cores.

Standard thicknesses are from 3 to 25 mm. ($\frac{1}{8}$ in. to 1 in.)

GRADES

Grading differs with various timbers and countries of origin but in general a dinghy builder would need plywood of Grades marked:

1, A, Good Two Sides, Good One Side, I, Premier, Gold or Marine

if the result was to be varnished.

For a paint finish the following grade marks might be acceptable:

2, B, BB, Solid Two Sides, S, Silver, II or III.

The following table gives the principal types of plywood, that may be found in the United Kingdom, which is of interest to dinghy builders but see also the table of timber characteristics.

Species	Producing Countries	Thickness (mm.)	Qualities	Adhesives
ANTIARIS	Ghana	3–25	B/BB	MR/WBP
(BONKONKO)	Nigeria	3–18	B/BB	MR/WBP
	Spain	3–25	B/BB	MR/WBP/BR

Species	Producing Countries	Thickness (mm.)	Qualities	Adhesives
ASH (Brown)	China	3–18	1/2	MR
BABOEN (or VIROLA)	Brazil	4–18	B/BB	MR/WBP
BASSWOOD	China	3–18	2	MR/WBP
BEECH	Austria	4–12	A/B/BB	MR/WBP
	Germany	3–25	I/II	MR/BR/WBP
	Japan	3–6	1/2	MR/BR
	Yugoslavia	3–18	A/B/BB	MR/WBP
BIRCH	Finland	3–24	B/BB	WBP
BIRCH (SPRUCE CORE)	Finland	9–27	B/BB	WBP
	Soviet Union	3–18	B/BB	WBP
DOUGLAS FIR	Canada	6.5–25.5	Good/Solid	WBP
	USA	6.5–25.5	A/B	WBP
GABOON (or OKOUME)	England	3–25	I/II	WBP
	France	3–25	B/BB	MR/WBP
	Gaboon	4–25	Premier	MR/WBP
	Germany	4–25	I/II	MR/BR/WBP
	Greece	3–22	B/BB	MR/WBP
	Holland	4–25	A/B/BB	WBP
	Israel	3–25	Super	WBP
	Spain	3–25	B/BB	MR/BR/WBP
HEVEA	Brazil	4–18	B/BB	WBP
ILOMBA	Cameroons	4–25	II	MR/WBP
	England	4–25	1/2	WBP
	Ghana	3–18	B/BB	MR/WBP
	Nigeria	3–25	II	MR/WBP
	Spain	3–25	B/BB	MR/BR/WBP
KERUING (or GURJUN or HOLLONG)	Malaysia Singapore }	3–25	B/BB	MR/WBP
	India	3–25	B/BB	MR/WBP

Species	Producing Countries	Thickness (mm.)	Qualities	Adhesives
LAUAN	China	3–18	2	MR/WBP
	Japan	3–6	2	MR/BR
	Taiwan	3–18	2	MR/WBP
LIMBA (or AFARA)	France	4–25	B/BB	MR/WBP
	Germany	4–25	I/II	MR/WBP
MAHOGANY (African types)	Cameroons	4–25	II	MR/WBP
	Eire	4–25	Marine	WBP
	England	5–25	1/2/Marine	WBP
	France	3–25	B/BB/Marine	MR/WBP
	Ghana	3–25	Gold/Silver/Marine/B/BB/2	MR/WBP
	Holland	4–25	A/B/Marine	WBP
	Israel	3–25	Super/Marine	WBP
	Italy	3–25	B/BB	MR/WBP
	Ivory Coast	4–25	B/BB	MR/BR
	Nigeria	3–25	Gold/Silver/Marine/II	MR/WBP
	Spain	3–25	B/BB	MR/BR/WBP
MAKORE	England	4–25	1/2	WBP
	France	3–25	B/BB/Marine	MR/WBP
	Ghana	4–18	Gold/Silver/Marine/2	WBP
	Holland	3–25	B/BB/Marine	WBP
MENGKULANG	Malaysia / Singapore	3–25	B/BB	MR/WBP
MERANTI	Malaysia / Singapore	3–25	B/BB	MR/WBP
MERSAWA	Malaysia / Singapore	3–25	B/BB	MR/WBP
OAK FACED (EUROPEAN)	Austria	3–18	1/2	MR/BR
	England	3–25	1/2	MR/BR/WBP
	Finland	4–25	1	MR/WBP
	France	4–25	1/2	MR
	Germany	4–25	1/2	MR/BR/WBP
	Italy	3–25	1/2	MR/BR

Species	Producing Countries	Thickness (mm.)	Qualities	Adhesives
OAK (JAPANESE)	Japan	3–12	1/2	MR
PINE (EUROPEAN)	Poland	4–18	B/BB	WBP
	Sweden	6.5–25	Good/Solid	WBP
PINE (PARANA or AURACARIA)	Brazil	3–30	B/BB	MR/WBP
POPLAR	Canada	6.5–25	Good/Solid	WBP
	Italy	3–25	B/BB	MR/WBP
SAPELE	Austria	3–18	1/2	MR/BR
	England	3–25	1/2	MR/BR/WBP
	Finland	4–25	1	MR/WBP
	France	4–25	1/2	MR
	Germany	4–25	1/2	MR/BR/WBP
	Italy	3–25	1/2	MR/WBP
SEN (or WHITE ASH)	Japan	3–12	1/2	MR
SERAYAH	England	5–25	1/2	WBP
	Sabah	3–18	2	MR
SPRUCE	Canada	8–25	Select	WBP
	Sweden	6.5–25	Good/Solid	WBP
STERCULIA (or EYONG)	Cameroons	4–25	II	MR/WBP
	France	4–18	B/BB	MR
	Spain	3–25	B/BB	MR
TEAK	Austria	3–18	1/2	MR/BR
	England	3–25	1/2	MR/BR/WBP
	Finland	4–25	1	MR/WBP
	France	4–25	1/2	MR
	Germany	4–25	1/2	MR/BR/WBP
	Italy	3–25	1/2	MR/BR
	India	3–18	1	MR
	Japan	3–18	1	MR/BR
	Malaysia	4–12	A	MR/BR
	Taiwan	3–18	1	MR

⚓ *Boatbuilding Timbers*

Based on information supplied by the Timber Research and Development Association Ltd., Stocking Lane, Hughenden Valley, High Wycombe, Bucks.

Timber	Description	Av. wt. lb/cu. ft. kg/m³ at 15% m/c
ABURA (*Mitragyna* spp.) Trop. Africa	Pale reddish brown to light brown, fairly fine even texture slightly interlocked grain. Medium hardness.	36 576
AFARA LIMBA (*Terminalia superba*) Trop. Africa	Pale straw colour to light yellow brown, occasionally with irregular greyish or blackish markings, straight grained, medium textured. Medium hardness.	35 560
AFRORMOSIA (*Afrormosia* spp.)	Yellowish brown with brown markings. Shallowly interlocked grain, and fine even texture. Moderately hard, but strong.	44 704
AFZELIA (*Afzelia* spp.) Trop. Africa	Light reddish brown, darkening to reddish brown. Grain irregular, commonly interlocked, texture coarse but even. Hard and strong.	48 768
AGBA TOLA BRANCA (*Gossweilerodendron balsamiferum*) Trop. Africa	Yellowish pink and yellowish brown. Grain similar to that of mahogany (*Khaya* sp.). Fairly fine textured. Medium hardness.	30 480
ALDER (*Alnus glutinosa*)	Pale brown to pinkish or light brown, often marked with irregular dark lines. Fine textured timber with smooth even surface.	33 530
ASH (*Fraxinus excelsior*) Europe	White with occasional pinkish tinge. Straight grained and rather coarse texture. Moderately hard, excellent bending properties.	44 704
BABOEN (*Virola* spp.)	Brown to deep reddish brown often with a purplish hue but sapwood is oatmeal in colour. Medium texture, straight grain and somewhat lustrous.	30 480
BASSWOOD (*Tilia* spp.)	Creamy white to light brown. Soft, even textured.	29 460
BEECH, EUROPEAN (*Fagus Sylvatica*)	Uniformly pale brown to reddish brown characterised by small brownish flecks, particularly prominent on quarter cut surfaces. Fine even texture. Moderately heavy.	45 720

Durability	Working qualities	Suitability
Not resistant.	Works fairly easily, takes good finish, glues, stains, and polishes well. Requires care in nailing and screwing to avoid splitting especially near edges.	Softwood alternative.
Not resistant.	Works easily and finishes clearly. Glues and stains well. Requires filling before polishing. Tendency to split in nailing. Stable.	Softwood alternative.
Very resistant.	Fairly easy to work, finishes smoothly. Glues and polishes well. Needs care in nailing, as it has a tendency to split. Stains when in contact with ferrous metals under moist conditions. Very stable.	Keels, hogs, etc.
Very resistant.	Moderately hard to work, takes a good finish. Difficult to nail and screw and recommended to be prebored. Glues and polishes satisfactorily. Very stable.	Keels, stems, hogs.
Resistant.	Works, nails, glues and screws well, stains and polishes satisfactorily. Should be selected free from gum, as this is sometimes troublesome. Stable.	Planking, decking, and many other purposes.
Not resistant.	Moderately hard. Highly suitable for veneering. Stains well and takes a good finish.	Plywood, veneering, panelling.
Not resistant.	Works fairly easily and finishes smoothly. Glues, nails screws and polishes well. Stains satisfactorily. Liable to distort.	Tillers, boathooks, cleats, paddles and spinnaker and jib booms.
Not resistant.	Good working properties. Takes stain well but rather absorbent due to porosity.	General utility
Not resistant.	Works exceptionally well, finishes smooth, takes paint well.	General utility, frames etc.
Not resistant.	Smooth, hard, clean surface. Excellent for veneer, staining and polishing.	Tillers, hard fillets and bones. Plywood.

Timber	Description	Av. wt. lb/cu. ft. kg/m³ at 15% m/c
BEECH, JAPANESE (*Fagus Crenata*)	Similar to European Beech but lighter.	40 640
BIRCH, EUROPEAN (*Betula* spp.)	Whitish with irregular light buff coloured lines. Moderately hard and fine textured.	42 670
CEDAR, CENT AMERICAN (*Cedrela* spp.) Trop. America	Pinkish to reddish brown. Usually straight grained, with a moderately coarse and uneven texture. Soft.	30 480
CEDAR, WESTERN, RED (*Thuya plicate*) Canada	Reddish brown, non-resinous wood. Straight grained, medium to coarse textured. Soft.	24 385
FIR, DOUGLAS (*Pseudotsuga taxifolia*) Canada, U.S.A.	Reddish yellow to light orange red-brown. Generally straight grained sometimes wavy or spiral, texture medium. Medium hardness.	33 530
ELM, ROCK (*Ulmus thomasi*) Canada, U.S.A.	Pale brown, straight grained with moderately fine texture. Hard, strong and elastic.	50 800
ELM, WYCH (*Ulmus glabra*) Europe	Medium brown with greenish tinge. Fairly straight grained and medium textured. Moderately hard, strong and elastic.	43 690
FRELIO (*Cordia goeldiana*) South America	Yellowish brown, with brown markings. Straight grained, rather coarse texture. Medium hardness.	37 590
FUMA (*Ceiba pentandra*)	Whitish, sometimes with yellow streaks. Cross grained and coarse textured.	17–28 270–450
GABOON (*Aucoumea Klaineana*) Gaboon, Fr. Congo, Sp. Guinea	A mahogany-like timber, but entirely distinct from this species. Often called Okoume. Colour light reddish brown. Light in weight. Straight grained with little figure, soft. Strong for its weight.	25 400
GUAREA (*Guarea* spp.) West Africa	Light pinkish or orange brown. Straight grained, fine textured. Medium hardness.	37 590
HEVEA (*Hevea braziliensis*)	Fairly light hardwood, white when cut turning to light brown. Even texture, moderately coarse, straight grain. Characteristic sour smell.	35–40 560–640

Durability	Working qualities	Suitability
Not resistant.	Similar to European Beech.	Same uses.
Not resistant.	Paints, stains and veneers well. Comparatively hard wearing but liable to rot.	Veneers and plywood but must be well protected. Cold moulding.
Resistant.	Easy to work and finishes well. Nails, screws and glues excellently. Varnishes, stains and polishes satisfactorily. Stable.	Skins of light craft, planking, etc.
Resistant.	Easy to work, takes good finish. Nails and screws fairly well, tends to stain ferrous metal under moist conditions. Glues and stains satisfactorily. Stable.	Planking, painted; canvas-covered decks.
Moderately resistant.	Fairly easy to work. Nails, screws and glues satisfactorily, requires various finishing treatments, as raised grain and resin may be troublesome. Medium stability.	Decking, planking, thwarts, floors, masts and spars, etc.
Moderately resistant.	Moderately hard to work, but takes a smooth finish. Takes nails screws and glues satisfactorily and paints, stains and varnishes well.	Rubbing strakes, framing and bent work.
Moderately resistant.	Fairly easy to work and takes a good finish. Nails, glues, stains and varnishes well.	Rubbing strakes, etc.
Resistant.	Easy to work and finishes well. Takes nails and screws easily. Paints, varnishes well. Very stable.	Hogs and keels, not readily available.
Not resistant.	Very light and easy to work.	Light framing. Plywood cores.
Not resistant.	Works well and finishes excellently. Veneers well and takes glue and paint without trouble.	Excellent for plywood and also substitute for Mahogany in brightwork.
Moderately resistant.	Works easily and takes good finish. Nails, screws and glues well. Gum present which may exude. Not particularly stable.	Hogs, keels, etc.
Not resistant.	Tends to split when nailed.	Veneers and plywood.

Timber	Description	Av. wt. lb/cu. ft. kg/m³ at 15% m/c
IDIGBO (*Terminalia ivorensis*) West Africa	Pale yellow to light brown. Grain variable, straight to shallowly interlocked, texture coarse and uneven. Medium hardness.	36 575
ILOMBA (*Pycnanthus angolensis*)	Greyish white to pinkish brown. Sapwood not clearly differentiated. Grain generally straight, texture coarse and even. Soft and light.	32 510
IROKO (*Chlorophora excelsa*) Trop. Africa	Light yellow brown when fresh, ageing to medium brown or dark reddish brown. Grain interlocked, texture coarse. Strong and hard.	41 655
KERUING (also called GURJUN, YANG, or HOLLONG) (*Dipterocarpus* spp.)	Generally light to reddish brown but can be deep pink, through orange pink to purply red. Sapwood is lighter tinged with grey. Coarse and even texture. Varies from soft to very hard.	45 720
LARCH, EUROPEAN (*Larix decidua*) Europe	Light orange red-brown. Normally straight grained, medium textured. Medium hardness.	35 560
LAUAN (*Shorea, Parashorea. Pentacme* spp.)	Pale red to reddish brown with greyish sapwood. Moderately coarse. Moderately hard and heavy.	37 590
MAHOGANY, AFRICAN (*Khaya* spp.) Trop. Africa	Reddish brown. Grain broadly interlocked, texture coarse, fairly even. Medium hardness.	35 560
MAHOGANY, AFRICAN (*Khaya Ivorenics*) Cent. Africa	The cheapest of the mahoganies. Of coarser texture than Honduras. Often has interlocked grain and can be well figured, but is more prone to warp. Good strength.	35 560
MAHOGANY, CENTRAL AMERICAN (*Swietenia Macrophylla*) Mexico, Cent. America, Peru, Brazil	Light reddish or yellowish brown in colour. Often called Honduras mahogany. Can be well figured, grain usually straight and the timber is very stable. Lighter and softer than Cuban. Very good strength.	34 545
MAHOGANY, CUBAN (*Swietenia Nahagoni*) West Indies, Florida, Cuba	Very close grained with a fine silky texture, and can be beautifully figured. Heavier than other types of mahogany. Good strength and able to bend.	48 770
MAKORE (*Mimusops heckelii*) West Africa	Pinkish to dark reddish brown. Grain generally straight, texture fine and even. Hard and fairly strong.	39 625
MENGKULANG (*Heretiera* spp.)	Red or dark reddish brown with almost black streaks. Sapwood lighter. Moderately coarse. Generally straight but sometimes slightly interlocking grain. Moderately hard.	44 700

Durability	Working qualities	Suitability
Resistant.	Works fairly easily. Glues, nails and screws moderately well. Requires filling before polishing. Very stable.	As an alternative to Oak, but needs careful selection and not so strong.
Not resistant.	Similar to Basswood but more brittle.	Veneers and framing. Plywood.
Very resistant.	Moderately easy to work, takes a good finish. Nails, screws and glues satisfactorily. Stable timber, though irregular grain may result in distortion.	Could be used as an alternative to Teak, with careful selection.
Moderately durable.	Straight grained hardwood. Sometimes exudes resin.	Unpainted decking. Structural framing.
Resistant.	Fairly easy to work, except when resinous. Nails, screws and glues well. Takes satisfactory finish. Medium stability.	Planking, decking and as for Douglas fir.
Moderately resistant.	Although coarse, can be worked to a fair finish.	Brightwork, framing veneers.
Moderately resistant.	Easy to work, takes a good finish. Nails, screws and glues well. Stable.	Planking, decking, framing and all solid parts of small boats.
Moderately resistant.	Difficult to work due to interlocked grain, but satisfactory if sharp tools are used. Veneers well.	Used for joinery and all types of boatwork.
Resistant.	Excellent timber to work with all types of tools. Good nailing and screwing properties. Takes glues and paints well. Finishes very effectively.	High-class joinery. All uses in boatbuilding. Planking.
Resistant.	Works well with all tools and finishes with an exceptionally smooth surface. Veneers easily and takes fine polish. Bending and compressive qualities greater than English Oak.	All uses for boatwork and planking. High-class joinery.
Resistant.	Works moderately well, but has blunting effect on cutting edges. Nails, glues and screws well. Takes an excellent finish. Stable.	Planking for underwater parts, etc.
Not resistant.	Superior quality general timber. Attractive face.	Veneers and plywood. Brightwork. Thwarts etc.

Timber	Description	Av. wt. lb/cu. ft. kg/m³ at 15% m/c
MERANTI (*Shorea*) Malaya, Borneo, Sumatra, Philippines	Light to dark red, but fades to light to dark yellow brown. Rather coarse but even texture. Light red Meranti is soft and also light and is often called Borneo red Seraya. Dark red Meranti is dense and hard and often called Oba Suluk.	25–45 400–720
MERSAWA (*Anisoptera* spp.)	Distinctive pale yellow to yellowish brown with lighter sapwood. Moderately coarse and even with shallowly interlocked grain. Moderately hard.	40 640
OAK, WHITE (*Quercus* spp.) Europe, North America	Light brown to medium brown. Grain commonly straight, texture coarse and uneven. Hard and strong with fairly good bending properties.	45 720
OAK, JAPANESE (*Quercus* spp. incl. *mongolica*)	Yellowish brown to brownish red. Slower growing than European Oak and hence more uniform. Lighter.	41 660
OBECHE (*Triplochiton scleroxylon*) West Africa	Creamy white to pale yellow. Grain often interlocked, texture medium soft, but has good strength properties for its weight.	24 385
PINE, EUROPEAN (*Pinus sylvestris*)	Creamy white to yellow. Distinguished from Sitka Spruce by prominent dark borders to annual rings. Moderately hard and fairly even.	32 510
PINE, PARANA (*Araucaria augustifolia*) Brazil	Pale straw coloured with brownish and reddish streaks. Straight grained, fine, even textured. Variable in density, generally moderately hard.	34 545
PINE, PITCH (*Pinus* spp.) U.S.A. and Brit. Honduras	Pale yellowish brown springwood, with reddish summerwood. Straight grained medium texture. Very resinous. Hard and strong.	41 655
PINE, OREGON. See FIR, DOUGLAS		
POPLAR (*Populus* spp.)	Varies from white to pale grey. Rather soft and woolly but with a fine even texture.	28 450
REDWOOD, EUROPEAN (*Pinus sylvestris*) Europe	Pale yellowish brown to light reddish brown. Straight grained, medium textured, fairly resinous. Moderately hard and strong.	31 495
SAPELE (*Entandrophragma cylindricum*) Trop. Africa	Pinkish to reddish brown, grain narrowly interlocked, texture fairly fine. Hard and strong	40 640
SEN (*Acanthopanax ricinifolius*)	Light cream to greyish brown; similar to Japanese Ash. Moderately coarse and uneven. Moderately hard.	35 550

Durability	Working qualities	Suitability
Fairly resistant.	Saws, planes and moulds easily and finishes to a good surface with sharp tools. Nails, paints and glues satisfactorily.	Different types of Meranti can be used for all purposes in small boat building.
Moderately durable.	Will dull saws and planes due to silica in the rays.	Veneers, plywood, general framing, carlins and brightwork.
Resistant.	Variable in working qualities, but generally medium in working. Nails, screws and glues well. Stains when in contact with ferrous metals under moist conditions.	Stems, framing, stringers, etc.
Moderately durable.	Easier to work than European Oak. Good bending properties.	Ribs, timbers, laminations, hogs, keels, tillers, etc.
Not resistant.	Works easily and takes a good finish. Nails and screws well, but its holding properties are not great. Has good staining and gluing properties. Fairly stable.	An alternative to softwood, interior work, and needs preservation.
Moderately resistant.	Top grades are easy to work. Glues and paints well. Liable to split when nailed.	Planking and spars when straight and clear grained.
Not resistant.	Easy to work, tends to split when nailed and screwed near edges. Takes smooth finish, stains, polishes well. Not particularly stable.	Wide widths available, little used in this field as yet.
Very resistant.	Moderately hard to work due to its resinous nature. Moderately hard to nail and screw. Needs careful preparation before finishing.	Not much used in dinghies, but could be used for underwater parts of boats kept afloat.
Not resistant.	Good bending.	Light laminates, frames.
Moderately resistant.	Fairly easy to work, takes a good finish. Nails, screws and glues well. Takes paint and varnish satisfactorily. Stable.	Planking, decking for canvas covering, thwarts, floors, etc.
Moderately resistant.	Works fairly well. Nails, screws and glues well, finishes and polishes excellently. Not particularly stable.	Hogs, keels, etc.
Not resistant.	Similar to Oak.	Hogs, keels, ribs, laminated frames.

Timber	Description	Av. wt. lb/cu. ft. kg/m³ at 15% m/c
SERAYA, WHITE (*Parashorea* spp.) North Borneo	Pale straw coloured. Grain straight, sometimes shallowly interlocked, texture medium to coarse. Medium hardness.	35 560
SPRUCE, SITKA (*Picea sitchensis*) Canada	Light pinkish brown, with high lustre. Straight grained, Uniform textured. Commonly free from resin. Moderately soft but strong for its weight.	28 450
SYCAMORE (*Acerpseudoplatnus*) Europe	Attractive creamy white to yellowish white colour which darkens on exposure to pale golden brown. Straight grained and fine texture with silky lustre. Curly-grain sycamore is available for veneering. Very strong, bends well.	39 625
TEAK (*Tectona grandis*) Burma, Siam, India and Java	Golden brown to medium brown. Grain generally straight, texture medium, sometimes coarse. Moderately hard, but strong.	41 655
UTILE (*Etandophragma utile*)	Very similar to Sapele	42 670

Durability	Working qualities	Suitability
Moderately resistant.	Easy to work. Nails, screws and glues well. Takes a good finish and polish. Stable.	Hogs, keels and all solid timber parts.
Not resistant.	Easy to work and takes fine finish. Nails, screws and glues well. Takes paint, varnish and other treatments readily. Stable.	Spars, oars, paddles, decking, canoes, canvas covered, etc.
Not resistant.	Use sharp tools. Figured material tends to pluck on planing. Finishes well.	Rubbing bands, breakwaters, and brightwork for boats and yachts. Excellent contrast to Mahogany.
Very resistant.	Moderately easy to work. Nails satisfactorily, tends to split near edges. Screws and glues well. Very stable.	Too well known to need comment. Does not need painting.
Resistant.	Similar to Sapele.	Plywood, planking, carlins, brightwork.

♩ Suppliers of Materials for Constructing G.R.P. Boats

There are a number of firms which give a comprehensive service to amateur boatbuilders. Some of these despatch materials from a central headquarters, such as GLASPLIES, while others rely on the chandlers and other retail outlets to reach the customer, such as RYPLAS. Still others have retail shops of their own in selected centres, such as BORDEN and STRAND GLASS.

Some firms issue more or less comprehensive instructions, hints and data sheets which are invaluable to amateurs who are not sufficiently technically minded to work through the manufacturers' information sheets.

The comprehensive suppliers have a wide range of ancillary equipment, tools, gloves, barrier creams, mould making materials, colour pigments, mixing vessels and measures etc.

Also listed are some specialist manufacturers who make items which might be needed for some applications.

* Suppliers of all or most of the materials needed for boatbuilding:

STRAND GLASS CO. LTD., Brentway Trading Estate, Brentford, Middlesex. Also to be found at 17 branches in the United Kingdom.
Comprehensive range of materials, tools and literature including Data Sheets and books. The firm also runs demonstrations including the showing of films.

BORDEN (UK) LTD.—Marine and Leisure Division, 61–67 Commercial Road, Southampton.
Manufacturers of Epophen Epoxide Resins, Cascophen Resorcinal Resin Adhesives and Cascover Nylon Sheathing systems.
They supply materials and accessories for these systems together with technical and practical information sheets. In addition to the above address they have another shop at Mr. Bosun's Locker, 63 East Street, Chichester.

RYPLAS DISTRIBUTORS LTD., Howard Chase, Pipps Hill Industrial Area, Basildon, Essex.
Distributors of materials for the amateur to retail shops and chandlers.
Handbook, price lists and lists of stockists are available.

GLASPLIES, office—2 Crowland Street, Southport, Lancs., yard—109 Moss Lane, Churchtown, Southport.
Mail Order suppliers of all materials, tools and equipment needed by amateur boatbuilders. Also supplied to callers at the yard every day of the week. Comprehensive duplicated sheets of instructions and hints including how to calculate quantities required.

BARTOLINE LTD., Barmston Close, Beverley, Yorkshire.
Small quantities of resin and other materials supplied.

WILSON'S (FIBREGLASS), 26 Scratchface Lane, Bedhampton, Havant.
Suppliers of the more popular types of resins, glass and other materials for amateur moulders.

BMS PLASTICS LTD., Higgins Lane, Birscough, Lancs.
Suppliers of Fibreglass Ltd. glass reinforcements, F.G. Industries' Fabmat and Rovcloth, B.P. Resins and Gelcoats, Laporte Catalysts, Novadel Accelerators, Plastichem Fillers and other equipment and materials. Also Polyspray equipment.

BONDAGLASS—VOSS LTD., 158/164 Ravenscourt Road, Beckenham, Kent.
Glass, resins, fillers, metal primers and polyurethane closed-cell foam.

Other suppliers can be found in trade advertisements in magazines.

* Specialist Manufacturers or suppliers who may be found useful in some cases are as follows:

MITCHELL & SMITH LTD., 54 Willow Lane, Mitcham, Surrey.

Epoxy Esters and also Polyester laminating and Gel-coat resins.

CIBA-GEIGY (UK) LTD., Duxford, Cambridge.

Araldite Epoxide resins and adhesives in various types (minimum quantities supplied—1 lb). Also casting resins, hardeners, accelerators, colouring pastes, fillers, mould releasers, sealers and plasticizers.

HERMETITE PRODUCTS LTD., Tavistock Road, West Drayton, Middlesex.

Hermetite double-bond Epoxide resin adhesives, in putty and cream grades.

Hermetite Kwikfill Polyester filler.

Hermetite silicone R.T.V. Rubber Sealant and adhesive for deck caulking and waterproof sealing.

T.B.A. INDUSTRIAL PRODUCTS LTD., P.O. Box 40, Rochdale, Lancs.

Glass Fibre reinforcements. Small quantities available via Strand Glass.

FIBREGLASS LTD., Reinforcements Division, St. Helens, Merseyside.

Chopped strand mats, woven roving and surfacing mat (minimum quantity one roll—approx. 30kg, 40kg and 100m² respectively). Rovings (minimum quantity one cheese—approx. 15kg).

BAKELITE XYLONITE LTD., Mitcham Road, Croydon.

Plastazote foamed cross-linked polyethylene and Evazote foamed cross-linked ethylene vinyl acetate for buoyancy.

BP CHEMICALS INTERNATIONAL LTD., Devonshire House, Mayfair Place, Piccadilly, London.

Resins—apply to G.R.P. (Southern) Ltd., Nutwood Close, Off Kiln Lane, Brockham, Surrey.

Solvents and Acetone—apply to Tennants Ltd., 69 Grosvenor Street, London W1.

LLEWELLYN RYLAND LTD., Haden Street, Birmingham, B12.

Paints, varnishes, laquers and colour pigments. Excellent colour pattern book. Small quantities sold through Strand Glass.

ALFRED JEFFERY & CO., Marshgate, Stratford, London E.15.

Mendex adhesive filler and 'Pour-it-yourself' foam. Leaflets available.

K Suppliers of Materials for Wooden Boat Construction

Local timber merchants are usually unable to supply hardwoods and softwoods of joinery quality and in suitable varieties. Timber should be ordered from mills or importers, some of whom are listed or who can be located from the Yellow Pages in a telephone directory or from trade advertisements.

Some mills specialise in partially converting timber to customers' requirements. Kit suppliers provide fully converted parts in the correct materials.

Boatyards will usually supply timber and plywood, often in small quantities but this can be the most expensive way of buying.

Certain other specialist manufacturers of interest to boatbuilders are also listed:

THAMES PLYWOOD MANUFACTURERS LTD., Harts Lane, Barking, Essex.
Anti-fracture ply sheets, Plydeck, Celply, Teakply, and Marineply using Makore (standard weight) and Gaboon (lightweight).

GLIKSTEN PLYWOOD LTD., P.O. Box 118, Carpenters Road, London E15.
Marinaply is available through trade distributors and local timber yards.

W. W. HOWARD BROS. LTD., Bitterne Wharf, Southampton.
Timber and veneers.

WILLIAM MALLINSON & SONS LTD., 130 Hackney Road, London E.C.2.
Timber and veneers.

COUSLAND AND BROWNE LTD., Piggery Wharf, Manor Farm Road, Alperton, Wembley, Middlesex.
Softwood and hardwood importers.

ROBBINS LTD., Cumberland Road, Bristol.
Hardwoods and Softwoods cut to size. Plywood in full, half or quarter sheets; Teakply and Plydeck.

M & J. REUBEN LTD., Essex Wharf, Barking Road, London E.16.
Timber.

UNION GLUE AND GELATINE CO. LTD., P.O. Box 14, Accrington, Lancs.
Seal brand wet-or-dry abrasive papers (minimum quantity one Quire (25 sheets))

BOWMAN BOATS, 54 Beacon Road, Chatham, Kent.
Alloy mast making kits and general chandlery and rigging.

CORNELIUS CHEMICAL CO. LTD., Ibex House, Minories, London E.C.3.
Flare fluorescent pigments and paints, Plexiglas acrylic sheeting and extrusions and many other materials.

W. MANNERING & CO. LTD., 180/182 Bermondsey Street, London S.E.1.
Large range of items made of rubber or neoprene. Also tube and sheet.

TUFNOL LTD., P.O. Box 376, Perry Bar, Birmingham B42.
Reinforced cloth laminates in many grades, thicknesses and sections.

ROWDEAN SUPPLIES, 12 Maple Lodge Close, Maple Cross, Rickmansworth, Herts.
Ferrous and Non-Ferrous fastenings, screws, bolts, machine screws.

BAKELITE XYLONITE, Enford House, 139 Marylebone Road, London N.W.1.
Microballons.

CIBA-GEIGY (UK) LTD., Duxford, Cambridge.
Aerolite 300 (liquid), Aerolite 306 (powder) separate application wood adhesives. Araldite epoxy adhesives.

METAL CENTRE LTD., Summer Road, Thames Ditton, Surrey.

Sheet, bar, rod, tube in stainless steel, brass, copper, alloys etc.

WHITELY PRODUCTS LTD., Ravensbury Mills, Mitcham, Surrey.

Shockcords, fittings and assemblies. Toestrap webbing.

ALLSCREWS LTD., 270/282 King Street, Hammersmith, London W.6.

Stainless steel fastenings.

TOWER MANUFACTURING, Diglis, Worcester.

Silicon Bronze barbed ring nails.

FREDERIK MOUNTFORD LTD., Warley, Birmingham.

Screws and bolts of all types.

Some Suppliers and Publishers of Boatbuilding Plans and Kits

WILLIAM PORTEOUS & CO., 9 Royal Exchange Place, Glasgow G1.

Sell the *Rudder* Catalogue of boat plans, though the plans themselves have to be obtained direct from the publishers in Greenwich, Connecticut.

FAREHAM BOAT PLANS, 88 Portchester Road, Fareham.

Large numbers of stock plans. Special designs undertaken for boats in ferro-cement, and all other materials.

YACHTING MONTHLY, Hatfield House, Stamford Street, London SE1.

Complete plans for YM Junior, 13 ft 6 in. and YM Senior, 16 ft family boats.

YACHTING WORLD, Dorset House, Stamford Street, London SE1.

Complete plans for Utility pram, 9-ft dinghy, Buccaneer, Bass Boat and Barbican.

PERCY W. BLANDFORD, Quinton House, Newbold-on-Stour, Stratford-upon-Avon, Warwicks.

Mostly plywood designs for prams, dinghies, canoes and outboard runabouts.

MICHAEL VERNEY, Hillsborough, The Parkway, Rustington, Sussex.

Large range of clinker planked designs suitable for traditional or glued plywood construction including rowing, sailing and motor boats from 6 ft 6 in. to 17 ft.

Also Mr. Verney's popular book *Complete Amateur Boat Building*.

ARDLEIGH LAMINATED PLASTICS CO. LTD., Wheaton Road, Industrial Estate East, Witham, Essex.

Large range of plans, materials and kits including some dinghies.

HARTLEY'S BOAT PLANS, The Croft, Polvarth Road, St. Mawes, Truro, Cornwall.

Large range of designs and kits which include cutting lists and quantities of materials.

Also books by Richard Hartley.

BELL WOODWORKING CO., 199 Narborough Road South, Leicester.

Supply kits for home completion of *Yachting World* pram, Heron, Enterprise, GP14, Mirror 16, Bell Seagull and Bell Seamew.

Also kits for Mirror 11, Mirror 14 and Mirror Miracle which are sold by I.P.C., 79 Camden Road, London NW1.

ROBERT TUCKER DESIGNS, 58 Southbury Road, Enfield, Middlesex.

A large range of designs for timber GRP and ferro-cement of which about 12 are under 20 ft.

YORK MARINE CRAFT, Worthington Street, Bradford 8, Yorkshire.

Wide range of plywood designs for which kits can be supplied.

E. G. VAN DE STADT & PARTNERS, Box 440, Zaandam, Holland.

Many designs for amateur builders.

Index

Figures in italics refer to pages on which illustrations appear